The Holy Spirit and His Ministry through the Scriptures

Brian Sherring

ISBN: 978-1-78364-551-0

www.obt.org.uk

Unless indicated otherwise, all Scripture quotations are from the ESV® Bible (The Holy Bible, English Standard Version®), copyright © 2001 by Crossway, a publishing ministry of Good News Publishers. Used by permission. All rights reserved.

****

Small superscript numbers in the text refer to additional notes at the back of this book.

****

The Open Bible Trust
Fordland Mount, Upper Basildon,
Reading, RG8 8LU, UK.

Contents

Page	
4	Preface
7	1. The Holy Spirit: Who is He?
18	2. 'Spirit': Translations and usage
21	3. The Holy Spirit and the world of 'men'
33	4. The Spirit of God and the Word of God
35	5. The Holy Spirit in the Old Testament
41	6. The Holy Spirit between the Testaments
43	7. The Holy Spirit in the New Testament
49	8. The Holy Spirit in the Synoptic Gospels
65	9. The Holy Spirit in John's Gospel
83	10. The Holy Spirit and the Preparation of the apostles for their coming mission (John 14-16)
101	11. The Holy Spirit during the Acts Period
115	12. Gifts of the Spirit during the Gospel and Acts Periods
126	13. The Holy Spirit in the non-Pauline Acts Epistles
143	14. The Holy Spirit in the Pauline Acts Epistles Part 1: 1 & 2 Thessalonians; 1 & 2 Corinthians
175	15. The Holy Spirit in the Pauline Acts Epistles Part 2: Galatians; Romans
192	16. One door closes; another door opens Philemon; Philippians; Ephesians; Colossians
231	17. Paul's final witness: The Holy Spirit in the Pastoral Epistles: Titus; 1 & 2 Timothy
240	Also on the Holy Spirit
241	About the Author
242	Also by Brian Sherring
244	Subject Index
251	Bibliography
254	Additional (superscript) Notes

Preface

Anyone who attempts to study the nature and being of God, especially if they intend to put that study into writing for the benefit of others, will soon realise that, "not only is our intellect too small to encompass him but also our language is too limited to explain him." So wrote Derek Tidball in his excellent book, *The Message of the Holy Spirit*: *The Bible Speaks Today* series. As to language, how do we refer to Him? 'A force'? 'An entity'? 'A person'? The last of these, as I intend to show, is in my view to be preferred, providing we explain what we mean by the word 'person'.

The problem with the English word 'person', is that it can so easily lead to the concept of three 'people', even three Gods, if we apply it also to the Father and the Son. And so we end up with the statement sometimes used of the Trinity in Christian circles, "God the Father, God the Son and God the Holy Spirit". If there is only one God, could this be misunderstood as suggesting three Gods. This is the very error that Jews, and some other religions, have accused Christians of at various times.

For Israel, there is one statement of fact that is the last word in their understanding of God. It is expressed in their great *Shema* (Hear), still proclaimed in Jewish synagogues today:

> *Shema Yisrael*, "Hear, O Israel: the LORD our God, the LORD is one. You shall love the LORD your God with all your heart ..." (Deuteronomy 6:4,5)

Israel's God is the God whose name is *Jehovah* (LORD) and '*Jehovah* our God is ONE'. In all three references to LORD in this call for Israel to 'hear' and to 'love Him', the Hebrew word translated into English 'LORD' (small capitals) is 'JEHOVAH'. I take this as a foundational statement that must condition our understanding of the Trinity. The Jewish conception of God as 'One', must never be lost sight of.

This brings us back to the usage of 'person' as a means of distinguishing between the Father, the Son and the Holy Spirit. If we use it in the sense of one playing a 'character' or 'role' in a play, which is what *The Concise Oxford Dictionary* gives as one of its meanings, then that difficulty is (partly) removed. We can then introduce it into the concept of the Trinity, and speak of the 'manifestation' of God in three 'persons', the Father, the Son, the Holy Spirit (more on this later).

This study is focused particularly on the Holy Spirit, but not in isolation from the Father and the Son for, as I hope to show, there is a unity of purpose in three 'manifestations' of God that demonstrate that *One God* is presented to us in three 'roles'. With that in mind, we could therefore quite happily sing the words, "God *in Three Persons*, Blessed Trinity" that appear at the end of the first and last verses of the hymn, "Holy, Holy, Holy! Lord God Almighty".

Another statement open to misinterpretation is when the Holy Spirit is referred to as "the *third* person of the Trinity". This seems to infer a kind of hierarchy:

(i) Father,
(ii) the Son and
(iii) the Holy Spirit.

In the Scriptures there is certainly the concept of a Triune God, where the '**Three**' work together in unity, for example in John 15:26:

> When the Helper comes, *the Spirit of truth*, whom I will send to you from *The Father*, he will bear witness about *me* (*Jesus the Messiah*).

Here, *The Father sends* the Spirit, *the Spirit comes* to the disciples, and He *bears witness to Jesus the Messiah.* This unity of purpose involves each of the '**Three**' playing their 'role' in calling the sinner to embrace "the salvation that is in Christ Jesus" (2 Timothy 2:10); a salvation that makes possible the fulfilment of God's plan and purpose for His people. Although the word 'hierarchy' sometimes has bad connotations, used in a good sense, could it indicate that the three 'persons' in the Trinity take different 'roles' necessary for the fulfilment of God's purpose for mankind? I will try to answer this and other questions that come to mind in this study.

The Trinity, and specifically the Holy Spirit, is related to 'man's' place in that purpose. I examine this initially in regard to *all* mankind, believers or otherwise, for I believe that His ministry involves not just Christians (as though they were some kind of exclusive club) but mankind in general. "(God) does not wish that any should perish, but that *all* should come to repentance"—He loved *the world*, and the sacrifice of His Son was the evidence of that love (2 Peter 3:9; John 3:16). *The Holy Spirit* is very much involved in making that salvation *known to all.*

There is a tendency to associate the Holy Spirit with the New Testament, in particular the giving of the Holy Spirit on the Day of Pentecost. This may be because there is an abundance of references to the Holy Spirit in the New Testament compared with the apparent lack of the same in the Old. And yet, "the Spirit of God" is referred to in the second verse of the English Bible, and (as I will show) "the Spirit of God" in Genesis 1:2 is one and the same as "the Holy Spirit" in the New Testament.

What has been revealed of the Holy Spirit, and our perception of Him, may have developed and changed with the unfolding of God's Word throughout the ages, but He himself has not—He is "the eternal Spirit" (Hebrews 9:14). Just like Jehovah: "I the LORD do not change" (Malachi 3:6) and Jesus: He "is the same yesterday today and for ever" (Hebrews 13:8). His ministry may vary according to the purpose God is pursuing; whether His purpose for the earth, and the Jews and their 'hope', or for those who are blessed in the heavenly places. However, He does not change.

In this respect I have tended to refer, even in quotations, to Jesus as 'Messiah' when considering God's purpose through Israel, and as 'Christ' when referring to Him in association with His purpose in the heavenly places.

Chapter 1.
The Holy Spirit: Who is He?

This question generally defines itself by two further questions: Is He a Person? Is He God? Without making any attempt to discuss the various answers that have been given to these questions, I will go directly to the Scriptures, observing that the New Testament writers have treated Him as both. Here are some examples of this.

A) The Holy Spirit is a Person

'Person' is a translation of the Greek *prosopon*, so the first thing is to establish the meaning of this word as used by the New Testament writers. *The Concise Oxford Dictionary* gives one meaning of 'person' as: "An individual human being", which, if we adopt that meaning, suggests that the Holy Spirit is *a separate individual with a separate existence* outside the Father and the Son. This could lead to the 'three Gods' concept, which contradicts the insistence of the Scriptures that there is 'one God'. Those who struggled with the wording of the early Creeds came up with an answer now resident in the Western version of the Nicene Creed:

> We believe in *the Holy Spirit*, the Lord, the giver of life, *who proceeds from the Father and the Son*. With the Father and Son he is worshipped and glorified. He has spoken through the prophets. (*Common Worship*)

Returning to the Dictionary, it gives another aspect of the definition of 'person'; "a *character* in a play or story". *Chambers Dictionary* puts it even more succinctly, "a capacity in which one is acting", in other words, a 'role' being played. This meaning is found also in Classical Greek.

Prosopon is rendered "person" several times in the *KJV*[1] and came to mean *the part played* by an actor on the stage, hence "what an individual *appeared to be*". In the Greek version of the Old Testament (*Septuagint LXX*) it is used above all for the "face" of the LORD (e.g. Numbers 6:25,26) and this is reflected in the New Testament in 2 Corinthians 4:6, "The light of the knowledge of the glory of God" is seen "in the *face* (*prosopon*) of Christ". (In everyday life it is generally a person's *face* that calls them to mind in our memory.)

In the New Testament it is evident that Peter believed that the Holy Spirit was both a 'Person' and 'God', in the language he used to condemn Ananias and Sapphira and their attempt to deceive him and the brethren (Acts 5:1-11). With the knowledge of his wife, Ananias sold a piece of property, but gave only part of the proceeds to the apostles. But he pretended that he had given all of it into the common pool. But Peter, acknowledging that sold or unsold, the land was at Ananias' disposal, pronounced judgement upon the couple because they had attempted to deceive the apostles, and he said to Ananias:

> "Why has Satan filled your heart to *lie to the Holy Spirit* ... you have not *lied* to men but *to God*". (Acts 5:3)

In common parlance, one can only *lie to* a person, and Peter equated lying to the Holy Spirit with *lying to God*. There was no doubt in his mind that the Holy Spirit was not only a 'Person' but God. The Scriptures also speak of '*grieving*' the Holy Spirit (Isaiah 63:10; Ephesians 4:30), and, again, one can only grieve a person.

In other places we find the Holy Spirit *saying*, "Set apart for me Barnabas and Saul" (Acts 13:2), and in another, we are told that, "*It seemed good to the Holy Spirit* and to us ..." (15:28). See also Acts 28:25, where the Holy Spirit is *said to have spoken the truth*. Here Paul goes on to quote Isaiah 6:9,10 which I refer to below.

'Lying to', 'seeming good to', 'speaking the truth' and 'grieving' can only be actions relating to a 'person'. Jesus referred to the Holy Spirit as a Counsellor (or Comforter, Helper, Advocate *parakletos* John 14:16,26; 15:26; 16:7), different translations that attempt to interpret this Greek word into English, but all suggesting a 'Person'.

B) The Holy Spirit is God

Some of the same Scriptures that demonstrate that the Holy Spirit is a

'Person', also show that He is God. Peter's words to Ananias in Acts 5:3 for example: "Why has Satan filled your heart to *lie to the Holy Spirit* ... you have not *lied to* men but *to God*". In Acts 28:25 Paul attributes the words of *the Lord* in Isaiah's prophecy (6:8-10) to *the Holy Spirit*. Similarly, in Hebrews 3:7 where the writer quotes Psalm 95:6-7:

> "O come, let us worship and bow down, let us kneel before *the LORD our Maker*! For *he is our God*, and we are the people of his pasture and the sheep of his hand. Today, if you will hear *his voice* ..."
>
> "Therefore, *as the Holy Spirit says*, 'Today, if you will hear his voice ..."

However, although we can compare passages of Scripture with each other to identify the Holy Spirit as both a Person and God, that does not mean that we have fathomed His depths. Keith Warrington's comment that, "our intellect is too small to encompass Him and our language too limited to explain Him", still stands.

The same commentator made another important statement which is worth repeating here: "The authors of the Bible were much more interested in the practical, dynamic consequences of encounters with the Spirit ... an exploration of His activity rather than a comprehensive survey of His actuality; i.e. His roles rather than His reality." They believed in His existence, acknowledged that they could not comprehend Him, but longed to be transformed by Him. We in our turn, are bidden to pursue the same path—"Be filled with (or by) the Spirit" (Ephesians 5:18).

C) The Holy Spirit within 'the Trinity'

The word 'Trinity' (Tri-unity) is an attempt to explain how one God can exist in three 'Persons' (Person understood as above). Christians have believed in a Trinity of Father, Son and Holy Spirit from the earliest days of Christendom, even though the word appears nowhere in the Scriptures. Without necessarily using the word in their declarations of belief, the Creeds have effectively accepted it. In the Western version of the Nicene Creed this is acknowledged:

> We believe in *the Holy Spirit*, the Lord, the giver of life, who proceeds from *the Father* and *the Son*. With the Father and Son

he is worshipped and glorified. He has spoken through the prophets. (*Common Worship*)

All three 'Persons' of the Trinity are here acknowledged as worthy of the same worship, and the same glory. And without suggesting that the word 'person' comprehends fully the Being and nature of God, it is, I believe, a useful concept of the threefold and co-equal manifestation of the one God, as Father, Son and Holy Spirit, and is justified by the Scriptures. An example of this "Trinity" is found in John 14:26:

> The Helper, *the Holy Spirit*, whom *the Father* will send in *my* (*Jesus*') name, he will teach you all things.

I have heard it said that, in the Old Testament we have the revelation of God as Father; in the Gospels, God as Son and in The Acts of the Apostles, God as The Holy Spirit—a Trinity! The following Scriptures might seem to support this:

> **O.T. Father:** The nation of Israel was looked upon by the LORD as His "firstborn son" (Exodus 4:22; see Hosea 11:1). He said in the days of Jeremiah, "I am a father to Israel and Ephraim is my firstborn"[2] (31:9). In the first century, the Jews continued to claim, "We have one Father—even God" (John 8:41).
>
> **Gospels: Son:** The Word was God, "became flesh and dwelt among us ... the only Son (Jesus) from the Father" (John 1:1-14; 1 Timothy 3:16); "Immanuel ... God with us" (Matthew 1:23).
>
> **Acts of the Apostles: The Holy Spirit:** Promised (John 14:16,17,26): Coming (Acts 2:4), Working (Acts 8:29, 39; 11:12; 16:7), Gifts from the Spirit of God (1 Corinthians 12 etc.).

It is evident from the Scriptures as a whole, however, that the revelation of any one of the 'Persons' of the Trinity is not confined to any of the above divisions. It might be better to say that *the emphasis* in the Old Testament is *largely* upon the Father, *largely* on the Son in the Gospels and *largely* on the Holy Spirit during the Acts Period. So what evidence is there for the teaching of and belief in the Trinity in the Old Testament?

D) The Trinity in the Old Testament

God as a 'Trinity' is not so obvious in the Old Testament as it is in the New. Nevertheless, the use of plural forms there when referring to God has suggested to some commentators a Trinity. This is seen very early on in the Scriptures. The very word for God, *Elohim*, is plural and the use of plural pronouns and verbs in passages in which He speaks, is considered also to suggest a Trinity.

When God determined to make man, He said, "Let *us* make man in *our* image". Later, after Adam had eaten of the forbidden tree, The LORD God said, "Behold, the man has become like *one of us* in knowing good and evil". At the Tower of Babel, when the LORD saw what man was doing He said, "Let *us* go down and there confuse their language" (Genesis 1:26; 3:22; 11:7). None of this is 'cast iron proof' that the Trinity is embodied in Old Testament understanding of God, but it is worthy of note. There are plenty of indications that it is in the New.

E) The Trinity in the New Testament

The best-known passage suggesting a Trinity in the New Testament, and used regularly at the end of Christian meetings, is Paul's benediction: "The grace of *the Lord Jesus Christ* and the love of *God* and the fellowship of *the Holy Spirit* be with you all" (2 Corinthians 13:14). This formula also formed part of the Lord's command to the disciples and their ministry among the nations;

> "Go and make disciples of all nations, baptising them in the name of *the Father* and of *the Son* and of *the Holy Spirit* ..."[3] (Matthew 28:19).

Here, "name" is singular and suggests the unity of Father, Son and Holy Spirit.

The same 'Trinity' is resident in Paul's words to the Corinthians concerning spiritual gifts:

> Now there are varieties of gifts, but the *same Spirit*; and there are varieties of service, but the *same Lord*; and there are varieties of activities, but it is the *same God* who empowers them all in

everyone. (1 Corinthians 12:4-6)

In that great Epistle to the Ephesians, chapter one verses 3-14 (a passage that J. Armitage Robinson described as, "A kaleidoscope of dazzling lights and shifting colours") the Trinity is seen in relation to the choice, salvation and sealing of the believer and his inheritance in the holy places. Known to some as 'The Charter of the Church',[4] it may be set out structurally so:

> 1:3-6 **The will of the Father**
> He *chose* us in Christ
> 1:7-12 **The work of the Son**
> In Him we have *redemption*
> 1;13,14 **The witness of the Spirit**
> Having believed you were *sealed* by Him[5]

The Holy Spirit is referred to in these passages as working with the other 'Persons' of this Trinity on an equal footing in every respect to the Father and the Son. But as with Christ, man's knowledge and understanding of Him has been the subject of *an unfolding revelation.*

> **Verses 1-6** *The Father chooses us* before the foundation of the world and *predestines us* to be adopted as sons "according to *the purpose of his will*".

> **Verses 7-12** In order to make that possible, *the work of the Son* gives us "redemption through his blood" and "the forgiveness of our trespasses". And to those "riches of (God's) grace" has been added "wisdom and insight" into "the mystery of his will" that has been "set forth *in Christ*", a plan that will come to fruition in "the fullness of time" and which unites "all things in (Christ), things in heaven and on earth".

> **Verses 13,14** We are taken back to the beginning of our faith, when we "heard the word of truth, the gospel of our salvation", and assured that having "believed (in Christ)" *the Holy Spirit* set His seal upon us and so "guaranteed our inheritance until we acquire possession of it".

This passage not only suggests a Trinity, but touches upon the different relationships of each 'Person' to the members of The Church which is the

Body of Christ. But perhaps the most significant passages that suggest both the unity and the diversity of the Trinity are found in chapters 14-16 of John's Gospel.

The disciples were gathered with the Lord before He made the one great sacrifice for mankind, and He comforts them and assures them with His promises on the eve of His 'going away'. All three 'Persons' are mentioned by the Lord as He prepares the apostles for His withdrawal from the earthly scene.

The Father will send:

- "I am going *to the Father* ... to him *who sent me*" (14:12; 16:5)
- "I will ask *the Father* ... he *will give you another Helper, to be with you for ever,* even the Spirit of truth ..." (14:16,17)
- "The Helper, the Holy Spirit, *whom the Father will send* in my name, will teach you all things and bring to your remembrance all that I have said to you." (14:26)
- "When the Helper comes, whom *I will send to you from the Father,* the Spirit of truth, *who proceeds from the Father*, he will bear witness about me." (15:26)

The Lord will return:

- "I go to prepare a place for you ... *I will come again* and will take you to myself." (14:2,3)
- "I will not leave you as orphans, *I will come to you.*" (14:18)
- "I am going away and *I will come to you.*" (14:28)

The Spirit will come:

- "*The Spirit* of truth ... he *dwells with you* and *will be in you.*" (14:17)
- "I (the Lord) will send him (the Helper, *the Spirit*) to you." (16:7)
- "When *the Spirit* of truth comes, he will guide you into all the truth ... he will take what is mine and declare it to you." (16:13,14)

The Lord was leaving His disciples to return to His Father; if He did not, the Holy Spirit would not come (16:7). Why? John 7:38,39 may have the answer: "the Spirit had not been given, because Jesus was not yet glorified". The coming of the Holy Spirit awaited the *glorification* of Jesus and so was after the death and resurrection of the Messiah, when Jesus "breathed" on the disciples and said to them, "Receive the Holy Spirit" (20:22).

Later, on the Day of Pentecost, those disciples were "all filled with the Holy Spirit and began to speak in other tongues *as the Spirit gave them utterance*" (Acts 2:4). The ministry of the Holy Spirit was to take the things of Jesus the Messiah and show them to the disciples. They were to declare those 'things' first to Israel, and hence *glorify Him* (John 16:12-15). In some ways this sums up the ministry of the Holy Spirit as Jesus said: "He will glorify me, for he will take what is mine and declare it to you" (John 16:14).

F) The Holy Spirit: An unfolding revelation

In his epistle to the Ephesians, Paul made the following claim:

> "When you read this (what he wrote earlier in the epistle) you can perceive my insight into the mystery of Christ, which *was not made known to the sons of men in other generations as it has now been revealed* to his holy apostles and prophets by the Spirit" (Ephesians 3:1-6)[6].

"The mystery of Christ (Messiah)" was unfolded throughout the Scriptures from the first hint in Genesis 3:14,15, where He is seen as the One who will bruise the serpent's head, to that passage that reveals Him as "Head over all things to the church, which is his body" and beyond (Ephesians 1:22,23)—"The mystery of Christ" was *an unfolding revelation.* (See the author's *Messiah and His people* OBT for more on this). I believe the same is true in respect of the Holy Spirit.

Not that either Jehovah (Malachi 3:6), Jesus Christ or the Holy Spirit have *changed* in any way for, as is said of the Messiah:

> Jesus Christ is the same yesterday and today and forever. (Hebrews 13:8)

However, *the ministry* of Christ may be different according to which aspect of the purpose of God He is ministering to; that for the earth or that in the heavenly places. In Ephesians above, Paul links "the mystery of Christ" with "the mystery" concerning a *changed* relationship between Jew and Gentile (3:6).

So it is with the Holy Spirit. He is "the eternal Spirit" (Hebrews 9:14). He is one and the same as the Spirit of God in Genesis 1:2 who "hovered" over the primeval waters, but His ministry in both the Old and New Testaments may be *different* according to God's will and purpose.

Our perception of Him may have developed and changed with the unfolding of God's Word as it has been revealed throughout the pages of the Bible, but the Spirit Himself has not. It is important to keep this in mind as we consider man's concept of Him throughout the ages, whether we see Him in relation to the creation (Genesis 1:2) or as the One who indwells the believer (Romans 8:9). More on this when we come to consider His ministry in detail.

G) The Trinity: Different 'roles'

Father, Son and Holy Spirit are presented to us in different 'roles' within the Trinity, but is there an 'order' (I hesitate to use the word 'hierarchy'). Take for instance John 14:28 where Jesus said to His disciples:

> "I am going to the Father, for the Father *is greater than I*."

This 'order' does not deny the Deity of the Son, as C.K. Barrett noted: "The Father is God sending and commanding, the Son is God sent and obeying" (*in loco*). Each has to be seen in the 'role' assumed. The Holy Spirit likewise assumes His 'role' within the Trinity. Of Him Jesus said (John 16:13,14):

> When the Spirit of truth comes, he will guide you into all the truth, for *he will not speak on his own authority*, but whatever he hears he will speak, and he will declare to you the things that are to come. *He will glorify me,* for he will take what is mine and declare it to you.

The Holy Spirit assumes a 'role' here as 'a spokesman' or 'messenger'. The Father, Son and Holy Spirit have to be seen as having different 'roles' within the "Godhead" (divine being)[7]. The interaction between the Father, Son and Holy Spirit, is nowhere better seen than in John chapters 14-16. Consider these three promises in chapter 14:

> "I (*Jesus*) will ask *the Father*, and he will give you *another Helper, to be with you for ever*, even *the Spirit of truth* ..." (14:16,17)

> "I will not leave you as orphans, *I* (*Jesus*) *will come to you* ... in that day you will know that I am in *my Father*, and you in me, and I in you." (14:18-20)

> "If anyone loves me (*Jesus*), he will keep my word, and *my Father* will love him, and *we* (*Father and Son*) *will come to him and make our home with him.*" (14:23)

Father, Jesus (Son) and Holy Spirit; all three would come and abide with the disciples, and with anyone who loves Jesus and keeps His word; a Trinity in unity. Later, in the knowledge of the revelation of Christ's relation to The Church which is the Body of Christ, Paul wrote of Christ: "In him the whole fullness of deity (*KJV* 'Godhead') *dwells bodily,* and you have been filled in him, who is the head of all rule and authority ..." (Colossians 2:9,10).

H) The Holy Spirit: A brief summary

The Holy Spirit is the invisible 'manifestation' of God, the spokesman and messenger of God. In Old Testament times He spoke through the prophets (Hebrews 1:1). He was sent by the Father in Jesus' name, to "teach (the disciples) all things and bring to remembrance all that (Jesus) had said (to them)."

This would include some "things" that Jesus had withheld from them because they were unable to bear them at the time. The Holy Spirit would reveal these "things" to them and guide them into "all the truth" (John 16:12,13). This takes us as far as God's purpose for the earth.

The Holy Spirit is working today through the Word of God in the Church which is the Body of Christ. He seals us and is the guarantor of our future inheritance in "the day of redemption" (Ephesians 1:13,14; 4:30). He waits to fill us with The Word of God (Ephesians 5:18; Colossians 3:16. (The connection between these two Scriptures and its relevance for today is considered more fully later.)

Today the Holy Spirit *speaks* through the Word of God, and this association of the Holy Spirit with the Word of God, 'Spirit' with 'Word', is perhaps the most important aspect of His teaching ministry for us today.

Chapter 2.
'Spirit': Translations and usage

A) The Hebrew and Greek words

'Spirit' and 'spirit' are *ruach* (Hebrew) and *pneuma* (Greek). The primitive origin of *ruach* is "a movement of air, wind, breath (especially of God)" and hence, "the *breath* of life" (Genesis 6:17; 7:15). *The Englishman's Hebrew Concordance* to the Old Testament under *ruach*, lists the various words the King James translators used to render it into English. Used of natural phenomena they are, "air, blast, breath, tempest, wind". It is also used of both "the Spirit of God" and man's "spirit" and of (ministering) angels (Psalm 104:4 quoted in Hebrews 1:7 where the Greek is *pneuma*). The Greek version of the Old Testament (Septuagint, *LXX*) almost always uses *pneuma* to translate the Hebrew *ruach*.

Rendered with a small 's' it is used in expressions such as, "a spirit of jealousy", "a spirit of wisdom", "a faithful spirit", "an evil or lying spirit"; even "the spirit" of a nation (Egypt, Isaiah 19:3). A person's 'spirit' can be overwhelmed, broken and vexed. A man's or a woman's 'spirit' is basically what they are in reality.

Used of the "Spirit of the LORD" coming upon mankind, (e.g. Samson and Saul), it is described sometimes as coming "mightily" upon someone (*KJV*); "rushed upon" (*ESV*) and the *NIV* has "coming in power" (Judges 14:6,19: 1 Samuel 10:6,10). These renderings are reminiscent of what happened on the Day of Pentecost when: "Suddenly there came from heaven a sound like *a mighty rushing wind* ... they were all *filled with the Holy Spirit*", a phenomenon described as "power from on high" (Luke 24:49; Acts 1:8).

But there is a difficulty when translating both the Hebrew and the Greek words, that is not often drawn attention to, or given the prominence it should have. Since the original languages are no help here, the English translator has to decide whether or not the word 'spirit' should begin with a small 's' as shown here, or a capital 'S' which signifies that the Holy Spirit is meant. So although it may seem a small problem, it can have wide ranging consequences. Let us look further at the problem.

B) An important decision: 'Spirit' or 'spirit'?

Before we look at the ministry of the Holy Spirit in any detail, we must recognise that the difficulty mentioned above **(A)** could greatly influence our interpretation of some passages of Scripture. The Old Testament was written in Hebrew, apart from a few places[8], and the New in Greek. The Hebrew word *ruach* has its equivalent in the Greek word, *pneuma*, generally translated "Spirit" and "spirit". The use of the capital 'S' in a particular version of the Bible, indicates that the translators are suggesting that the Holy Spirit is meant; a small 's' that it is used in another way. This difference is noted in commentaries, but rarely explained at any length.

It may not be realised that there is no indication in the original documents from which the English Bible has been translated, as to whether the Hebrew word *ruach* and the Greek word *pneuma*, should be rendered "Spirit" or "spirit" in any particular instance. So the use of 'S' or 's' is effectively left to the translator, and (it almost goes without saying) they do not always agree amongst themselves. In respect of the New Testament, this difficulty, was dealt with at length by Dr. E.W. Bullinger in his book originally published as *The Giver and His Gifts*. It now appears under the title, *Word Studies on the Holy Spirit* (see Bibliography).

Ruach:

Languages develop according to the environment in which people live and their need to communicate with each other and differentiate between things. The ancient Hebrews, living 'cheek by jowl' with the natural world had (e.g.) seven words for 'lion' (five of them appear in two verses in Job 4:10-11—see *KJV*), and yet one word, *ruach* did service for 'wind', 'breath' and 'spirit', whether the spirit of man or of God

> In the earliest understanding of *ruach* there was little or no distinction between natural and supernatural. The wind could be

described poetically as the blast (*ruach*) of the LORD's nostrils, Exodus 15:8; 2 Samuel 22:1. (*New Bible Dictionary*)

Initially 'the wind' as a 'natural' force was seen as just another aspect of the 'divine' spirit that came upon men of God, such as Joseph (Genesis 31:48), the judges that ruled when Israel had no king (Judges 3:10; 6:34 etc.) and David (1 Samuel 16:13; Psalm 51:11).

Pneuma:

Such 'ambiguity' is seen in the use of the words 'wind' and 'spirit' (*pneuma*) in the New Testament, where the Lord, speaking to Nicodemus says, "The wind (*pneuma*) blows where it pleases. You hear its sound, but you cannot tell where it comes from and where it is going. So it is with every one that is born of the Spirit (*pneuma*)" (John 3:8; cp. Ecclesiastes 11:5).

Hence it is important to distinguish between when the Scriptures are referring to "The Holy Spirit" and when it is used in another way, such as of 'a gift', given by Him. This should be clear by the simple use of a capital 'S' when referring to the The Holy Spirit, but as we shall see, it is sometimes not as easy as that. Hence, Bible versions and commentaries often differ over which it should be in specific cases.

C) Spirit/spirit and 'the calling to which you are called'

A second factor that is taken into consideration in this study is the need to differentiate between The Holy Spirit's ministry as it is relevant to *each and every* calling, in other words a 'foundational ministry', and His ministry towards those who are blessed in *specific* callings, who have different 'hopes'. This second factor draws a distinction between **a)** God's purpose for the earth, which is to come to fruition through Israel, and **b)** His purpose in the Church today, the Body of Christ, which is not dependent on Israel as a channel to declare God's salvation. This, I trust, will become clearer as we proceed.

Chapter 3.
The Holy Spirit and the world of 'men'

A) 'Man' and 'the natural man': Definitions

In this study, the words 'man' and 'men' in single quotes includes both male and female, a usage established in the opening chapter of the Scriptures when, "God created *man* in his own image ... *male and female* he created them" (Genesis 1:27).

And I use the term, 'Natural Man' of all 'men' without reference to their beliefs or way of life. Paul referred to such using the term, "in Adam", whereby all are *identified* with Adam in his death and *identified* with Christ in His resurrection. (1 Corinthians 15:22; cp. Romans 5:12-21).

B) The Holy Spirit and 'all men'

There is a tendency for Christians to consider the ministry of "the Holy Spirit" only in relation to believers. This might be inferred from Peter's words to his brethren on the Day of Pentecost: "Repent ... be baptised ... in the name of Jesus Christ for the forgiveness of your sins, and you will receive *the gift of the Holy Spirit*" (Acts 2:4,38). Does this teach that an individual has to be a believer before the Holy Spirit has anything to do with them? I think not.

As we will see, whilst the *gift* of the Holy Spirit spoken of here (it could be anything from the ability to "speak in other tongues", to any of the "spiritual gifts" listed in 1 Corinthians 12) *was given only to believers*, the Holy Spirit was involved in the lives of every 'son of Adam', believer or unbeliever.

Consider the following prophecy given to the disciples in John 16:8 when preparing them for their coming ministry. Jesus said:

> "When he (the Helper, *the Spirit truth*) comes, *he will convict the world* concerning sin and righteousness and judgement: concerning sin, because *they do not believe in me*; concerning righteousness, because I go to the Father and you will see me no longer; concerning judgement, because *the ruler of this world* is judged." (John 16:8-11)

Here, the promised Holy Spirit convicts 'the *world* of men'. The Greek *kosmos* 'world', is *defined* by E.W. Bullinger here as, "the abode of humanity, or that order of things in which humanity moves or of which 'man' is the centre" (*Critical Lexicon and Concordance*).

John has much to say of "the world" (*kosmos* 79 occurrences) in his Gospel. It was a 'world' into which the Messiah came; a world He had made but which did not recognise Him (1:10); a world (*kosmos*) under the control of "the ruler of this world" (John 14:30). Perhaps above all is the statement that "God so loved the world (*kosmos*), that he gave his only Son, that whoever believes in him should not perish but have eternal life" (John 3:16).

Another passage that bears upon this is John 12:27-31. In the context of "this hour", when Jesus foresaw the one great sacrifice that He was about to make for the world (*kosmos*) that God so loved He said:

> "Now is the judgement of *this world* (*kosmos*); now will the ruler of *this world* (*kosmos*) be cast out. And I, when I am lifted up from the earth, will draw *all people* to myself. He said this to show by what kind of death he was going to die."

When Jesus walked this earth, The Holy Spirit spoke through Him to many *unbelieving* Jews living in "this world". Later, that same Spirit was at work through the disciples who spoke to the wider world, to "all people", Jews and Gentiles believers and unbelievers. It is therefore wrong to consider the work of the Holy Spirit only in regard to Christians. The Holy Spirit's ministry is world-wide. The Lord is "not wishing that any should perish, but that ***all*** should reach repentance" (2 Peter 3:9).

C) The Holy Spirit in the man of dust

The Holy Spirit first appears in the Scriptures at the creation of this present earth; He was the 'prime mover'—"the Spirit of God was hovering (*KJV* 'moved') over the face of the waters" (Genesis 1:2). And it was He who gave life to the lifeless body of Adam and continues to do so for 'all men'. Consider the following Scriptures:

> The LORD God formed the man of dust from the ground and *breathed* into his nostrils *the breath of life*, and the man became *a living creature.* (Genesis 2:7)

> "In his hand (the LORD) is *the life of every living thing*, and *the breath of all mankind.*" (Job 12:10)

Of particular significance were Paul's words to the idolaters in Athens, where, speaking of "the God who made the world", he observed:

> "In him *we live and move and have our being.*" (Acts 17:28)

Paul made no difference between himself and the Athenians by using the word 'we', since all—believers, unbelievers, even idolaters—were included in the gift of life given to them by God. In fact Paul also drew attention to the 'oneness' of 'man', insofar that,

> "He made from one man every nation of mankind to live on all the face of the earth ... that they should seek God, in the hope that they might feel their way towards him and find him. Yet he is actually not far from each one of us." (Acts 17:26,27)

The Psalmist wrote:

> "O LORD, how manifold are your works! In wisdom you have made them all ... When you send forth your *Spirit* (*ruach*, margin "or breath") they are created." (Psalm 104:24,30)

Insofar that 'the spirit of life' is in all men, so the Holy Spirit is related to 'all men'.

But this is only half the story; when He takes it away, they die; "the spirit (*ruach*) returns to God who gave it" (Ecclesiastes 12:7). Formed from the

The Holy Spirit and His Ministry

dust of the earth, man was just flesh and bones. It was the "breath" of God that made him a "living soul (or creature)" (Genesis 1:26; 2:7). This earthly life was later forfeited through sin, and the withdrawal of that life is described as, "the *spirit* returns to God who gave it" (Ecclesiastes 12:7).

This 'life and death' situation can also be seen nationally in the experience of Israel. Judged by the LORD, they are seen in a vision by the prophet Ezekiel as "dry bones" in "The valley of dry bones". But the LORD promised the nation, "I will ... put *breath* (*ruach*) in you, and you shall live ... I will put *my Spirit* (*ruach*) within you, and you shall live" (Ezekiel 37:6,14).

D) The Holy Spirit: 'Man' and his conscience

Every 'man' has a conscience, or so it is believed; although it is difficult to believe that is true of some! Paul certainly believed that they do in Romans 2:14-16 when he referred to the Gentiles "who do not have the law (of Moses)", but had a conscience, a conscience that "bears witness" when they have conflicting thoughts. Hence, those who "do not have the law" can "*by nature* do what the law requires".

What is a conscience and where did it come from? The obvious answer is that, together with the ability to think and speak, 'man' was given a conscience, although it may have been dormant in Adam and Eve until that one act of disobedience triggered it into life.

Immediately following their disobedience, when our first parents "heard the sound of the LORD God walking in the garden in the cool of the day ... the man and his wife hid themselves from (His) presence"—they exhibited *all the evidence of a guilty conscience* (Genesis 2:16,17; 3:1-12). It was only then, that Adam and his wife "knew that they were naked" and tried to hide it with a bodily cover, and also "hid themselves from the presence of the LORD" (Genesis 3:7,8).

Alexander Cruden's definition of 'conscience' is as good as any I have come across:

> That faculty within us which decides as to the moral quality of our thoughts, words and acts. It gives consciousness of the good of one's conduct or motives, or causes feelings of remorse at evil-doing.

Cruden goes on to say that the conscience can be educated, or trained to recognise good and evil. Three verses of Scripture came to mind when I read this last statement:

> Before the boy knows how *to refuse the evil and choose the good* ... (Isaiah 7:16)

> Train up a child in *the way he should go*; even when he is old he will not depart from it. (Proverbs 22:6)

> Solid food is for the mature, for those who have their powers of discernment trained by constant practice *to distinguish good from evil.* (Hebrews 5:14)

Adam's sin was the result of desiring to partake of "the tree of the knowledge of good and evil", with the temptation that it was a tree "to be desired to make one wise"(Genesis 2:16,17; 3:6,7); the two opposites that underlie the three verses quoted above. As a person moves from childhood to adulthood, training is necessary for them to be able to choose good and eschew evil, not least by example. The first two quotations suggest that there is a point in life at which a child is able to make a decision as to right and wrong, and that 'training' is involved, the lessons learned remaining with the 'trainee' all their life.

The third quotation, using the example of weaning a child off mother's milk on to solid food, was directed by the Hebrews writer to Jewish believers urging them to move on from 'basic principles' and a 'foundational' repentance and to grow to maturity (Hebrews 5:12-14; 6:1). The word 'conscience' is not actually used in any of the above quotations, but it is implied in the ability to distinguish good from evil.

Such knowledge was withheld from our first parents in the Garden of Eden, but it was within reach in "the tree of the knowledge of good and evil". That tree was evidently put there, not just to test their obedience, but for a future day when they were 'mature' enough to cope with such knowledge. That they chose to disobey God and partake before they had reached that maturity was the biggest tragedy in the history of man (Genesis 2:9; 3:1-7). So what is the relationship between conscience that all possess, and the work of the Holy Spirit in the believer?

E) 'Conscience': The word as used in the Scriptures

In the New Testament the word 'conscience' is associated with various aspects of life. It may reflect different degrees of morals and be influenced by outside forces and circumstances; what we learn in word and deed from our parents and others, what we read, and (today) what we hear or see on the media. In the New Testament we read of[9]:

A good conscience	A perfect conscience	A pure conscience
A witnessing conscience	A weak conscience	A wounded conscience
An evil conscience	A defiled conscience	A seared conscience
A convicting conscience	An accusing conscience	An excusing conscience

The King James translators never used the English word 'conscience' when translating the Old Testament, although they did use the word many times in the New. Other versions have used the English word in both Testaments. In the Old Testament, the terms, "the fear of God" and "the fear of the LORD", seem to connect with the idea of the conscience.

The *NIV* translators use the word 'conscience' in Genesis 20:5,6, on the occasion when Abraham told king Abimelech that Sarah was his sister, not his wife, which led to the king pleading his good conscience. Misled by Abraham, the king "took" Sarah.

The truth came to light after God had spoken to the king warning that his life could be forfeited because he had taken a man's wife. But, having been deceived he said to the LORD, "I have done this with *a clear conscience* and clean hands". The *KJV* and the *ESV* have here, "in *the integrity of my heart* and the innocence of my hands I have done this". He had acted in all good faith; his conscience was clear.

In the New Testament, Paul, testifying before the Council in Jerusalem said, "I have lived my life before God *in all good conscience up to this day*" (Acts 23:1), and later in Caesarea before Felix he said, "I always take pains (strive) to have *a clear conscience* towards both God and man"

(Acts 24:16). He claimed that having a clear conscience was true of him both before and after he became a Christian.

The conscience of an unbeliever may lead them to live 'a good Christian life', without acknowledging Jesus Christ as Saviour. Paul acted according to his conscience in his pre-Christian days, even as "a persecutor of the church". He could write in all good conscience that he was, "under the law, blameless" (Philippians 3:6), and to Timothy he said, "formerly I was a ... persecutor ... I received mercy because I had acted ignorantly in unbelief" (1 Timothy 1:13).

But praise God, Christians can rest on the truth that, "the blood of Christ, who *through the eternal Spirit* offered himself without blemish to God", *cleanses the conscience* "from dead works to serve the living God" (Hebrews 9:14).

Our modern idea of 'conscience' comes to us through Greek thought and is not always seen as related to God. In the Scriptures it always is. In all its occurrences in the New Testament it is the Greek word, *suneidesis*, literally, 'to see or know together', 'co-perception'. There are 32 references to this word here, mostly in Paul's writings, but also in Hebrews where it is applied to the sacrifices required, year by year on the Day of Atonement.

They served only as a "reminder of sins" but never satisfied "the conscience" in respect of sin: if they had, it would not have been necessary to continually offer them. Those animal sacrifices, just types and shadows, are contrasted with the one sacrifice of Christ that sanctifies "through the offering of the body of Jesus Christ *once for all*" (Hebrews 10:1-10).

So the conscience, whilst it is not described as a 'law', does work in conjunction with given laws that are to be obeyed. It is seen at work in Adam and in the Gentiles who do not have the law but who, by nature, do the things contained in it. And it worked alongside the laws given to Israel who had the Ten Commandments; a covenant between them and God.

The Holy Spirit and His Ministry

F) Conscience: 'Light' and 'responsibility'

Our actions in this life are largely (if not totally) conditioned by how we react to our conscience. As already noted, Paul assumes everyone has a conscience. But it is evidently possible to have a conscience that has been deadened, such as Paul referred to in respect of some in his own day: "Liars whose consciences are seared with a hot iron" (1 Timothy 4:2 *KJV*), but generally, as for example when Paul referred to the Gentiles "who do not have the law", he assumes that all have a conscience. That conscience "bears witness" as a kind of arbiter when there are conflicting thoughts in a person's mind. Hence, those who "do not have the law" can "*by nature* do what the law requires", and hence, on that day when "the secrets of men" are revealed at the judgement of God, can be judged fairly.

This seems to be a general principle of the way that God deals with mankind, a judgement that is based upon how much 'light' an individual has. The more we know, the greater *our responsibility*, and the greater will be *our accountability* to God.

Prior to Paul's words in Romans on the conscience of Gentiles, he has given an example of some who were not lacking in 'light' but who nevertheless chose to "suppress the truth". This is an example of the principle; 'responsibility begets accountability', and consequently, judgement. We might wonder about the conscience of the men Paul is referring to here:

> The wrath of God is revealed from heaven against all ungodliness and unrighteousness of men, *who* by their unrighteousness *suppress the truth*. For *what can be known about God is plain to them, because God has shown it to them.* For his invisible attributes, namely his eternal power and divine nature, *have been clearly perceived*, ever since the creation of the world, *in the things that have been made. So they are without excuse.* (Romans 1:18-20)

These verses are part of a longer passage that stretches from 1:18 to 1:32. To understand the enormity of the sin of these men and the consequences, the whole passage should be read. Three times we read that they *exchanged* God's wisdom for a 'wisdom' of their own, and three times that He therefore, "gave them up":

The Holy Spirit and His Ministry

i) They knew God but did not honour him as the immortal God ... they *exchanged* His glory for idolatry.
> God gave them up to ... lusts of their hearts ... impurity ... dishonouring of their bodies.

ii) They *exchanged* the truth about God for a lie.
> God gave them up to dishonourable passions ... shameless acts.

iii) They did not see fit to acknowledge God
> God gave them up to ... a debased mind ... doing what not ought to be done.

And the final judgement is pronounced: "Though they knew God's decree that those who practice such things deserve to die, they not only do them but give approval to those who practice them" (Romans 1:32).

See more on this passage in the author's *Paul's Letter to the Romans* OBT (pages 45,46) where I suggested that this passage might look back to Babel and the rebellion there.

G) Three categories of 'man'

'Man' may be looked upon under three 'heads' who have emerged since the fall of Adam.

> **(i)** those who believe in God's only Son.
> **(ii)** those who do not believe in Him. (John 3:16)

But the Scriptures suggest a third category:

> iii) Those multitudes *who have never heard of His Son and the good news about Him*, and hence have never had the opportunity to believe or disbelieve. (Romans 2:14-16)

Expanding this we read:

> "When Gentiles, who do not have the law, *do by nature what the law requires*, they are a law to themselves, even though they do not have the law. They show that *the work of the law is written on their hearts*, while *their conscience also bears witness, and their conflicting thoughts accuse or even excuse them* on that day when, according to my gospel, God judges the secrets of men

by Jesus Christ."

Although this passage had specific reference to the Jew/Gentile situation during the Acts Period, underlying it there is a principle here that is universal and relevant to all ages and callings. It is that reaction to one's conscience, influenced by the 'light' and responsibility they have received, is taken into consideration in any final judgement on an individual.

H) Conscience and The Holy Spirit

The conscience is spoken of in the Scriptures as being something different from the Holy Spirit, but as working together in the individual with Him. Here is Paul's testimony to his own conscience at work in himself and its relation to the Holy Spirit:

- **Paul to the Council in Jerusalem:** "Brethren, I have lived my life before God *in all good conscience* up to this day" (Acts 23:1).
- **Paul to Felix in Caesarea:** "I always take pains to have *a clear conscience* towards both God and man" (Acts 24:16).
- **Paul to the Roman Christians:** "*The Spirit himself* bears witness with *our spirit* that we are children of God" (Romans 8:16).
- **Paul to the Roman Jews:** "I am not lying; *my conscience bears me witness in the Holy Spirit* ... I have sorrow ... unceasing anguish ... for the sake of my brethren, my kinsmen according to the flesh ..." (Romans 9:1-3).
- **Paul to the Roman Christians (Jew and Gentile):** "Be subject to the governing bodies ... instituted by God ... not only to avoid God's wrath but also *for the sake of conscience*" (Romans 13:1,5).

There are two 'spirits' here; "the Spirit of God" and "our spirit" and both 'influence' the conscience. Although we would not speak of God as having a conscience, "our spirit" is almost a synonym for "our conscience". Our spirit is *who and what we really are,* seen or unseen. And that is largely conditioned by what our conscience dictates; how we live our daily lives.

However, for the believer there is another factor to be considered; the presence of the "Spirit of God" *indwelling* him or her (Romans 8:9). And the Holy Spirit "bears witness" with our "spirit" and *acts together with* our conscience as an 'arbiter' within.

A person's conscience is conditioned by many outside influences, but in the believer the Holy Spirit exerts His influence also. In Romans 8:9 Paul makes the bald statement that defines the Christian (and the unbeliever) once and for all. Confident that the Romans he is addressing are bona fide Christians, he writes:

> "You, however, are not in the flesh but in the Spirit, if in fact the Spirit of God dwells in you. Anyone who does not have the Spirit of Christ does not belong to him."

This is probably the most direct statement made by Paul that defines a Christian and a non-Christian—the dwelling or not of the Holy Spirit within, having or lacking "the Spirit of Christ". For Paul the indwelling Spirit and the Spirit of Christ are one and the same. "It is implied that possession of the Spirit is the common denominator of all who belong to Christ, not the special prerogative of some over against the rest." And in respect of the conscience, the presence of the Holy Spirit in the believer "has become the most important factor at the level of primary *motivation and enabling*" (James D.G. Dunn *Word Biblical Commentary* in loco).

When prior to His resurrection and ascension, the Messiah spoke to the apostles of the coming of the Holy Spirit, He promised that He would send to them another "Helper" (Comforter *KJV*). He was "the Spirit of Truth, whom the world cannot receive" (John 14:16,17). If "the world" here is taken as the world of unbelief, we might remember that the unbeliever has a conscience that may lead him/her to become a great philanthropist or even to lay down their life for their country or friends (John 15:13); especially for a just cause. We cannot dismiss this as counting for nothing before God because he/she is not a Christian.

The Christian has no monopoly on good works or martyrdom. The Christian is not alone in doing good works; the unbeliever may match the Christian, good work for good work, the difference being that it is the conscience that influences the unbeliever's actions, but the conscience *plus* the influence of the Holy Spirit, "the Spirit of truth", that drives the Christian. It is this fact that makes the difference between the believer and the unbeliever.

The 'natural man' has a conscience influenced by factors like upbringing, teaching and the beliefs of others, and his experiences in everyday life. On the other hand, the believer (i.e., the one who has "received" Jesus Christ, John 1:12) who has the indwelling of the Spirit of God, is 'twice blessed', not only with a conscience, but in that "*The Spirit himself* bears witness with *our spirit* that we are children of God" (Romans 8:16).

Here lies the heart of the Holy Spirit's ministry in all ages and dispensations. (I think it was John Wesley who spoke of the Christian as having "the inward witness".) Such a 'witness' is especially relevant for us today in a calling whose hope is in "the heavenly places" (Ephesians 1:3).

Chapter 4.
The Spirit of God and the Word of God

The connection between "the Spirit of God" and "the Word of God", and to a lesser degree, between 'spirit' and 'word', is perhaps the most important connection revealed in the Scriptures. That connection is particularly important for the believer today to understand, who lives under a calling that is without the "signs and wonders" of the Acts Period. It appears on the first page of the Scriptures where such a relationship is suggested (Genesis 1:1-26):

> In the beginning, God created the heavens and the earth.
> The earth was without form and void,
>   and darkness was over the face of the deep.
> And *the Spirit of God* was hovering over the face of the waters.
> And *God said*, "Let there be … light ... expanse ... earth ... life."
> Then *God said*, "Let us make man in our image, after our likeness."

If the words, "without form and void" refer to the judgement of a previous creation on this earth,[10] we might wonder whether God was hesitating to begin again! Some believe that the state of the earth at this point in time ("without form and void") was the result of a previous creation, destroyed by the judgement of God, and referred to by Peter as "the world that then was". He contrasted it with, "the heavens and earth which are now", and which await the day of judgement by fire (2 Peter 3:5-7, 10,11). As Isaiah said (45:18), the LORD did not create the (original) earth formless and empty, it became so as a result of His judgement upon a previous creation. *The Companion Bible* suggests further that "Fossils and Remains", found from time to time, belong to this previous creation (Genesis 1:2 *in loco*).

Over this dark and lifeless world, *the Spirit of God* "hovered", waiting in anticipation for *the Word of God*—and it came—**God said**,

The Holy Spirit and His Ministry

"Let there be light", and there was light. And God saw that the light was good. And God separated the light from the darkness. God called the light Day, and the darkness he called Night. And there was evening and there was morning, the first day ... "Let there be an expanse ... dry land ... life ... man" ... and it was so. (Genesis 1:3-30)

The opening of John's Gospel looks back to this time when it records (John 1:1-14):

> In the beginning was the Word
> > and the Word was with God,
> > and the Word was God ...
> All things were made through him ...
> In him was life and the life was
> > the light of men ...
> and the Word became flesh and dwelt among us.

In Genesis we have God and *the Spirit of God*; in John we have God, the Word of God and *the Spirit of God* who descended upon Jesus, authenticating Him as the Son of God who came to "dwell among us" as the Messiah (1:14, 32-34). The relationship of Jesus, *the Word of God* (who speaks *the words of God*) to *the Holy Spirit*, is further emphasised by John the Baptist who exalted the Messiah as the Son of God:

> "He whom God has sent utters *the words of God*, for he gives *the Spirit* without measure. The Father loves the Son and has given all things into his hand." (John 3:34,35)

As we proceed, we find that there are many Scriptures that link *the Spirit of God* to the Word and words of God. This makes the Scriptures, that are "*breathed out* by God" (2 Timothy 3:16 *ESV*), a most important part of our Christian life. We are bidden, "Be filled by *the Spirit*" in Ephesians 5:18, and in the parallel passage in Colossians 3:16 we read, "Let the word of Christ dwell in you richly. (The relationship between these two Scriptures is considered later.)

Chapter 5.
The Holy Spirit in the Old Testament

The ministry of the Holy Spirit did not begin in the New Testament. He did not confer his 'gifts' upon His people for the first time on the Day of Pentecost. We read of His activity from the very beginning of creation; there He is referred to as "the Spirit of God." Also, just as The LORD "changes not" (Malachi 3:6) and Jesus "is the same yesterday today and forever" (Hebrews 13:8), so the Holy Spirit does not change. *Our understanding* of Him may deepen and change as we observe the unfolding of God's Word, learn more of His ministry and observe how He sometimes ministers differently to mankind in different callings, but He remains the same—He is "the eternal Spirit" (Hebrew 9:14).

The Holy Spirit's ministry in the Old Testament is largely confined to specific individuals or small groups of prophets, and this is much in contrast to the New Testament where, especially after Pentecost, His ministry is widespread amongst all believers as we shall see. Even there His ministry varies in some respects towards a people whose hope lies in earthly blessings promised to Abraham and his seed (Genesis 12:1-3: Acts 3:25) and those blessed "in the heavenly places" (Ephesians 1:3; 2:6). Both of these callings are part of the Holy Spirit's ministry and must not be confused together as though they are one and the same. More on this later.)

In the *KJV* version of the Old Testament, "Holy Spirit" occurs only three times[11]; the term "The Spirit of God" seems to have been preferred when referring to Him. That the two refer to the same 'Person' is confirmed when we read of "The Spirit of God" in Genesis 1:2 (Septuagint *LXX*), and "the Spirit of God" who dwells in the believer in Romans 8:9.

> The Spirit of God (*pneuma theou*) was hovering over the face of the waters. (Genesis 1:2)

> You ... are not in the flesh but in the Spirit, if in fact the Spirit of God (*pneuma theou*) dwells in you. (Romans 8:9)

A) The Spirit of God: Pre-Moses

"The Spirit of God" was at work in the creation (Job 26:13; Psalm 33:6) and He also gives newness of life to the believer. He was the agent when, "The LORD God formed man of dust from the ground and breathed into his nostrils ... the breath of the *spirit of life*", and "the man became a living creature" (Genesis 2:7; see also 6:17; 7:15,22 lit.). The Spirit of God gave life to Adam and to all "in Adam", as Paul said to the Athenian idolaters:

> "The God who made the world and everything in it, being Lord of heaven and earth ... gives to all mankind life and breath (*pnoen*) and everything ... 'In him we live and move and have our being', as even some of your own poets have said, 'for we are indeed his offspring.'". (Acts 17:24-28)

The ministry of the Spirit of God/the Holy Spirit, begins on the first pages of the Scriptures. He is introduced as brooding/ moving over the dark primeval waters that covered the earth, and that led to the forming of the present earth "by the word of God" (Genesis 1:3; 2 Peter 3:5). On this earth God put creatures in whom was the breath of God, of which man was the zenith.

"The Spirit of God", "the Spirit of the LORD" and "My Spirit" are all terms used in the Old Testament that have been preferred to "the Holy Spirit" and occur more frequently there. We have already seen the first of these used in relation to the creation in Genesis 1:2. "My Spirit" then occurs some 1650 years later in Genesis 6:3, where the LORD, seeing the wickedness of man in the days of Noah, said: "My Spirit shall not contend with (*ESV* margin[12]) man for ever, for he is flesh: his days shall be 120 years." This fixed the date of the Flood.[13]

The LORD is seen here "striving" (*KJV*) with man and his wickedness, and He prophesies, "*My Spirit* shall not abide in man for ever". He gives mankind 120 years of grace (presumably to give them a chance to change their ways) before the great Flood inundated the earth, and "all flesh died that moved on the earth ... everything in whose nostrils was the *breath of life*" (Genesis 6:1-3, 17; 7:15, 21-23). Only Noah and those with him in the Ark survived. Noah stepped out on to the 'cleansed' earth, and from then on references to "the Spirit of God" are mainly associated with His 'gifts' to individuals.

In the Patriarchal period the only reference to "the Spirit of God" was when Joseph was recognised by Pharaoh as a man, "in whom is *the Spirit of God*" (Genesis 41:38).

B) The Spirit of God: Post-Moses

As I have noted (above) in the Old Testament *KJV* version, "Holy Spirit" occurs only three times. It was used by David in his prayer of repentance after being convicted by Nathan of his adultery with Bathsheba and (effectively) the 'murder' of her husband, Uriah the Hittite. David pleaded with God:

> "Cast me not away from your presence, and take not *your Holy Spirit* from me." (Psalm 51:11)

"The Spirit of the LORD" had come upon David when he was chosen from amongst Jesse's sons to reign over Israel, and the Spirit remained with him. Now, condemned by his actions, he feared that the Spirit would be taken away from him, as that had happened to Saul when he had been rejected (1Samuel 10:1-6; 11:6; 16:13,14).

The only other passage where "Holy Spirit" is used (twice) is Isaiah 63:10,11. It looks back to the generation of Israel during Moses' time who "grieved (God's) *Holy Spirit*" (*ESV*) in the wilderness, when "*the Holy Spirit* ... dwelt in their midst" (*ESV*):

> They rebelled and *grieved his Holy Spirit*; therefore he turned to be their enemy, and himself fought against them. Then he remembered the days of old, of Moses and his people. "Where is he who brought them up out of the sea with the shepherds of his flock? Where is he who put in the midst of them *his Holy Spirit*?"

Although there can be no doubt that the LORD dwelt in the midst of His people, firstly in the Tabernacle and then in the Temple, Moses was given a special 'gift of the Holy Spirit' that enabled him, as a shepherd of his flock, to lead Israel from Egypt to the borders of The Promised Land. (See below for others who were given special gifts during this period.)

The rebellion of Israel in the wilderness is described in Psalm 78:40,41 as grieving and provoking "the Holy One of Israel", a term used many times in the Old Testament. (Later, in our own dispensation, it is still possible to "grieve the Holy Spirit of God"; Ephesians 4:30.)

C) Old Testament gifts of the Spirit

As noted (above) one of the more obvious things about the Holy Spirit's ministry in the Old Testament is that it seems to have been largely confined to specific individuals or small groups of men (prophets). This is in contrast to the New Testament where, following Pentecost, His ministry is widespread amongst all believers.

In the Old Testament, "the Spirit of God/the LORD" is said to have been in Joseph, where Pharaoh said to his servants, "Can we find a man like this, in whom is the Spirit of God?". This 'gift' enabled him to take charge of all Egypt's affairs, holding a position second only to Pharaoh (Genesis 41:38-44).

In Moses' day, the LORD gave gifts to various men who were involved in the making of the furniture for the Tabernacle and its erection. He said to Moses:

> "I have called by name Bezalel ... of the tribe of Judah, and I have *filled him with the Spirit of God,* with ability and intelligence, with knowledge and all craftsmanship ... to work in every craft ... I have appointed with him Oholiab ... of the tribe of Dan ... I have given to all able men ability, that they may make all that I have commanded you ... the Tabernacle ... the ark of the testimony ... the mercy seat ... the furnishings ..." (Exodus 31:1-8: see also 35:30-35)

The coming of "the Spirit of God" upon a craftsman and other able men, *endued them* with both the knowledge and the skill to do their work to a standard fit for the LORD Himself; the mercy seat and even down to the furnishings. He "filled them with skill to do every sort of work", whether it be artistic designs, working in gold and silver, cutting stones, embroidery or weaving (Exodus 35:30-35). Here is a lesson for us today, that only the best is good enough for the Lord, the 'best', that is, that we can do, inspired by the fact that it is for Him.

The Ark of the Covenant, and later the Temple itself with all its furniture, had to be of the highest quality, and if they were to be consecrated to the LORD, needed the very best men to work on them "in every craft"; it was not just animal sacrifices that had to be "without spot or blemish". (Was something of this 'spirit' behind the building of magnificent cathedrals dedicated to the Christian worship of God?)

The Spirit of God gave certain men in Moses' day the knowledge and ability to produce such magnificence—He was "the Giver". In our own day, although some do acknowledge the 'gift' they have is "God's gift", all Christians should use their 'gifts' in His service to "glorify the Lord" (John 16:13,14).

D) Anointing, the Spirit of the LORD and "The Lord's anointed"

'Messiah' (the anointed One) is a translation of the Hebrew word *mashiach* and the Greek word *Messias*. It is translated as such only twice in the *KJV* Old Testament, and in some versions (e.g. *ESV, NIV*) "an anointed one" (Daniel 9:25 & 26). It occurs only twice in the New Testament in its Aramaic form, "Messias" *KJV* and "Messiah" *ESV* (John 1:41; 4:25). The Hebrew *mashiach* actually occurs some 40 times in the Old Testament, and is used of Prophets, Priests and Kings[14].

In the Greek translation of the Old Testament *(LXX)* it is always translated by the word *christos:* Saul was "the LORD's *anointed*" and David, "the *anointed* of the God of Israel" (1 Samuel 12:3,5; 2 Samuel 5:3). It is also used of Cyrus, king of Persia who was, in a sense, a 'redeemer' of Israel (Isaiah 45:1,13): "Thus says the LORD to *his anointed*, to Cyrus ... He shall build my city and set my exiles free".

Saul and David were given, *by the Spirit*, the authority and the ability to rule over God's people, 'gifts' which were signified by 'anointing', but the most significant anointing of all was that of the Lord himself. The same "Spirit of the LORD" who anointed Saul and David (1 Samuel 10:1-6; 16:12,13) also anointed Jesus, who is "the LORD's anointed", the Messiah[15]. Old Testament prophecies looked forward to Him in that office and recognised Him as the Son of God.

In Psalm 2:2, "the kings of the earth ... and the rulers take counsel together,

The Holy Spirit and His Ministry

against the LORD and *his Anointed*"; a passage that resonated in the prayer of the believers gathered together after the release of Peter and John from before the Council in Jerusalem (Acts 4:25,26 see 10:38).

Another reference to the Messiah quoted in the New Testament is Isaiah 61:1, a passage read out by Jesus himself in the synagogue in Nazareth and which He applied to Himself. He read from the scroll:

> "*The Spirit of the Lord God* is upon me, because *the LORD has anointed me* to bring good news to the poor; he has sent me to bind up the broken-hearted, to proclaim liberty to the captives, and the opening of the prison to those who are bound; to proclaim the year of the LORD's favour ..." (Luke 4:18,19)

At this point Jesus rolled up the scroll indicating that He was finished. In fact, He had left out the next part of this passage that spoke of "the day of vengeance of our God". By this action He indicated that "the year of the LORD's favour" was upon His hearers, and that *He was "the LORD's anointed"*. These were "the days of the Messiah"[16]; the next part of this passage referred to the day of judgement which was still future.

Isaiah 61:1,2 (quoted above) is a particularly significant usage of the word 'anointed' where the emphasis is on the Messiah as a prophet, proclaiming the blessings that accompanied His presence among them, but with the added warning that a day of vengeance would follow. Jesus was claiming that since this prophecy was *now being fulfilled*— "Today"—**He** was the promised "Anointed (One)", the promised Messiah.

However, the year was acceptable (*dektos* lit. 'welcome') to the LORD, but Jesus was not 'acceptable' to His brethren; "no prophet is acceptable in his home town". He was eventually driven out of the town, and an attempt made on His life, but which failed (Luke 4:24-30).

Chapter 6
The Holy Spirit between the Testaments

> Zedekiah ... did what was evil in the sight of the LORD his God ... all the officers and the priests likewise were exceeding unfaithful ... they polluted the house of the LORD that he had made holy in Jerusalem ... they kept mocking the messengers of God, despising his words and scoffing at his prophet, until the wrath of the LORD rose against his people, until there was no remedy. (2 Chronicles 36:11-16)

These words occur on the last page of the Hebrew Bible. They sum up the situation that existed when the last king of Israel (Zedekiah) ruled over the kingdom of Israel (specifically Judah). He reigned in Jerusalem for eleven years, and together with the authorities and the people, incited "the wrath of the LORD ... **until there was no remedy**". The result was that "The LORD rose against his people" and allowed the Babylonians to burn the Temple, destroy its precious vessels and break down the walls of Jerusalem. Many of the people were taken into exile.

So began that long period during which the people of Israel were dominated by Babylon, then Persia, Greece and, when the New Testament opens, under the dominance of Rome. Records relating to Israel's history made during this period, are not accepted by the Jews into the Hebrew Canon, nor considered by many Christians to be part of the Word of God, as the other books of the Hebrew Bible are[17].

However, this period of Israel's history is recorded in the Apocryphal books and they are included in some Bibles, but not considered by many as part of the God-breathed Scriptures. The prophecy of Malachi is therefore generally considered by many Christians to close the Old

Testament writings, and no further prophet sent by God arose for over 300 years, until John the Baptist appeared in the wilderness of Judea. Malachi prophesied:

> "Behold, I send my messenger, and he will prepare the way before me. And the Lord whom you seek will suddenly come to his temple; and the messenger of the covenant in whom you delight, behold, he is coming, says the LORD of hosts." (Malachi 3:1)

What of the Holy Spirit during this period between the close of the Old Testament and the opening of the New? It is difficult to believe, given the LORD's words in Jeremiah 31:35-37, where He compares *the permanence of His care for Israel* with *the permanence of the universe*, that the Holy Spirit was inactive. There are few occurrences of the Greek *pneuma*, however, in the Apocryphal books. Here are some examples.

> The holy *spirit* of discipline will flee deceit and remove from thoughts that are without understanding, and will not abide when unrighteousness comes in ... wisdom is a loving *spirit* ... The Spirit of the Lord fills the world. (*The Wisdom of Solomon* 1:5,6,7)

Could this final reference be to **The** Holy Spirit? It could well be so.

In *2 Maccabees* 14:46 there is a reference to "the LORD of life and *spirit*"; in *4 Maccabees* 7:14 we read of "a *spirit* of reasoning" and in *4 Maccabees* 11:11 of one whose "*breath* ... is confined".

Chapter 7.
The Holy Spirit in the New Testament

A) Background and context of the New Testament

The Scriptures encompass God's twofold purpose, for 'the earth' and 'the heavenly places far above all'. It goes without saying that these need to be distinguished, and so does the ministry of the Holy Spirit. But, as I have already noted, the LORD "changes not" (Malachi 3:6) and Jesus "is the same yesterday today and forever" (Hebrews 13:8). That permanence is also true of the Holy Spirit. *Our understanding* of Him may deepen and change as we observe the unfolding of God's Word, learn more of His ministry and observe how He sometimes ministers differently to mankind in different callings, but He remains the same—He is "the eternal Spirit" (Hebrew 9:14).

The fulfilment of both aspects of God's purposes for mankind was of course only made possible by the one sacrifice, "once for all" of Jesus Christ (Hebrews 7:27). To illustrate the difference between the two spheres within which the ministry of the Holy Spirit is revealed in the Scriptures, here is a brief outline of the two.

Timeline:

Purpose for the earth: Abraham to end of Acts, 1876 B.C. to A.D. 61 (dates approximate).

> **Scriptures:** Genesis 12 to Acts 28; Old Testament, Gospels, Acts of the Apostles, letters written *during Acts*.
> Jewish: James, Peter (2), John (3), Jude, Hebrews, Revelation.
> Pauline: Romans, Corinthians (2), Galatians, Thessalonians (2).

Purpose: The salvation and *blessing of all mankind on earth* through Abraham's seed and the nation of Israel.

Scriptures:
- "The LORD said to Abram ... I will make of you a great nation ... and in you all families of the earth will be blessed" (Genesis 12:1-3).
- "I, (the Lord), have made you (Jews) a light for the Gentiles, that you may bring salvation to the ends of the earth" (Acts 13:47; Isaiah 49:6).
- "Salvation is of the Jews" (John 4:22).

Purpose for the heavenly places: After A.D. 61. Post-Acts and release of Paul (?) to death A.D. 64 to 68.

Scriptures: Letters written *post-Acts 28* by Paul: (Prison) Ephesians, Philippians, Colossians, Philemon, (Freedom) 1 Timothy, Titus, (Reimprisonment) 2 Timothy.

Purpose: The salvation and *blessing of the Church which is the Body of Christ.*

Scriptures:
- "Blessed be the God and Father of our Lord Jesus Christ who has blessed us in Christ with every spiritual blessing in the heavenly places" (Ephesians 1:3).
- "By grace you have been saved ... God ... raised us up with him (Christ) and seated us with him in the heavenly places" (Ephesians 2:5,6).
- "Your life is hidden with Christ in God. When Christ who is your life appears, then you also will appear with him in glory" (Colossians 3:3,4).

Looking back over the Old Testament that occupies some 4000 years of scriptural history, it may seem that *the Spirit of God* was not very active during this time. But if we take Israel's history alone, beginning with Abraham, the LORD is constantly watching over His people and speaking to them through the prophets many times. They were moved by *the Holy Spirit* to speak the word of God; blessing, chiding, warning, judging (Hebrews 1:1; cp. Ezekiel 2:1-7; Zechariah 7:8-12; Acts 28:25; 1 Peter 1:10-12).

Two facts emerge from the closing stages of the Old Testament that must influence our understanding of the ministry of *the Holy Spirit* in the New.

> i) Israel had *lost their kingdom* to Gentile powers who now controlled and dominated their lives.
>
> ii) Malachi's prophecy, promising the coming of the Lord, preceded by His "messenger" to prepare the way, remained unfulfilled. The "messenger" was identified later in that prophecy as "Elijah the prophet" (Malachi 3:1; 4:5).

The first of these found its expression in the question the apostles asked Jesus just before His ascension: "Lord, will you at this time *restore the kingdom* to Israel?" (Acts 1:6). This is one of the most important questions raised in the whole of the New Testament, and interpretations of it that do not take it literally have led to a misunderstanding of the Acts of the Apostles.[18]

B) The restoration of the kingdom to Israel

Israel's kingdom 'died' with the death of its last king, Zedekiah, and when our Lord came to the earth Israel was under the Roman yoke, but with many looking for the Messiah who would deliver them from it. That 'hope' was bound up in The Lord's Prayer which asked of the Father, "your kingdom come, your will be done, on earth as it is in heaven" (Matthew 6:9.10). They were praying for an earthly kingdom where God's will prevailed as it did in heaven. Such 'a kingdom' was later defined in the apostles' question to Jesus just before He ascended to heaven: "Lord, will you at this time *restore the kingdom to Israel*?"

The apostles were not rebuked for having completely misunderstood the Lord's mission, as some people think they should have been. Are we expected to believe that they learnt nothing from His 2 to 3 years of teaching whilst with them, and the "forty days" during which He spoke to them about "the kingdom of God" (Acts 1:3)? The Lord's reply was not a rebuke but, "It is not for you to know times and seasons that the Father has fixed by his own authority." (Acts 1:6,7). That Israel's 'kingdom' would be restored was not in question, but the 'timing' of it was.

Further light is thrown on the 'hope' of Israel's restored 'kingdom' when we see how Paul described it to Agrippa:

> "I stand here on trial because of my hope in the promise made by God to our fathers, to which our twelve tribes hope to attain, as they earnestly worship night and day." (Acts 26:6,7)

Those twelve tribes would be settled in their allotted portion of The Promised Land, according to the closing chapters of Ezekiel (which see). In this 'new world', when the Messiah sits on His throne of glory, the twelve apostles would sit on twelve thrones judging the tribes of Israel, as promised by the Lord Himself when on earth (Matthew 19:28). These two facts are very much part of "the hope of Israel" (Acts 20:20) and Israel will recognise Jesus as their Messiah. That day will be heralded by His return to the Mount of Olives, from which He left shortly after the question concerning the restoration of the kingdom to Israel:

> Behold, he is coming with the clouds, and every eye will see him, even those who pierced him, and all tribes of the Land will wail because of him. (Revelation 1:7; see Zechariah 12:10-13:1)

It is against this background that the Gospel and Acts Periods should be understood: the restoration of Israel's kingdom and the coming of the Messiah to redeem the nation—"the hope of Israel". Two verses of Scripture in particular emphasise this belief. Those two disciples who met Jesus on the road to Emmaus, said to Him, as they thought back over the events of the last days:

> "We had hoped that he was *the one to redeem Israel*." (Luke 24:21)

And the apostles who accompanied Jesus to the Mount of Olives, from where He was about to ascend into heaven, asked Him the question:

> "Lord, will you at this time *restore the kingdom to Israel*?" (Acts 1:6)

The second 'fact' (above) was raised by the priests and Levites sent from Jerusalem to where John was baptising. Who was he? What authority did he have? Was he the Messiah?

The expectations of the Jews at the opening of the New Testament, based on the prophecy of Malachi and other prophecies, influence and help to explain all that is recorded of the Gospel and Acts Period, and are a key to understanding those periods. They can be summed up in the words, "The Hope of Israel". What was that hope? It can be defined by

- the expectations of those living at the time,
- the work of *the Holy Spirit* in their lives, and
- other references to that 'hope' in the New Testament.

C) Expectancy of the coming of the Messiah

The period just prior to the birth and coming of Jesus the Messiah, was a time when the thoughts and hopes of some (perhaps many) Jews turned to the expectancy that He was soon to come to His people (cp Luke 2:36-38). This expectancy was realised by the presence of *the Holy Spirit* in the lives of four people recorded by Luke in his Gospel:

- **Zechariah** was told that his wife, who was "advanced in years", would have a son who would be *"filled with the Holy Spirit*, even from his mother's womb". This was fulfilled in the birth of **John the Baptist** (1:15).   Whilst naming that son "John", he was himself *filled with the Holy Spirit"* (1:67).
- **Mary** was told by the angel Gabriel that *the Holy Spirit would come upon her* and her firstborn would be named Jesus—"the Son of God" (1:35).
- **Elizabeth** was *"filled with the Holy Spirit"* during Mary's visit to her (1:41).
- **Simeon**, was a righteous man who was looking for the coming of the Messiah. *The Holy Spirit came upon him* with the promise that he would see the expected One before his death, and he did (2:25-28).

The 'hope' of the people of Israel, made real in the lives of those mentioned here by the activity of the Holy Spirit, was to be realised by the coming of the Messiah. They all actually saw Him. But what was their 'hope'?

With hindsight, we know that at the end of His earthly ministry, Jesus of Nazareth Himself, led by the Holy Spirit to do the will of the Father (John 14:25,26; 16:12-15), was rejected and crucified. That 'hope' died for some—"We had hoped that he was the one to redeem Israel" (Luke 24:21), but made alive again by the resurrection of the Messiah, and to this the Acts of the Apostles testifies. But with the second rejection by the nation of Israel and the judgement of God that followed (Acts 28:25-28), that 'hope' remains to this day in abeyance.

Chapter 8
The Holy Spirit in the Synoptic Gospels

> When the fullness of time had come, God sent forth his Son, born of woman, born under the law, to redeem those who were under the law. (Galatians 4:4)

Chronologically, the first references in the New Testament to *The Holy Spirit* that relate to the 'hope' of the people "who were under the law", i.e. the 'hope of Israel', occur in the opening chapters of Luke's and Matthew's Gospels. They concentrate our thoughts on the One who is coming to make the fulfilment of that 'hope' possible—the long-awaited Messiah. In the first instance He *is* that 'hope', and in these references we read of the promise of His 'coming', His birth and His preparation for the ministry that lies ahead. For the purpose of this study I have divided the four Gospels into two parts:

> i) Matthew, Mark and Luke. Since much of the records in these Gospels covers the same events and teaching of the Lord, they have been dubbed 'the Synoptics' by commentators.

> ii) John's Gospel, where even a casual reader might notice how different much of this record is from the other three in content and presentation.

This has led to the belief that whilst the first three Gospels are 'Jewish', John's Gospel had a Gentile destination. But John's Gospel is just as much a record of the life and teaching of Jesus the Messiah as the other three. And as J.B. Lightfoot has observed of John's Gospel,

> It is the most Hebraic book in the New Testament, except perhaps

> the Apocalypse. (*Biblical Essays* page 135)

He also observed that:

> The chronology of our Lord's life can be gathered from John alone. In the other Evangelists the incidents are often grouped together with little or no reference to their chronology ... the minute exactness of St. John's chronology ... arises in great measure from the part which he himself has in the drama. (*Biblical Essays* pages 180,181)

In respect of the Holy Spirit, all four Gospels record the descending of the Spirit upon Jesus at His baptism by John the Baptist.[19] And hence all four authenticate Jesus as the Son of God, and set the scene for all that follows. But it is John who takes us into the 'inner sanctum' of Jesus' teaching to prepare the apostles for His departure and the coming of the Holy Spirit and His ministry to the apostles.

All we know about the ancestry, virgin birth and events surrounding the early life of Jesus the Messiah is contained in **Matthew 1 & 2 and Luke 1-3**. Both Matthew and Luke give the genealogy of the Messiah; Matthew takes that genealogy back to Abraham and David; Luke goes back to Adam.[20]

However, 'Synoptic' these two Gospels are, even these genealogies suggest that the two Evangelists had, in some respect, different motives in recording them. Matthew is evidently concerned with showing the relationship of Jesus to Abraham and David, around which the 'hope' of Israel is vested. Luke goes back to Adam, to the very beginning of mankind, demonstrating the relationship between Jesus and all mankind (and incidentally, laying the foundation for Paul's teaching in Romans 5:12-21; all 'in Adam', all 'in Christ').

A) The birth and early days of John and the Messiah

i) The Holy Spirit in the Gospel of Luke

Luke 1:13-17: The angel of the Lord tells Zechariah the priest that his wife Elizabeth will have a son,

> "Who will be filled with *the Holy Spirit*, even from his mother's womb ... he will turn many of the children to the Lord their God ... he will go before him in the spirit and power[21] of Elijah."

Zechariah, as a priest, would almost certainly see this as a reference to the prophecy of Malachi, where the coming of Elijah was foreseen by the prophet: "Behold, I (the LORD) will send you Elijah the prophet before the great and awesome day of the LORD[22] comes" (Malachi 4:5). Was his son the "messenger" who was coming to herald the arrival of the Messiah to Israel, "in the spirit and power of Elijah"? The angel instructed Zechariah to name that son 'John'.

Luke 1:34,35: The angel Gabriel told Mary:

> "*The Holy Spirit* will come upon you, and the power of the Most High will overshadow you; therefore the child to be born will be called holy—the Son of God."

This epithet was equivalent to 'Messiah' in Jewish thought. J.B. Lightfoot in *Biblical Essays* made the point that the three titles, 'Messiah', 'Son of God' and 'King of Israel' were understood at the time as referring to the same person. (This is confirmed by Scripture, as Lightfoot observes in *Biblical Essays*.)

How Jesus could be both God and man is outside the remit of this book, as is the biological implications of a 'virgin birth'. See the author's booklet *Jesus: God and Man* OBT, for some thoughts on this. It is evident, however, that the Son of Man could not be implicated in the sinful nature that Adam passed down to his descendants. Hence, as both Luke 1:34,35 and Matthew 1:20 record, "that which is conceived in her is *from the Holy Spirit*". Joseph was excluded, Mary was passive and God alone was active through His Spirit.

Luke 1:39-55: Elizabeth, with child herself, was "filled with *the Holy Spirit*" when, during a visit from Mary, she heard of the promise of Mary's child and referred to Him as "my Lord". This led to Mary's famous "Magnificat", which began, "My soul magnifies the Lord, and my spirit rejoices in God my Saviour", and ended with:

> "He has helped his servant Israel, in remembrance of his mercy, as he spoke to our fathers, to Abraham and his offspring for ever."

Mary looked back to the LORD's ancient promise and covenant to Israel via Abraham, Isaac and Jacob, that all peoples (nations) would be blessed through her people. Later both Peter and Paul were to remind their brethren of this in their ministries to the Jews:

> "Men of Israel ... *You are the sons of the prophets and of the covenant that God made with your fathers, saying to Abraham, 'And in your offspring shall all the families of the earth be blessed*'..." (Acts 3:12-25)

> *Abraham is the father of us all, as it is written, "I have made you the father of many nations."* (Romans 4:16,17)

Luke 1:67-80: At the birth of John, Zechariah was *filled with the Holy Spirit* and prophesied, saying,

> "Blessed be the Lord God of Israel, for he has visited and redeemed his people and has raised up a horn of salvation for us in *the house of his servant David*, as he spoke by the mouth of his holy prophets from of old ... to remember *his holy covenant, the oath that he swore* to our father Abraham ..."

Luke 2:25-28: *The Holy Spirit* came upon Simeon, described as, "a righteous and devout man, waiting for the consolation of Israel". It had been revealed to him by *the Holy Spirit* that he would not see death before he had seen the Lord's Messiah. *He came in the Spirit* into the temple where Jesus was being presented to the Lord, according to the Law of Moses. He took Him up in his arms and blessed God and said,

> "Lord, now you are letting your servant depart in peace, according to your word; for my eyes have seen your salvation ... a light for revelation to the Gentiles, and for glory to your people Israel."

Simeon's words refer back to Isaiah 42:6 and 49:6, both passages referring to 'the Servant of the LORD' (an epithet for the Messiah) and were quoted later by Paul to the Jews in Pisidian Antioch (Acts 13:47). In the latter passage, Paul interprets the relationship between Israel and the nations that was operating throughout the Gospel and Acts Periods, quoting Psalm 49:6 to the Jews, "I (the Lord) have *made you* a light for the Gentiles, that *you may bring* salvation to the ends of the earth."

In these verses at the beginning of Luke's Gospel, the *Holy Spirit* lays the foundation for the fulfilment of "the hope of Israel" based on Old Testament promises and its relationship to the nations at this time. And that 'hope' rested upon the coming Messiah who was 'the salvation of God'. Matthew takes up the story.

ii) The Holy Spirit in the Gospel of Matthew:

Matthew 1:18-24: "The birth of Jesus Christ took place in this way" Mary was:

> Found to be with child from *the Holy Spirit* ... Joseph was told by the angel of the Lord, "that which is conceived in her is from *the Holy Spirit*".

The Holy Spirit's ministry is seen here in the conception and miraculous virgin birth of the Messiah, fulfilling Old Testament prophecy (Matthew 1:23; Isaiah 7:14). This was necessary as the Son of Man could not be implicated in the sinful nature that Adam passed down to his descendants. Hence, as both Matthew (here) and Luke (1:34,35) record, "what is conceived in her is *from the Holy Spirit*". As I have already noted, Joseph was excluded, Mary was passive and God alone was active *through His Spirit*.

A passage of Scripture that may help in some way to an understanding of the virgin birth is 1 John 3:9 (*KJV*). John refers to a 'seed of God' lit. "the seed of Him" (*sperma autou*) planted in a Christian, where sin is excluded because he/she is "born of God":

> Whosoever is *born of God* does not commit sin; f*or his* (God's) *seed remains in him*; and he cannot sin, because *he is born of God*.

This does not mean that becoming a Christian makes us sinless, but that the 'seed' God has planted in us, the beginnings of the new "eternal life", "cannot sin" because we are "born of God". That is, the believer is "born of the Spirit" (John 3:5,8) and has a new nature from God, (cp. Romans 8:8-11); a "seed" remains in him—God's seed. So we might look upon the Holy Spirit, God's Spirit, *as God's seed.* Compare 1 Peter 1:23:

> You have been born again, not of perishable seed, but of

imperishable (*seed*), through the living and enduring word of God. (The connection between the Spirit and the Word of God was considered on page 33.)

In his second epistle Peter speaks of becoming "partakers of the divine nature" (1:4 *KJV*). Whichever way we look at it, the Spirit of God was active in the birth of Jesus and likewise in us when we believed. In our case we speak of it as "born again" (John 3:3-8: 1 Peter 1:3,23), "partakers of the divine nature" (2 Peter 1:4) or "a new creation" (2 Corinthians 5:17).

B) John the Baptist: God's messenger

i) Was John Elijah?

John the Baptist was sent as the forerunner to the ministry of the Lord; of John it had been prophesied:

> "He will be *filled with the Holy Spirit*, even from his mother's womb. And he will turn many of the children of Israel to the Lord their God, and *he will go before him in the spirit and power of Elijah* ... to make ready for the Lord a people prepared." (Luke 1:15-17)

John the Baptist was a Colossus who stood, as it were, with one foot in the Old and one foot in the New Testament. The Lord's testimony of him was: "I tell you, among those born of woman none is greater than John" (Luke 7:28). He was a link between the Old and New Testaments, so much so that he may be looked upon in one sense as the last of the Old Testament prophets. But was he Elijah or even the Messiah?

His ministry caused quite a stir, so much so that the Jews in Jerusalem sent priests and Levites to the Jordan to find out who he was (John 1:19-28). Given their knowledge of the prophecies in the Hebrew Bible, they asked him, "Who are you?" He confessed that he was neither the Messiah nor Elijah nor the Prophet (spoken of by Moses in Deuteronomy 18:15 see Acts 3:22). John's testimony to himself was simple, but he related it to the prophecy of Isaiah (40:3), not to the prophecy of Malachi that spoke of the coming of Elijah.

> "I am the voice of one crying out in the wilderness, 'Make

straight the way of the Lord', as the prophet Isaiah said." (John 1:19-23)

The next day, (presumably after the Jerusalem party had left) John said even more significantly:

> "For this purpose I came baptising with water, that he (Jesus, the Lamb of God) *might be revealed to Israel.*" (John 1:29-31)

On another occasion when he again denied that he was the Messiah, John referred to himself as "the friend of the bridegroom, who stands and hears him, and rejoices greatly at the bridegroom's voice ... he must increase, but I must decrease" (John 3:25-30). John never claimed he was the Elijah promised by Malachi, but he did confess that he was the "voice" prophesied by Isaiah (40:3; John 1:23) preparing the way of the Lord.

The confusion that surrounded whether or not John was the Elijah prophesied by Malachi (4:5) was clarified (if that is the right word) by the Lord Himself when He said of him:

> "All the Prophets and the Law prophesied until John, and *if you are willing to accept it*, he is Elijah who is to come. He who has ears to hear, let him hear."[23] (Matthew 11:13-15)

ii) "If you are willing to accept it"

The words, "If you are willing to accept it", are amongst the most significant ever recorded in the New Testament, not just in their relation to John, but in relation to the whole of the Gospel and Acts Periods. Properly understood, these words are one of the keys to an understanding of the period and the 'hope' of believers at that time, and why that 'hope' was never realised *at that time.*

A certain historian (his name escapes me) once observed that we can often learn as much about history by what *did not* happen, as we can from what did happen. Applying that to prophecy in the Scriptures, and specifically to John the Baptist, John seemed to have had all the 'outward signs' necessary to be the 'Elijah' of Malachi 3:1 as well as "the voice" of Isaiah 40:3; Jesus even said, he *could have been* Elijah—"If you are willing to accept it, he is Elijah who is to come" (Matthew 11:14). But to accept John as Elijah would mean accepting his testimony to Jesus that

The Holy Spirit and His Ministry

He was the Messiah (John 1:29-31). This, nationally, Israel never did.

On a later occasion and following the transfiguration (Matthew 17:1-8), during which Moses and Elijah had appeared in a vision, the disciples were querying whether Elijah must come first. The Lord referring back to the death of John at the hands of Herod, answered:

> Elijah does come, and he will restore all things. But I tell you that *Elijah has already come,* and they did not recognise him, but did to him whatever they pleased ... Then the disciples understood that he was speaking to them of John the Baptist. (Matthew 17:9-13).

John the Baptist appeared to fit all the 'requirements' of the promised 'Elijah', but since the Jews did not recognise him and were unwilling to accept him and his testimony, he was not reckoned to be Elijah. However, the prophecy made to Zechariah concerning his son John was surely fulfilled in one sense by his ministry, "*he will go before* (*the Lord*) *in the spirit and power of Elijah*" (Luke 1:17).

This 'IF' principle is seen in other places in the Scriptures, most significantly in the situation that developed during the Acts Period. The Jews had been forgiven their denial of Jesus and His subsequent crucifixion, as it was reckoned they had "acted in ignorance". Now they were given a second chance to repent (Acts 3:17) but *nationally* there was no repentance.

But what IF there had been? Presumably Israel's sins would have been blotted out, and all those blessings that Peter drew their attention to from Moses and the Prophets, would have come to pass (Acts 3:17-26). But it did not happen and eventually God's judgement was pronounced upon them, and this 'hope' went into abeyance. What happened next is vital to our understanding of the New Testament (see page 193).

iii) John and baptism with fire

Matthew 3:1-12; Mark 1:2-8; Luke 3:2-17; John 1:6,7: John, on seeing "many of the Pharisees and Sadducees coming to his baptism" said to them:

> "Who warned you to flee from the wrath to come ... I baptise you

with water for repentance, but he who is coming after me is mightier than I ... He will baptise you *with the Holy Spirit and fire.*"

This warning occurs in the context of the Messiah's first coming, and it reminds us that His appearance on earth was (and will be the second time) not only to bring blessings to the faithful but accountability to the unjust as prophesied by Malachi:

> Behold, I will send my messenger, and he will prepare the way before me. And the Lord whom you seek will suddenly come to his temple, and the messenger of the covenant in whom you delight, behold, he is coming, says the LORD of Hosts. But who can endure the day of his coming, and who can stand when he appears? For he is like a refiner's fire and like fuller's soap ... *Then I will draw near to you for judgement* ... (Malachi: 3:1-5).

The prophet goes on to name those who will come under His judgement; they have broken His laws ... were adulterers ... have sworn falsely ... have oppressed the widow and the fatherless ... have thrust aside the sojourner ... and generally "do not fear me ... the LORD of Hosts".

In modern usage, "a baptism of fire" has been likened to a soldier finding himself for the first time in the trenches, knee deep in mud and under enemy fire. Such was the *fear* endured, that an officer during the First World War remarked, "There are no atheists in the trenches!"

When Jesus baptises *with the Holy Spirit and fire,* it is a baptism that includes a judgement, separating the good from the bad, as prophesied (Matthew 3:11,12; Malachi 3:2,3; cp. Isaiah 4:4; 1 Corinthians 3:13-15).

(Baptism is a subject in its own right. See the author's *Baptisms in the Scriptures* OBT where this subject is considered at length.)

C) "This is My beloved Son"

Matthew 3:13-17; Mark 1:9-11; Luke 3:21,22; John 1:32-34: When Jesus was baptised by John:

> Immediately he went up from the water, and behold, the heavens were opened to him, and he saw *the Spirit of God* descending like

a dove and coming to rest on him; and behold, a voice from heaven said, "This is my beloved Son, with whom I am well pleased."

In all four accounts *the Holy Spirit* is seen descending upon Jesus and authenticating Him as the "Son of God"; the first three have "beloved Son" and John adds that "this is he who baptises with *the Holy Spirit*". Another difference between John and the three Synoptics is that in the latter the testimony to Jesus is by "a voice from heaven", in John it is the testimony of John the Baptist based upon *his observation* of the event.

This difference is in accordance with the reason John wrote his Gospel, and was 'the testimony of men'; the Baptist, Andrew, Philip, Nathanael, etc. (John 1:32-34; 40-49), and of the apostle himself who wrote:

> Jesus did many other signs in the presence of his disciples, which are not written in this book; but these are written so that you may believe that Jesus is the Messiah, *the Son of God*, and that by believing you may have life in his name. (John 20:30,31)

"The Son of God" together with "the King of Israel" were titles given to "the Messiah" at the time (J.B. Lightfoot *Biblical Essays*). These all come together in John's Gospel at the calling of the first disciples in (1:41-49):

> Andrew said to his brother Simon (Peter): "We have found *the Messiah*." (v.41)

> Nathanael, on meeting Jesus, said to Him, "Rabbi, you are *the Son of God*! You are *the King of Israel*." (v.49)

The resting of the Holy Spirit upon Jesus (the Son of David) is reminiscent of the experience of His famous ancestor, when Samuel anointed him and *"the Spirit of the LORD rushed upon David* from that day forward". The Spirit of the LORD *authenticated* David as the chosen one to be king over all Israel (1 Samuel 16:13). In a less spectacular, but no less important way, the Holy Spirit *authenticates* an individual who believes in Christ, as "a Christian" when He comes upon them when they believe the gospel of salvation (Ephesians 1:13-14).

D) The temptation of Jesus

Matthew 4:1-11; Mark 1:12,13; Luke 4:1-13: After forty days fasting,

> Jesus was led up by *the Spirit of God* into the wilderness to be tempted by the devil.

Matthew 4:1-11; Mark 1:12,13; Luke 4:1-14: The final act of the 'preparation' of Jesus for His ministry was the temptation He had to endure at the hands of the devil in the wilderness. Here Luke describes Jesus as "full of *the Holy Spirit*" on His return from Jordan. That same *Spirit* now *led Him* into the wilderness to be temped of the devil for forty days.

The Synoptics use three different words to describe the action of *the Holy Spirit*, but John does not record the temptations. *The Revised Version* which "is most faithful to the original Greek" (H.F.D. Sparks, *A Synopsis of the Gospels*) recognises this difference. Matthew has *anexthe eis* "*led up* of the Spirit"; Mark *auton ekballei* "the Spirit *driveth him forth*" and Luke *egeto en* "*led by* the Spirit".

Whether or not we are intended to see a difference here I cannot say. Mark's "driveth" may suggest that Jesus, was under some pressure, just as He was in Gethsemane when He prayed, "My Father, *if it be possible* let this cup pass from me, nevertheless, not as I will, but as you will."

Jesus was subjected to three temptations by the evil one, all of which He countered by referring him to the Scriptures. Jesus had been authenticated as the Messiah, the Son of God. He is put to the test by His most powerful adversary, Satan. The first temptation is to turn "stones into bread" as a demonstration of His miraculous powers. The second was to reveal Himself as "the Son of God" by casting himself from the pinnacle of the temple, entrusting His survival to the interception of the angels. Put bluntly, the devil wanted Him to 'show off'!

Having failed in these two temptations, the devil now offers Him, not just the kingdom of Israel, but "all the kingdoms of the world and their glory" in exchange for one act of worship. (Luke adds that this was not an idle promise as the devil claimed to have had "all this authority and their glory" delivered to him and he could give it to whom he will Luke 4:1-13). This, like the other temptations, Jesus counters by quoting the Scriptures against the devil who, thus defeated, leaves Him and the angels come and minister to Jesus (Matthew 4:1-11). Luke records (4:13,14):

> When the devil had ended every temptation, he departed from him until an opportune time. And Jesus returned *in the power of the Spirit* to Galilee.

The words "an opportune time" remind us that the devil's departure was only temporary, the Lord was to encounter him more than once during His ministry (cp. Luke 22:53; John 14:30). But, "The hope of Israel" was 'on course', and remained so throughout the whole of the Gospel and Acts Periods (even as late as Acts 28:20-24).

Having looked at the references to *the Holy Spirit* that refer to the 'preparation' of Jesus the Messiah for His ministry, I now move on to references to *the Holy Spirit* following that 'preparation'.

E) The ministry of Jesus in the Synoptics

i) His commissioning and warning to His disciples

Matthew 4:12 records that Jesus began His ministry when He heard that John the Baptist had been arrested, and then called His first disciples, who heard what was at the heart of His ministry in 'The Sermon on the Mount' (chapters 5-7). He then went about healing many (chapters 8 & 9) and in chapter 10 He is recorded as sending out the twelve disciples into the world where He warns them they will be like "sheep in the midst of wolves". It is in this context that the Holy Spirit is again mentioned.

Matthew 10:16-20; Mark 13:11-13; Luke 21:12-19: As they go about proclaiming "the kingdom of heaven is at hand", healing the sick and even raising the dead, they will inevitably be called before courts and synagogues to account for their beliefs and actions. But He tells them:

> "When they deliver you over, do not be anxious how you are to speak or what you are to say, for what you are to say will be given to you in that hour. For it is not you who speak but *the Spirit of your Father speaking through you.*" (Matthew 10:16-24)

The ministry of *the Holy Spirit* here looks forward, I believe, to the time when the Lord would no longer physically be with His disciples. Whilst

He was 'the ringleader' He would be the centre of that persecution. And, whilst we cannot rule out that the disciples did suffer when they were with Jesus, and before Pentecost, it was only after that event that they were "delivered over to courts ... dragged before governors and kings". In Acts 4:1-22 we have an example of this when Peter, appearing before the council in Jerusalem to defend his preaching in the name of Jesus, was "filled with the Holy Spirit" (verse 8 cp. Stephen in Acts 6;10; 7:55).

ii) Blasphemy against the Holy Spirit

Matthew 12:22-32; Mark 3:22-30; Luke 11:14-20: Jesus said:

> "If it is by *the Spirit of God* that I cast out demons, then the kingdom of God has come upon you." (Matthew 12:28; Luke 11:20 has *"the finger of God"*.)

This was the Lord's answer to those who accused Him of casting out demons by Beelzebub, the prince of demons, and it led to the Lord's warning about blasphemy. In Matthew 12:32, "blasphemy (*NKJV*) against *the Holy Spirit* will not be forgiven". Mark's record says, "Whoever blasphemes against the Holy Spirit never has forgiveness, but is guilty of an eternal sin" (3:29).

The first reference in the New Testament to "blasphemy" (evil speaking especially against God) is Matthew 9:3 (Mark 2:5-7) when Jesus was accused of such for saying to a paralytic, "your sins are forgiven you". This was the province of God alone. "Who can forgive sins but God alone" (Luke 5:21 *NKJV*).

However, Jesus claimed, "I cast out demons by *the Spirit of God*" (Matthew 12:22-32), countering what the Pharisees had said; "It is only by Beelzebub, the prince of demons, that this man casts out demons" (*ESV*). It is in that context that Jesus went on to say:

> "Every sin and blasphemy will be forgiven men; but the *blasphemy against the Spirit* will not be forgiven men. Anyone who speaks a word against the Son of Man, it will be forgiven him, but whoever *speaks against the Holy Spirit*, it will not be forgiven him, either in this age or the age to come." (Matthew 12:22-32 *NKJV*)

The foundation for the sin of blasphemy was laid in the Ten Commandments, where the LORD said that He would "not hold him guiltless who takes *his Name* in vain" (Exodus 20:7). In Leviticus 24:10-16 we have an example made of the son of an Israelite woman who "blasphemed *the Name* and cursed"; he was put to death—no forgiveness; he had to "bear his sin". There is no suggestion of forgiveness here. In his book *The Giver and His Gifts*, in loco, Dr. Bullinger summed up Matthew 12:31,32:

> What this blasphemy was is clearly explained in verse 24. It is ascribing to Beelzebub (*i.e.*, Satan himself) that which was wrought by the Holy Spirit.

Whether it has any application to members of the Church which is the Body of Christ seems doubtful, as Michael Penny noted (*in loco*) in his *40 Problem Passages* OBT. He wrote:

> The words which Christ uttered were to a very specific group of people, at a very special point in time. What He said was to certain people who heard what He preached and taught and who had seen how He healed and helped. They were in a unique situation. If they had rejected it all, and left it at that, they could have had another chance. However, they attributed all Christ's miraculous powers to the prince of demons, and that was unforgivable. However, as we shall see, it is possible for us today to "grieve the Holy Spirit of God" (Ephesians 4:30).

iii) David's Son and David's Lord: A Conundrum

Matthew 22:41-45; Mark 12:35-37; Luke 20:41-44: The Pharisees were often asking the Lord questions hoping to catch Him out, and His teaching often contradicted their 'traditions'. But now it was His turn. Taking the opportunity when many of them were gathered together He asked:

> "What do you think about the Messiah? Whose son is he?" They said to him, "The son of David." He said to them, "How is it then that David, *in the Spirit*, calls him Lord, saying,
> 'The Lord said to my Lord,
> Sit at my right hand
> until I put your enemies under your feet'?

If then David calls him Lord, how is he his son?"
And no one was able to answer him a word, nor from that day did anyone dare to ask him any more questions. (Matthew 22:41-45)

"David, *in the Spirit*, called Him (the Messiah) Lord", and David spoke with divine inspiration (2 Samuel 23:2), so how could David acknowledge the Messiah as Lord and yet the Messiah be his son? Jesus quoted Psalm 110:1, a Messianic psalm, which must have been well known to the Pharisees, and He challenges them to explain that conundrum; David's Son *and* David's Lord, how could that be?

This passage is best seen against the background of the constant testing of Jesus by both the Pharisees and the Sadducees, trying "to entangle him in his words" (Matthew 22:15). But it 'backfired on them' and shut them up, it would seem, for good (Matthew 22:46). The Pharisees had no answer for Jesus, and He never enlightened them.

Chapter 9
The Holy Spirit in John's Gospel

Whether it is right to say that one part of the Scriptures is more important than others I do not know. But it would seem in respect of the Holy Spirit, that John's Gospel has more to say about His ministry than the other three. Hence it is important to place this Gospel in its right context and that involves considering who wrote it, when, and with what purpose. My own view is that the belief that the apostle John wrote this Gospel in his old age has not helped towards our understanding of it. And it also impinges on how we understand the ministry of the Holy Spirit as recorded by John.

A) Authorship and date of the Gospel

That the apostle John wrote this Gospel is not in my mind in any serious doubt. Apart from the *internal* evidence that may be gleaned from the Gospel itself, the two great Cambridge scholars B.F. Westcott (*Gospel of St. John*) and J.B. Lightfoot (*Biblical Essays*) exhibited a weight of *external* evidence in favour of John's authorship, both from the Fathers of the orthodox Church, and perhaps surprisingly, also from heretical writers. As to the *internal* evidence they detailed at length their reasons for believing that:

> The author was a Jew ... A Jew of Palestine ... An eye-witness ... An Apostle ... St. John.

Many scholars agree with this, but *when* it was written is another matter. Most give the Gospel a late date, in the old age of the apostle, towards the end of the first century. But in view of the content of the Gospel on the one hand, and the unlikelihood of John waiting sixty odd years before making a written record of the Lord's ministry, with not even a suggestion that the temple in Jerusalem was not still standing on the other, I find this difficult to accept.

The destruction of Jerusalem and its temple by the Roman Army in *Anno Domini* 70 (bringing to an end institutional temple worship) was, and remains, one of the most important events in the history of God's dealings with man. It was not just far reaching for the Jewish nation, but for the Gentiles, in particular the Christians. Its implications continue to impinge upon many aspects of Christian belief and practice today, and throw light on the future history of the Jews in relation to unfulfilled prophecy. It was the *de facto* 'proof' of the *de jure* judgement pronounced upon Israel at the end of the Acts Period (Acts 28:25-28, see page 193).

There have been those, however, who recognising that not one of the New Testament writings, including John, shows any indication that that momentous event in A.D.70, *had already taken place*—it was prophesied, yes, but taken place, no. Hence, in the study of the New Testament, nothing like enough attention has been given to the significance of the events of A.D. 70, in dating and understanding the content of its various writings. How did this most datable and climactic event of the period come to be almost ignored from the first century onwards, and continues to be so? James Moffatt in his *Introduction to the Literature of the New Testament* first published in 1911 wrote:

> We should expect that an event like the fall of Jerusalem would have dinted some of the literature of the primitive Church ... It might be supposed that such an epoch-making crisis would even furnish for determining dates of some of the N.T. Writings. As a matter of fact, the catastrophe is practically ignored in the extant Christian literature of the first century.

And at least two other respected commentators that I know of, drew attention to this event as having been neglected in the dating of the New Testament books:

John A.T. Robinson (1919-1983)
Anglican Bishop of Woolwich/ Dean of Trinity College:
    Re-dating the New Testament, Published 1976.
    The Priority of John, Published 1985.
`John Wenham (1913-1996)
Anglican biblical scholar:
    Re-dating Matthew, Mark and Luke (with references to John and Acts) Published 1991.

Many ignore the significance of A.D. 70, others treat it as being secondary in this respect, and date the writings of the New Testament on the basis of tradition. In doing so they fail to see a distinction between those writings that minister to the 'hope' of the blessings of a kingdom upon earth and those where the blessings are in the heavenly places). This in turn smudges the overall picture and the fact that the New Testament writings minister to two different 'callings'.

A.D. 70 was the 'proof' that the judgement of God had come upon Israel in accordance with the words of the Holy Spirit spoken through Isaiah's prophecy, and it has led to the "salvation of God" being sent to the Gentiles (Acts 28:25-27). Any overview of the New Testament must take the above prophecy and the events that followed into consideration. This will help us to distinguish between God's purpose for the earth through Abraham and Israel on the one hand, and His purpose in the heavenly places for the Church which is the Body of Christ on the other.

B) Destination of the Gospel

It would take up many pages of this book on "The Holy Spirit", to give my reasons for when John wrote his gospel and for whom he wrote it. I therefore refer the reader to my booklet, *The Gospel of John and the Samaritans*, which deals at length with some of the arguments that indicate **a)** that this Gospel was written *during the Acts Period* and **b)** the consequent implications of that. It was not written much later in the first century as some believe. Hence my position is that:

> The Gospel was written early in the first century rather than later. *At that time*, the fulfilment of "the hope of Israel" (Acts 26:6,7; 28:20) and the imminent return of the Messiah was a real possibility, as most of the New Testament letters written during this period suggest.[24]

John practically tells us this with his urgent call to believe that Jesus is the Messiah; a necessary belief for Jews living during the Acts Period, but not for Gentiles living at the end of the first century. The latter would accept without question the connection between the name 'Jesus' and the title, 'Christ', whether they believed what was claimed of him or not; for the Jew the connection was vital. John gave as the reason for his Gospel:

> Jesus did many other signs in the presence of the disciples,

> which are not written in this book;
>> but these are written so that you may believe:
>> (i) That Jesus is the Messiah, the Son of God, and
>> (ii) That by believing you may have life in his name.
> (John 20:30,31)

The tendency to place more emphasis on the second clause of these verses than the first, hides the true original intention of John. Hence, John's original purpose is inclined to be forgotten, and the key to an understanding of the whole Gospel is lost. The Gospel was originally written to Jews (and Samaritans), with an appeal that would have made much more sense to a Jew living *during the Acts Period*, than the average Gentile of that time, or indeed to Gentiles living near the end of the first century. The message that John was urging his readers to grasp, was the very same as that of the apostles during the Acts Period, as Peter said in closing his appeal to the Jews on the Day of Pentecost:

> Let all the house of Israel therefore know for certain that God has made him *both Lord and Messiah, this Jesus* whom you crucified. (Acts 2:36)

This appeal to the Jews that "Jesus is the Messiah" continued throughout the Acts Period. Even when Paul, the apostle to the Gentiles, came on the scene he preached the same to Jews (Acts 9:20,22; 17:1-3). In contrast to his appeal to the Jews, when Paul encountered Gentiles, his message was very different. He spoke to them of God as Creator, a Giver of all good things, and presented Christ as having been appointed the Judge of all men (see Acts 14:15-18 and 17:22-31).

John recorded eight out of the many miracles that Jesus did, but referred to them as "signs". These signs were his evidence that "Jesus is the Messiah" and completely in accord with that message to Jews during the Acts Period. Israel were the "sign" people—"The Jews require a sign, and the Greeks seek after wisdom" (1 Corinthians 1:22).

All that John records must be considered from that premise, and especially here in relation to the ministry of the Holy Spirit, *in the context of the time*, before we ask what relevance its teaching has to us today. For example, what of the spiritual gifts and miracles that seem to have been almost 'commonplace' at the time, but (rarely) occur today (see pages 117-125).

The original destination of this Gospel was to Jews (and Samaritans[25]) living at that time (Acts Period) and was written in order to convince them that Jesus is (not was) the promised Messiah. This was demonstrated by the many "signs" that He did, of which John recorded eight in detail:[26] John states clearly that the prime object of his Gospel was for his readers to believe and accept that Jesus was the long expected and prophesied Messiah. Hence, first and foremost, the ministry of *the Holy Spirit* as recorded by John, must be considered in that context.

John's Gospel has of course, been a great blessing to many throughout the ages, and I have no intention here of detracting from that fact. But I do believe that it is important to see the Gospel, as with all Scripture, first and foremost in the context of the setting in which John wrote it, and to whom it was first addressed.

The Gospel of John has much to say about The Holy Spirit and His witness to the Messiah; in particular in chapters 14 to 16. I have earlier quoted some of the verses from these chapters that relate to the Holy Spirit when considering His 'role' within the Trinity. If I repeat them here, it is because we cannot separate our understanding of the Holy Spirit (and in fact of the Father and the Son) from His relationship to mankind, and in particular the believer. If (e.g.) He is called "the Helper", that implies there is someone that needs help and so on.

C) References to the Holy Spirit in John's Gospel

We might have expected in a Gospel which begins with a revelation of God and the creation, with the opening words of Genesis, and that speak of the Spirit moving and God creating, there would be some reference to the Holy Spirit, but there is not. The first time He is mentioned is when John observes the Spirit descending and remaining on Jesus (1:33). However, what we do have is a reference to "the Word" (1:1) and this brings us back to the important connection in the Scriptures that I have already noted between the Spirit of God and the Word of God (page 33).

Without repeating too much of what has already been said, or anticipating too much of what we will see of this connection in our own calling today (Ephesians / Colossians), I believe the relationship between the "the Word of God" and "the Spirit of God" (and between 'word(s)' and 'spirit', *pneuma*) to be one of the most important keys to our understanding of *the Holy Spirit's ministry*, especially today.

To anticipate, what does it mean to be "filled by the Spirit" and how can we recognise it? Can others recognise it in us? Do we exhibit signs of emotion? Do we speak in tongues? How, if at all, have we become different in any way? Let us take an example from the Scriptures recorded in Luke 24:13-32; the experience of the two disciples on the Road to Emmaus who met Jesus and conversed with Him. After what must have been one of the greatest Bible Studies ever, they said to each other (v.32):

> "Did not our hearts burn within us while he talked to us on the road, while he opened to us the Scriptures?"

They had *an inward emotion* as a result of an exposition of the Word of God. I expect many Christians have experienced something similar, either during an exceptional sermon, or more likely, when reading God's Word in the quietness of their own studies—I know I have. This is analogous to being "filled with (or by) the Spirit"—letting the Word of God dwell in us richly (Ephesians 5:18 / Colossians 3:16).

D) The Baptist reveals the Messiah to Israel

The "strong Jewish nature" of John's Gospel (Lightfoot *Biblical Essays*) is nowhere more evident than in his record of the ministry of John the Baptist, that the Messiah "might be *revealed to Israel*" (1:29).
John 1:29-41: John the Baptist was in a sense, the last of the Old Testament prophets who called upon Israel to repent and turn back to the LORD, but with the added call to them that *now* … "The kingdom of heaven is at hand" (Matthew 3:1,2). In John's record, however, the apostle testified of the Baptist that he said of his own ministry:

> "For this purpose I came baptising with water, *that he* [Jesus v.29] *might be revealed to Israel.*" (John 1:31)

This important aspect of John the Baptist's ministry is sometimes overlooked to the detriment of a proper understanding of that ministry. John saw *the Spirit* descend upon Jesus and declared Him firstly to be "the Lamb of God who takes away the sin of the world", (John 1:31,36: cp. Isaiah 53:7).[27] He then refers to Him as "the Son of God" who "baptises with *the Holy Spirit*" (1:33,34), and from this testimony He is declared by (at least) three of His disciples to be

> "The Messiah" by Andrew (John 1:41).
>
> "Him of whom Moses in the Law and also the prophets wrote" by Philip (John 1:45; Deuteronomy 18:15).
>
> "The Son of God ... the King of Israel" by Nathanael (John 1:49)

J.B. Lightfoot noted that the titles applied to Jesus as, Messiah, Son of God and King of Israel are coincident with each other (*Biblical Essays* pages 148,149). They are all titles of "Him of whom Moses in the Law and also the prophets wrote". These confessions made by the first of the disciples, demonstrate that the Baptist's ministry was already, at least to some, "revealing Him to Israel", and is coincident with John's purpose in writing his Gospel; "That you may believe that *Jesus is the Messiah, the Son of God*" (20:30,31). (For more on the Baptist's ministry and baptism in general see the author's book *Baptisms in the Scriptures*.)

E) The Lord's ministry in John

i) "You must be born again"

John 3:1-15: The new birth: "born of water and *the Spirit*".

From Genesis 3 onwards, when "through one man (Adam) sin entered the world" (Romans 5:12) until the purpose of God for man reaches its fulfilment, every human being (except Jesus, the Son of Man) will have been in need of "the salvation that is in Christ Jesus" (2 Timothy 2:10). He has paid the price of sin, and the believer who has accepted Him and this great salvation has become "a new creation ... born of God ... born again (from above) ... *born of the Spirit*" (2 Corinthians 5:17; John 1:13; 3:3,7,8). This aspect of the Holy Spirit's ministry is relevant in all ages and for all callings, earthly or heavenly, for all are in need of the new birth, "*born of the Spirit*".

The Lord's conversation with Nicodemus goes on to declare, what is to many, the most loved and well-known verse of Scripture:

> God so loved the world, that he gave his only Son, that whosoever believes in him should not perish but have eternal life.

(3:16)

There are some differences of opinion as to whether these words and what follows (John 3:17-21) were spoken by Jesus to Nicodemus or were part of John's expansion of 3:1-15. Westcott (*The Gospel of St John*) says that they are the Evangelist "unfolding the meaning" of the conversation that has gone before. My feeling is that Westcott's view is right.

John draws a parallel between an event in Israel's history; "**as** Moses lifted up the serpent in the wilderness, **so** must the Son of Man be lifted up" (3:14). This event would have been well known to Nicodemus (and to Jews in general), and was a pointer to the sacrifice that was necessary to bring about God's salvation.

There is much in John 3:1-15 that is applicable universally, but there is one statement in John's record that is, I believe, not relevant today. This can only be understood by comparing the differences between the 'calling' during which John was writing and the 'later revelation' made by Paul in Ephesians 3 (see page 193).

What Jesus set before Nicodemus was: "Unless one is born *of water and the Spirit*, he cannot enter the kingdom of God" (3:5). Does this suggest that water baptism was necessary to enter the kingdom of God?[28] Peter laid this requirement upon his own people on the Day of Pentecost:

> *Repent and be baptised* every one of you in the name of Jesus the Messiah *for the forgiveness of your sins*, and *you will receive the gift of the Holy Spirit.* (Acts 2:38)

Peter was obviously referring here to a water baptism first, followed by a Spirit baptism ("the gift of the Holy Spirit"). 'Baptism by the Holy Spirit' is another way of referring to the gift of the Holy Spirit coming upon a person as Acts 11:15-17 makes clear. Peter recalls his experience with Cornelius and company:

> "As I began to speak, *the Holy Spirit fell on them* just as on us at the beginning. And I remembered the word of the Lord, how he said, 'John baptised with water, but *you will be baptised with the Holy Spirit*'. If then God gave the same gift to them as he gave to us when we believed in the Lord Jesus Christ, who was I that I could stand in God's way?"

Here then, as in John 3, we have water baptism and Spirit baptism linked together. This water/Spirit connection, sometimes with certain reservations, is still seen as relevant by some today. (See the author's book, *Baptisms in the Scriptures* OBT for more on this.)

ii) The Spirit given without measure

John 3:25-36: John the Baptist testifies of Jesus: "He whom God has sent utters the words of God, for he gives *the Spirit without measure*." C.H.C. Macgregor's suggestion here seems to get to the nub of verse 34.

> The words 'not by measure' (*KJV*) mean ... beyond the measure experienced by all who are sent by God ... for each of His messengers God has given a measure of His Spirit proportionate to his task, and that this is surpassingly true of Christ. (*The Gospel of John*)

iii) Worship in spirit and truth

John 4:19-26: It has always surprised me that Jesus should reveal this important truth about worship to a Samaritan, and to an adulterous woman at that, and yet spoke to "the ruler of the Jews" (Nicodemus) about the most basic fact of salvation; "you must be born again". Should it not be the other way around? (For the relationship between The Gospel of John and the Samaritans see the author's book of that name published by OBT.) Following the question of where the right place was at which to worship, Jesus said to the woman:

> "The hour is coming when neither on this mountain nor in Jerusalem will you worship the Father ... the hour is coming, and **is now here**, when the true worshippers will worship the Father in spirit and truth, for the Father is seeking such people to worship him. God is spirit, and those who worship him must worship in spirit and truth." (John 4:21,23

The three Greek words, *kai nun estin*, "and now is" (John 4:23 *KJV*) in the Lord's statement, have been understood in two main ways. How we read them will affect our understanding of the Gospel of John, particularly as to when it was written; during the Acts Period as I maintain, or post-Acts towards the end of the first century.

First of all we must ask, did Jesus *actually* use these three words "and now is", to the Samaritan woman, or are they John's comment added much later, when the centre of Jewish institutional worship, Jerusalem, had been destroyed (A.D. 70)? ('True worship' in the Church which is the Body of Christ is, "in spirit and truth". It is not in question here; more on that later). But how were these three words, "and now is" understood originally by the Samaritan woman?

Did they, or more accurately, *should they* have been reflected in the actions of those who worshipped in Jerusalem *at that time*? If Jesus actually spoke these 'three words', how did believers at that time respond to the concept that worship in the Jerusalem Temple was now apparently irrelevant? Even a casual look at the actions of the apostles in The Acts of the Apostles, show that they never gave up worshipping in the Temple and even continued to keep the feasts and vows just as they had always done as required by the Law.

Peter and John went up to the Temple at the hour of prayer (Acts 3:1); the apostles were found every day in the Temple where they taught and preached that Jesus is the Messiah (Acts 5:42); Paul took two Nazarite vows in which he had cut his hair, a vow that had to be completed in Jerusalem (Acts 18:18; 21:23-26 see Numbers 6); Paul hastened to be in Jerusalem on the Day of Pentecost (Acts 20:16) and Paul prayed in the Temple (Acts 22:17) and said to Felix that he went up "to worship in Jerusalem" (Acts 24:11).

I am not saying that these Christian Jews either ignored or did not understand "worship in spirit and truth", I am only saying that *at that time* (Acts Period) keeping the Law and its requirements was not done away with. So if Jesus said these words to the Samaritan woman whilst the Jerusalem Temple was still standing, what did He mean by, "and now is"? Are we forced into believing that these words were not spoken by Jesus but that John added them some time after A.D. 70, when it was impossible to continue institutional worship in a Temple that lay in ruins?

I believe that these 'three words' (*kai nun estin*) were spoken by Jesus to the Samaritan women *at that time*. Let us then read them *in the context of that time*. The Temple is still standing and Jesus and His disciples are preaching, "the kingdom of heaven *is at hand* ... the coming of the Lord *is at hand* ... the Judge is *standing at the door*" (Matthew 3:2; James 5:8,9). There was an urgency during the Gospel and Acts Periods described here, and in many other places in the Scriptures written during the Acts Period. Many of them reflect the belief that the Messiah would soon be returning (see note 24) and, as Peter promised He would, restore "all things spoken by the prophets", if Israel would repent (Acts 3:17-21):

> Brethren ... Repent ... turn again, that your sins may be blotted out, that times of refreshing may come from *the presence of the Lord*, and that *he may send the Messiah* appointed for you, Jesus, whom heaven must receive until the time for restoring all the things about which God spoke by the mouth of his holy prophets long ago.

It is only by interpreting the Gospel and Acts Periods within this context, that we can see the place of "worship in spirit and truth" *at that time*. The words "is now here", spoken by the Lord to the Samaritan women, were said *in the light of 'the season'* and the imminence of the return of the King and Him setting up the kingdom: it was "at hand". And this becomes clearer when we see how the Acts Period was understood by a Jewish Christian writer who defined it for his own people in **the epistle to the Hebrews**. In this epistle, the writer sets the Old Covenant of Law with its "copy of the heavenly things" over against the New Covenant based upon "heavenly things with better sacrifices" (Hebrews 9:23), which was ready *at that time* to replace it:

> In speaking of a new covenant, he makes the first one obsolete. And what is *becoming obsolete* and growing old is *ready to pass away*. (Hebrews 8:13)

When Hebrews was written this was the situation; the Old Covenant was "becoming obsolete" and was "ready to pass away". But this awaited the repentance of the nation of Israel (Acts 3:19-21). Hence worship *at that time* continued to be made according to the Old Covenant, as the Acts story relates. However, the sad story is that repentance never came, leading to the consequences of Acts 28:25-28.

True worship "in *spirit* and truth ... for God is *spirit* ... true worshippers will worship the Father in *spirit* and truth". These words were said to a Samaritan woman; the Samaritans also looked for the coming of the Messiah. To her Jesus confessed that He was the Messiah—"**I who speak to you am he**" (John 4:24-26).

God is spirit: The *KJV* translates John 4:24: "God *is* a Spirit (*pneuma*), and they that worship him must worship him in spirit (*pneuma*) and in truth." But as E.W. Bullinger (*The Giver and His Gifts*[29]) points out, the *Revised Version* margin has "God is spirit" (small 's'), as does the later version I am using (*ESV*) and others. Hence strictly speaking, I believe the Holy Spirit is mentioned in the verse only insofar that the nature and Being of God is "spirit", making the point that true worship is not in the realm of the flesh—"that which is born of the flesh is flesh" (John 3:6)—but in spirit; our spirit in tune with His spirit.

iv) Spirit, the words of Jesus and eternal life

John 6:58-63: Jesus had fed five thousand of those who had followed Him and this was to lead to His discourse on "the bread of life". He made the contrast between the miraculous experience of the Moses generation who "ate manna in the wilderness and *they died*", and Himself as "the living bread that came down from heaven" where those who ate of it would "*live for ever*" (John 6:41,51).

But many of His disciples found this idea of feeding on Jesus, especially when He defined it further as, feeding on His flesh and drinking His blood, as "a hard saying" (John 6:55,56,60), and so He continued:

> "*The Spirit* gives life … The *words that I (Jesus) have spoken* to you are *spirit* and life." (John 6:63)

However, eventually many of His disciples turned back and deserted Him, and so Jesus said to the twelve, "Do you want to go away as well?" Simon Peter answered him,

> "Lord, to whom shall we go? You have *the words of eternal life*, and we have believed, and come to know that you are *the Holy One of God*." (John 6:66-69)

v) Jesus; The Holy One of God

I have already drawn attention to the important connection between the Spirit of God and the Word of God (Chapter 4).

Here, Jesus is recognised by Peter (and the other disciples—"we"?) as having "the words of eternal life" and declared to be "*the Holy One of*

God". The latter expression was used by the man with an unclean spirit who recognised Him to be just that. Upon seeing Jesus, he cried out,

> "What have you to do with us Jesus of Nazareth? Have you come to destroy us? I know who you are—*the Holy One of God*." (Mark 1:24)

Jesus rebuked the spirit, saying, "be silent and come out of him". And the unclean spirit came out of him, and that led to His fame spreading throughout all the surrounding region of Galilee (Mark 1:21-28).

In 1 John 2:20 the apostle reminds his readers that they "have been anointed by *the Holy One* and have all knowledge". Jesus was described in a similar way by Peter when referring to what the "Men of Israel" had done to Jesus, denying "*the Holy and Righteous One*" (Acts 3:14). And John in Revelation 3:7 wrote "He who has the key of David" and He is again referred to as "*the Holy One*".

When the birth of Jesus was foretold, Mary was told by the angel Gabriel that He "will be *called Holy—the Son of God*" (Luke 1:35; cp. also Hebrews 7:26). In some places it is difficult to distinguish between Jesus, as "the Holy One", and "the Holy Spirit", but then that is the mystery of the Godhead. What we should have no difficulty with, however, is that the words of Jesus whilst on earth, and those spoken through His faithful apostles by the Holy Spirit, are life, and life abundantly (John 10:10).

vi) Living Water = the Holy Spirit

John 7:37-39: Earlier the Lord had said to the Samaritan woman:

> "Whoever drinks of the water that I will give him will never be thirsty again. The water that I will give him will become in him *a spring of water welling up to eternal life*." (John 4:14)

Later He said to those present at the Feast of Tabernacles:

> "If anyone thirsts, let him come to me and drink. Whoever believes in me, as the Scripture has said, 'Out of his heart will flow *rivers of living water*.'" Now this he said about the Spirit, whom those who believed in him were to receive, for as yet the (Holy *KJV*) Spirit had not yet been given, because Jesus was not

yet glorified. (John 7:37-39)

"Living water" was identified by the Lord as "the Holy Spirit". The *KJV* has 'Holy' (omitted in some texts) in the second occurrence of 'Spirit' in these verses. The Lord's reference to 'Scripture' may be a reference to drawing "water from the wells of salvation" (Isaiah 12:3) and/or the water that flows out of the new temple to which the Shekinah glory will one day return (Ezekiel 47:1; see 43:1-4).

During the Feast of Tabernacles ("Booths" *ESV* John 7:2) priests, carrying water taken from Siloam, would process around the altar seven times. Jesus standing up and crying out in the midst of this ceremony, "If anyone thirsts, let him come to me and drink", would have had an electric effect on the crowd gathered there. And it made a deep impression on some people who said, "This really is the Prophet", and others who said, "This is the Messiah", although some doubted (John 7:37-43).

The connection of living waters with the Holy Spirit in Isaiah 12:3 is not just a Christian conviction, but was cited by Jewish teachers who interpreted it in relation to the water-drawing rite. *Sukka* 5:55a cites Jehoshua ben Levi who, when referring to the court of the women, said, "Why did they call it the place of drawing water? Because it was from there that they drew the Holy Spirit, according to the word: 'With joy you will draw water ...'"

In John 7:38 the living water is said to flow "out of his heart" and this was thought by some Christians to point to the incident when a Roman soldier pierced the side (heart?) of the crucified Jesus with a spear and, "at once there came out blood and water" (John 19:34); "the Lord becomes the source of living water when he is 'lifted up' on his cross and so to heaven" (John 3:14; 8:28; 12:32,34; *The Gospel John: Word Biblical Commentary* in loco, Beasley Murray).

Another example of water from Israel's history that may reflect on this connection with the Spirit, is where Paul looks back to the water that came from the rock in the wilderness and the actions of the Moses generation, with whom "God was not pleased". They "all drank the same *spiritual drink*. For they drank from the spiritual Rock that followed them, and the Rock was Christ." Paul reminded his own generation of this incident as a warning against idolatry (Exodus 17:6; Psalm 105:41; 1 Corinthians 10:1-11).

We have also a connection between the baptism of water and the baptism of the Holy Spirit, as promised to the apostles by the Lord shortly before He left them:

> "Wait for the promise of the Father", which he said, "you heard from me; for John baptised with water, but you will be baptised with the Holy Spirit not many days from now." (Acts 1:4,5) (For more on baptism see the author's Baptisms in the Scriptures OBT.)

vii) Jesus anticipates His coming sacrifice

John 13:21: Jesus was "troubled in *his spirit*" in anticipation of His coming betrayal and crucifixion. The *spirit* of Jesus is referred to later when on the cross, "Jesus, knowing that all was now finished ... bowed his head and gave up *his spirit*" (John 19:28-30; cp. John 11:33; 12:27-30).

This reference to the *pneuma*, 'spirit' of Jesus, prepares us for what is the 'Jewel in the Crown' of the Lord's teaching and preparation of the apostles for their coming ministry without His physical presence. They will not be left like orphans, for there is another Comforter, the Spirit of truth, promised and ready to take over. This pre-resurrection ministry occupies chapters 14 to 16 of John's gospel and I will come to it after looking at the final references to *pneuma* in the Gospel.

viii) Post-resurrection: "Receive the Holy Spirit"

John 20:19-23: During one of His post-resurrection appearances, when the disciples were locked away "for fear of the Jews", Jesus stood among them, and said, "As the Father has sent me, even so I am sending you" ... He breathed on them (*enephusesen*) and He said to them:

> "Receive *the Holy Spirit*. If you forgive the sins of any, they are forgiven them; if you withhold forgiveness from any, it is withheld." (John 20:22,23)

Did the Lord really give, even to the Twelve, the authority and ability to forgive sins? I look later at the connection of the 'gift' of the Holy Spirit with the authority to forgive and withhold forgiveness (page 94). But Jesus 'breathing' on His disciples is reminiscent of Genesis 2:7, where the Septuagint (*LXX*) version reads:

> God formed the man of dust of the earth, and breathed upon (*enephusesen*) his face the breath (*pnoen*) of life, and the man became a living soul.

B.F. Westcott's comment is, "The same image which was used to describe the communication of the natural life, is here used to express the communication of the new, spiritual, life of re-created humanity." He refers to Augustine's observation that 'by breathing', the Lord showed that the Spirit was not the Spirit of the Father only, but also His own (*Gospel of St. John*).

The 'gift' of the Holy Spirit here was to the disciples as a body, and we cannot be sure whether this consisted only of the apostles or included other Jewish believers, such as some of the 120 referred to in Acts 1:14,15. John records a later 'appearing' of Jesus when "Thomas, one of the Twelve" (v.24), was present, which might suggest that the Twelve were in mind here, including Matthias, selected later to make up their number to twelve (Acts 1:23-26).

The apostles had been prepared for their ministry; Jesus had breathed upon them and called upon them to "receive the Holy Spirit", and the Lord had said to them: "Peace be with you. As the Father has sent me, even so I am sending you." All was now ready.

ix) John's Epilogue (chapter 21)

The final reference to *pneuma* in John's Gospel is in John 20:22. Its absence in chapter 21 reminded me that many commentators hold the view that John's Gospel originally ended at 20:31, where John tells us his purpose in writing this Gospel: "These are written ... that by believing you may have life in his name." Then later, though not too much later (Lightfoot reckoned very soon after) he added this last chapter.

In this chapter John refers to an appearance of the resurrected Messiah to seven of His disciples, during which the miracle (sign?) of the 153 fish takes place. All night the disciples had fished and caught nothing, but when Jesus appeared He told them to cast their net on the other side of the boat and they caught this large quantity[30].

The meaning of this "sign" is open to different interpretations. It may indicate what was going to happen around the middle of the Acts Period when, because many Jews were rejecting Jesus as Messiah, God opened the door to the Gentiles, with the object of making Israel jealous. Together with the "remnant" of Jews who did believe (Romans 11:1-14), the Gentiles who believed at this time might be "those who did receive" the Messiah that John refers to in 1:12,13.

The rest of this chapter is about Peter, and John the apostle, author of the Gospel, and may have been added to the Gospel to 'clear up' misunderstandings that had arisen. John had recorded Peter's *threefold* denial of Jesus (18:5-27), now, to put the record straight, he reports Peter's *threefold* 'love' for Jesus (21:15-19). Also, John attempts to put an end to the rumours that he himself would not die, but remain alive to the Lord's second coming (21:20-24).

Chapter 10
The Holy Spirit and the Preparation of the apostles for their coming mission (John 14-16)

In approaching these chapters, we should take care not to assume arbitrarily that "the bulk of the discourse is addressed to the disciples *as representatives* of the Church that is to be" (Beasley Murray *Word Biblical Commentary* p.263). The first priority is to recognise that the apostles were being prepared for a ministry that was based on Old Testament promises to the Fathers, the restoration of the kingdom to Israel and their place in God's purpose for the earth that goes back to Abraham (Genesis 12:1-3). The tendency to spiritualise Scripture when it seemingly cannot seem to fit in with a literal sense, has not helped in our understanding of these chapters, or other Scriptures[31].

A) John chapters 14-16

These chapters are bounded on one side by the Lord's anticipation of His coming crucifixion, and on the other by the fulfilment of that event. "Troubled in his spirit", He knew that "his hour had come". He had prayed, "Father, save me from this hour", but knew that it was God's purpose for Him to "come to this hour". He had "glorified" the Father's name, and He would continue to do so, whatever was required of Him (John 12:27-30; 13:1).

The twelve apostles were together with Jesus at table. Following the foot washing incident, and the important example that it taught—that they were to act as 'servants' as He had done—He says to them, "one of you will betray me" (13:1-21). His betrayal by Judas Iscariot was at hand. Judas leaves the table and goes to do his dreadful deed. Jesus now addresses the Eleven (Chapters 14-16).

To begin with, it would seem that Jesus and the apostles were still seated in the room where they had eaten together. It is not until John 14:31 that Jesus says, "Rise, let us go from here." Their conversation was possibly continued on the way to the Mount of Olives where Jesus prays the High Priestly prayer that begins in chapter 17.

The Lord told the apostles they were not to be "troubled", either by things they had already heard and seen, or by what He was about to tell them. Jesus was "going away", leaving them so as "to prepare a place" for them in one of the many "rooms" in His Father's house. He would return and "take them to himself". He was about to prepare them for His 'departure' and their coming ministry (they had already spent 2 to 3 years with Him and that must also count as part of that preparation). But in one sense, He would still "work with them" (Mark 16:20). But how?

B) The promise of "another Helper" (John 14:15-17)

The Lord continued His discourse to the apostles promising that during His absence He would not leave them alone like orphans (John 14:14-18). He would send "another Helper" (Greek *Parakletos*)[32], the Holy Spirit, One to be 'alongside them ... called to their aid'. He was "the Spirit of truth"; He would be their teacher in Jesus' place (14:1-31). Effectively, the Holy Spirit's ministry would be, "the Lord *working with them*" (Mark 16:19,20). This ministry, with its outward signs, took place and was recorded by Luke in The Acts of the Apostles. (And this ministry of the Holy Spirit will surely be continued by Christian Jews at the return of the Messiah to His people, Israel, in a future mission to the nations, when God resumes His purpose for the earth through His chosen people, Genesis 12:1-3.)

The Holy Spirit was given to the apostles *to continue* the work of the Messiah after His departure. But as Westcott observed, "the efficiency of

His action for them depends upon their fellowship with Him through *their loving obedience*" (Westcott *in loco*):

> "*If* you love me, you will keep my commandments. *And* I will ask the Father, and he will give you another Helper, to be with you for ever." (John 14:15,16)

In John 14:12 Jesus promised the apostles, "Whoever *believes in me* will also do *the works* that I do; and *greater works* than these will he do, because I am going to the Father". Then, in verse 15, He calls for *love and obedience to His commandments.* In the first place, *faith* issues in works of power—even greater works—in the second the thought is more *of devotion to Him* that is based upon obedience; "obedience is the necessary consequence of love" (Westcott).

i) Greater works than these because I go to the Father

Jesus said to the apostles:

> "Truly, truly, I say to you, whoever believes in me will also do the works that I do; and *greater works than these will he do, because I am going to the Father.*" (John 14:12)

> "I tell you the truth: *it is to your advantage* that I go away, for *if I do not go away, the Helper will not come to you.* But if I go I will send him to you." (John 16:7)

Jesus is going away:

There will be differences between the Lord's ministry whilst on earth and the Holy Spirit's ministry through the apostles after His ascension. It seems that the latter was more 'advantageous' and 'greater' than the former, and that the presence of the Lord (physically) *hindered* the coming of the Holy Spirit. That the apostles would do "greater things" than Jesus Himself was doing somehow doesn't seem to be right. In regard to the latter it may be noted that Jesus said something similar of Himself:

> "The Son can do nothing of his own accord, but only what he sees the Father doing ... the Father loves the Son and shows him all that he himself is doing. And *greater works than these* will he

show him, so that you may marvel." (John 5:19,20)

We know of course, that in the final analysis, whether these works be by the apostles or by Jesus Himself, all are dependent upon the Father; all "works" in these contexts, whether they be "greater" or not, are "the works of God" (cp. John 6:28,29). They derive from God; the apostles are but the 'agents' through whom God's power is seen at work. But this does not satisfactorily answer the implications behind these statements. So I explore it further.

In John 16:7 the *KJV* has, "it is *expedient* that I go away"; *Moffatt*, the *NEB* and the *NIV* have "my going is *for your good*". Elsewhere the Greek *sumphero* has been rendered "profitable" (e.g. Matthew 5:29 *KJV*). In John it occurs here (16:7), and in 11:50 where Caiaphas the high priest said to the Council, "It *is better for* you that one man should die for the people, not that the whole nation should perish", and in 18:14 when these words are recalled at the trial of Jesus.

There is no suggestion as used here, that the word *sumphero* conveys the idea that there is no alternative, but simply that something is the best or advisable course—expediency. So when the Lord said, "If I do not go away, the Helper will not come to you", He is not saying that His presence on earth *precludes* the Holy Spirit from being there at the same time, but that the Holy Spirit's ministry through the apostles, *after He had gone to the Father*, would be for *their good* and *more profitable*. Turning to the other reference ...

The apostles' "greater works":

In John 14:12 the Lord promises that the apostles will do "greater works" than Jesus was doing; in what way 'greater'? The English word is generally understood in two ways, greater in number, or greater in kind or quality. So in what way will the ministry of the Holy Spirit working through the apostles, do *greater* works than those Jesus did during His ministry on earth? Are they miracles of *a greater nature*? Or is the meaning that they will do *more than* the Messiah did on earth? And what does "works" refer to?

"**Greater**", *meizona*. Liddell and Scott Greek-English Lexicon gives its meaning as "in a greater degree", and its usage in John 15:13 is probably the best example of this: "*Greater* love has no one than this, that someone lay down his life for his friends." Here "love" is more intense; the very zenith of 'love'. Other examples in John demonstrate its usage in this way:

- The Samaritan woman asks of Jesus, "Are you *greater* than our father Jacob?" (4:12)
- Speaking of Himself Jesus says, "The Father is *greater than* I." (14:28)
- Jesus to the apostles, "A servant is not *greater* than his master." (15:20)

If we compare the miracles done by the Lord whilst on earth with those done by the apostles during the Acts Period, we cannot honestly say that the apostles did "greater works" *at that time*. Compare for example what was probably the greatest miracle of all—'raising the dead'—as done by Jesus (Gospel Period) and Paul (Acts Period).

Jesus *raised Lazarus after he had been entombed four days* (John 11), and Paul brought Eutychus back to life *very shortly after his fall from the third storey of a building* (Acts 20:9). Both were miracles, but which was the "greater"? I think most would choose the raising of Lazarus, who was brought back to life well after rigor mortis would normally have set in, the corpse already decomposing with the accompanying odour (John 11:39).

I confess that I, in common with many others, do not know the answer to this problem, but I do think it has a lot to do with the contrast between the Gospel and Acts Periods, which were a kind of 'firstfruits' and a 'taste' of a coming age, and the arrival on earth of that coming (millennial) age itself. Something like this:

- **Covenants:** Gospel Period, Old Covenant; Acts Period, New Covenant 'ready' to replace the Old; Coming age of the millennial kingdom on earth, New Covenant in operation (Hebrews 8:13).
- **Works:** Gospel Period, 'good'; Acts Period, 'greater'; Coming millennium age, 'greatest'.

The importance of distinguishing between these three periods, will, I trust, become clearer as we proceed, and will, I hope, put "greater works" done by the ministry of the Holy Spirit at that time into perspective.

"Works", Greek *erga*. *Liddell and Scott* give its basic meaning as, "work, a man's business ... later of all kinds of works." It is evidently an all-inclusive word covering all that a person does or even says. John uses the noun many times; some examples in John are:

- This is the judgement; the light has come into the world, and men loved the darkness rather than the light because their *works* were evil. (John 3:19)
- Jesus, "My food is to do the will of him who sent me and to accomplish his *work*." (John 4:34)
- The Jews: "What must we do, to be doing the *works* of God?" (John 6:28)
- Jesus: "This is the *work* of God, that you believe in him whom he has sent." (John 6:29)

It is evident that the word is used here of the whole 'business' of man, not only his deeds but his beliefs. The ministry of the apostles will include miracles of healing, signs to authenticate their ministry and what they preach, but above all, those "works" will glorify the Lord. That ministry is recorded in the Acts of the Apostles and in those epistles written by five of the apostles during this period that have been preserved in the Scriptures. They are:[33]

- The epistles of James, Peter, John and Jude.
- Paul's epistles to the Galatians, Corinthians, Thessalonians, Romans and Hebrews (assuming it to be Pauline).
- Revelation, with its letters to the churches, is a special case (see the authors *Apocalypse* OBT).

All these epistles were written against the background of the Holy Spirit's ministry during the Acts Period, and contain things in them that are specifically relevant to that period. They do also, however, contain much that is relevant for us today in "The Church which is the Body of Christ".

In respect of the latter, I cannot emphasise enough, that whether the ministry of the Holy Spirit is seen at work during the Acts Period, or the post-Acts Period, that ministry is based solidly on the gospel that Paul spoke of in 1 Corinthians 15:1-4. Having reminded the Corinthians that it was the gospel which he had preached to them, he went on to describe it as, "the gospel ... by which you are being saved" and continued:

> I delivered to you as of first importance what I also received:
> > That Christ died for our sins in accordance with the Scriptures,
> > that he was buried,
> > that he was raised on the third day in accordance with the Scriptures.

Paul could add the testimony of many still living at that time, who could confirm Christ's resurrection. The Lord had appeared to Peter, then to the Twelve and then to more than 500 of the Jewish brethren, most still alive at the time. And lastly, the evidence of his own testimony to his meeting with Jesus on the Damascus road (Acts chapter 9; 1 Corinthians 15:5-10).

ii) He will guide you into all the truth

In John 16:12, Jesus had said, "*I* still have many things to say to you, but you cannot bear them now." Now, referring to the Holy Spirit's ministry, He promised the apostles:

> "When the Spirit of truth comes, he will guide you into all the truth, for he will not speak on his own authority, but whatever he hears he will speak, and he will declare to you the things that are to come. He will glorify me, for he will take what is mine and declare it to you." (John 16:13,14)

Some versions (e.g. *KJV*) read "all truth" here leaving out the definite article. Westcott (*in loco*) observes that,

> He leads them not (vaguely) 'into all truth', but 'into all *the* Truth', into the complete understanding of and sympathy with that absolute Truth, which is Christ himself.

As Jesus said "*I am* the way and *the truth* and the life" (John 14:6). He is the embodiment of 'truth'.

"The Truth" derives originally from the Father and is the perfect expression of the will of God. Some of its teaching had been given to the disciples whilst the Lord was on earth, but some they would not have been able "to bear" at that time. Now, with the ministry of the Holy Spirit, they were to be guided into "all the truth", and whatever that involved, it was given to "glorify" the Son of God—"He will glorify me" (John

16:14).

iii) The Truth: Then and now

"'What is truth?' said jesting Pilate; and would not stay for an answer" (Francis Bacon *The Advancement of Learning* referring to John 18:38). I doubt that Pilate was jesting, but more likely speaking against the background of the many voices that had claimed to answer this question in the age of philosophy in which he lived. Jesus had said to him, "Everyone who is *of the truth* listens to *my voice*", and well they might, for He is "the way, and *the truth*, and the life" (John 14:6; cp. 1:14,17).

In Scriptural terms we can compare "the truth" with "*the faith* that was once for all delivered to the saints", a deposit committed to Christians to keep and *contend* for (Jude 3). However, it is not just summed up in a written code of belief and practice, but in a Person, Jesus Christ. And far from being a series of things to believe and do, and not to believe and not to do, "the truth will set you free" (John 8:32). Nevertheless, seen as a 'body' of facts, what may be 'true' for some (e.g. the Jews of the Old Testament and Gospels) may not necessarily be relevant for others (e.g. Gentiles after the Acts Period) who are in a different calling.

Today, questions concerning 'the Truth' arise for those who see a difference between God's purpose for the earth through Abraham and Israel, and His purpose for the Church which is the Body of Christ and whose hope is in the heavenly places. With that in mind, I ask, 'What relevance does the Holy Spirit's ministry, revealed in John's Gospel (especially in chapters 14-16) and the Synoptics, have for us today who are members of The Body of Christ?'

As I have often tried to make clear in my writings on the Scriptures, it is both obvious and vital that "the truth" relating to the crucifixion, death and resurrection of Christ, and the importance in believing Jesus of Nazareth as the Saviour of the world, is relevant to all 'callings', earthly or heavenly. That is *the* Gospel of Christ.

But what of other aspects of the ministry of the Holy Spirit, such as (e.g.) spiritual gifts? Can we claim some of the promises given to the apostles who were assured they would do greater works than Christ (John 14:12), and promised "*Whatever you ask* in my (Jesus') name, this *I will do*" (John 14:13; 15:16), and "*Ask*, and *you will receive*, that your joy may be full" (John 16:24)?

Promises made by the Lord to the apostles (John chapters 14-16), have often been taken in commentaries, and by ministers and Christians, to apply to 'the Church' *carte blanche*. They see the apostles simply as 'representatives' of the 'Church' in all ages. In some cases, this has caused some to lose their faith in the Bible as they see the promises are not fulfilled in their lives. In other cases, this has led to certain sections of the 'Church' claiming the right to give absolution from guilt and the binding and loosing from sin according to Matthew 16:19.

Hence before we claim the Lord's promises to the apostles for ourselves, particularly in the latter case, I list (below) the different facets of the Holy Spirit's ministry as given to the apostles *at that time*. Are the things promised by the Lord to the apostles relevant *en bloc* to ourselves? We must remember that they were being prepared for a ministry, 'earth-shattering' in its claims, challenging as it did, a form of Judaism that had been practised for many years. They were claiming that *they* knew and possessed "The truth"?

Here, briefly is *what the Scriptures say* of the Holy Spirit, and *what the Scriptures record* He would do for the apostles as they remained in loving obedience to Jesus Christ (John 14:15,16).

iv) The Holy Spirit and the promises: A summary (John 14-16)

The Holy Spirit is the Spirit of truth ... another Helper ... although He was unseen, the apostles "knew him" ... He   "dwelt with them" (in the person of Jesus?) ... He "would be in them" (John 14:16,17).

- He would come "in the Father's name" ... "teach them all things ... bring to their remembrance all that Jesus had said to them" (John 14:26).
- Proceeding from the Father, when He comes "he will bear witness about (the absent) Jesus" (John 15:26).
- Unless Jesus went away the Holy Spirit, the Helper, would not come to them; His departure would be to their "advantage" (John 16:7). See below page 85.
- When He comes He will convict the world of sin, righteousness and judgement (John 16:8-11).

- When He comes He will "guide (the apostles) into all the truth".
- "Whatever he hears he will speak (presumably through the apostles) but not on his own authority" (John16:13).
- He will declare to the apostles "things that are to come" (John16:13).
- He will glorify Jesus, taking what is His and the Father's, and declaring it to the apostles (John 16:14,15).

(I have assumed throughout these chapters that the Lord was actually with the Eleven apostles when He spoke these things. It may be that other disciples, such as Matthias and Joseph Barsabbas (Acts 2:23), were present at some or all the time, in which case the above would have been addressed and relevant to them also. However, what we must be cautious of and ask is … how much of the Holy Spirit's ministry revealed here has relevance to the wider audience of the Acts Period Christians, and more to the point today, to us living after the Acts Period? This will, I trust, become clearer as we proceed.)

C) "The Great Commission" (so called)

i) The Twelve Apostles and their authority

Apart from the veneration given by the Church to the Twelve apostles down the ages, the specific commission and authority given to them through the ministry of the Holy Spirit has largely been considered to have been passed on to the Church. This has been done by treating those apostles simply as 'representatives' of that Church. But that detracts from the unique position of the Twelve, who were so important to the purpose of God that the Lord spent two to three years with them on earth, opened their minds to understand the Scriptures (Luke 24:32) and, "presented himself alive to them after his suffering by many proofs, appearing to them during forty days and speaking about the kingdom of God" (Acts 1:1-3). And in addition to this He promised them that:

> "In the new world (lit. in the regeneration) when the Son of Man will sit on his glorious throne, you who have followed me will also sit on twelve thrones, judging the twelve tribes of Israel." (Matthew 19:28)

Here is a promise that none apart from the apostles, not even the Church, can take to itself. Hence we don't often, if ever, hear a sermon on it. And commentaries are not far behind in their reluctance to comment on it in relation to God's purpose for the Church today. This promise was for the future 'new age'. However, what we should ask is ... what authority was given to the apostles, after Christ had "breathed upon them" and given them the Holy Spirit, which was relevant for their Acts Period ministry?

Excursus: Degrees of authority:

The priests and Levites, at the bidding of the Pharisees in Jerusalem, questioned John the Baptist as to who he was and what *authority* he therefore had to baptise. And in the Gospel and Acts Periods, it is evident that some disciples had the authority to baptise (e.g. John's disciples John 4:1,2), but what of the authority to give the Holy Spirit? Only apostles seem to have such authority.

For example, Philip (not an apostle) could baptise the believing Samaritans, but it was Peter and John who were sent and "laid their hands on them and they received the Holy Spirit" (Acts 8:4-8,12-16). Paul, as an apostle, also had this authority, as was demonstrated in Ephesus, when he met some disciples who knew only the baptism of John, and had "not even heard that there is a Holy Spirit". They were then "baptised in the name of the Lord Jesus. And when Paul had laid his hands on them, *the Holy Spirit came upon them*, and they began to speak in tongues and prophesying" (Acts 19:1-6).

These apostles were given authority as 'human channels', but it is evident that the Holy Spirit had come upon these Gentile believers without the need for the laying on of hands. This happened in the case of Cornelius and his friends on whom the Holy Spirit "was poured out" as Peter was declaring the gospel to them (Acts 10:44). Here the 'norm' was reversed; the Holy Spirit was received first and water baptism took place afterwards (vs. 47,48). The lesson to be learnt here is that we cannot confine the work of the Holy Spirit to a set 'formula'.

The authority to forgive sins was also given to the Twelve, and we must now look at this in some detail.

ii) Authority to forgive sins: binding and loosing

Before His ascension the Lord "breathed" on them (the apostles) and said to them, "*Receive the Holy Spirit*". He went on to say:

> "If you forgive the sins of any, they are forgiven them; if you withhold forgiveness from any, it is withheld." (John 20:19-23)

Earlier He had said something similar to His disciples. Did this include the forgiveness of sins?

> "Truly, I say to you, whatever you bind on earth shall be bound in heaven, and whatever you loose on earth shall be loosed in heaven." (Matthew 18:18)

The Lord's words in the second passage are almost identical to those that followed His promise to give to Peter "the keys to the kingdom of heaven" (Matthew 16:19), given to him exclusively and which he used to open that kingdom to the Jews at Pentecost (Acts 2) and Gentile God-fearers in Caesarea (Acts 10). Even if these passages in John and Matthew should not be read together, we still have the apostles apparently given authority to forgive sins.

Were the Pharisees not absolutely correct when they said to Jesus, "Who can forgive sins but God alone?" Was it not blasphemy to make such a claim? Jesus' answer to such was "the Son of Man has authority to forgive sins", which He claimed was proved when He healed a paralysed man (Luke 5:17-24; and see Isaiah 35:4-6). Hence, by giving His apostles *the power* to do miracles, did He pass on also *the authority* to forgive sins, when He, "breathed on them and said, '*Receive the Holy Spirit*'"?

However, there appears to be no record in the New Testament that Peter or any of the other apostles claimed to be able to forgive sins, even though they also did miracles. So how do we read John 20:22,23? Let us look beyond this question and look at the authority that we know for certain was given to them.

iii) Twelve apostles, twelve thrones of judgement

Jesus said to the Twelve:

> "In the new world (lit. in the regeneration) when the Son of Man will sit on his glorious throne, you who have followed me will also sit on twelve thrones, *judging the twelve tribes of Israel*." (Matthew 19:28)

The Acts Period, into which these apostles were about to enter, was an *anticipation* of this "new world." And as I hope to show, Jewish believers during this period were a kind of 'firstfruits' being called out and urged to "save yourselves from this crooked generation" (Acts 2:40). These 'firstfruits' were later described by Paul as a "remnant" (Romans 11:1-5). And the day would come when this remnant would increase in number to become a full harvest, and this is anticipated in the same passage (Romans 11:11,12,25,26).

James also, writing at this time to his brethren in the Jewish Dispersion (James 1:1), described them as "a kind of *firstfruits* of his creatures" (James 1:18). And the Hebrews writer, speaking to Jewish believers during the Acts Period and reminding them of their blessings, told them that they had:

> *Tasted* the heavenly gift, and have *shared in the Holy Spirit*, and have *tasted* the goodness of the word of God and *the powers* (*dunamis*, miracles) of the age to come. (6:4,5)

The situation at that time should become clearer when we look at the true meaning of Pentecost and the Acts Period. But if Jewish believers living at during the Acts Period had only "*tasted* ... the powers of the age to come", that is obviously very different from enjoying the "fullness" that would be theirs when that millennial age comes. And therefore, in regard to the "greater works" (see page 85) promised to the apostles (and other Jewish believers), they awaited the arrival of that age upon the earth. When this age dawned, however, these "greater works ... *the powers* of a coming age" would be part of that "fullness". In the same way, the Twelve would have the *authority* to pronounce judgement from twelve thrones "in this regeneration" (Acts 3:20,21).

What was said and what took place during the Gospel and Acts Periods can only be fully understood when seen against the background of what that period actually was. It was **not** a new beginning, but a continuation of God working through Israel to bring His purpose for the earth to fruition. It was intended to lead to the consummation of God's purpose for the earth through His chosen channel Israel. It rested on the LORD's promise to Abraham (Genesis 12:1-3; Acts 3:24-26), the return of "the kingdom to Israel" (Acts 1:6), the placing of that nation in their own Promised Land, tribe-by-tribe (Acts 26:6,7)—in short, the fulfilment of "the hope of Israel" (Acts 28:20).

To sum up, as to the authority to forgive sins, the twelve apostles had been promised:

> In the new world (*KJV* 'regeneration'), when the Son of Man will sit on his glorious throne, you who have followed me will also sit on twelve thrones, *judging the twelve tribes of Israel*. (Matthew 19:28)

This does not actually say that the Twelve will have the authority to forgive sins, but when the Messiah returns, the apostles will be given authority to dispense justice in Israel, no doubt under the inspiration of the Holy Spirit, which is the connection made in John 20:19-23:

> "*Receive the Holy Spirit*. If you *forgive the sins* of any, they are forgiven them; if you withhold forgiveness from any, it is withheld." (John 20:19-23)

But as I have remarked, there is no record in the New Testament of Peter, or any of the other apostles, actually pronouncing the forgiveness of sins *on their own authority*. And neither is there any suggestion that such an authority was passed on by 'Apostolic Succession'[34] to a series of bishops (or Popes) down to the present day. The authority to forgive sins, or withhold forgiveness of sins, was at most relevant only to the twelve apostles, and then only insofar that it anticipates their future role as 'judges' over the tribes of Israel (Matthew 9:28; Luke 22:30).

Thus fully equipped, the Twelve were ready for their witness, beginning in Jerusalem.

iv) The apostles are sent forth[35]

The title, 'The Great Commission', has been coined and used by Christians to describe the missionary efforts starting with the apostles and, following them, made by men and women of God in all ages, who have carried the Christian Gospel to "the ends of the earth". I rejoice with them all in their success, and have admiration for their faithfulness to the Lord under all circumstances. So if I draw some conclusions in this study that don't quite fit in with some Christian interpretations of the apostles' ministry, that is in no way intended to be a criticism of the efforts both in the past and now made by those who are attempting to bring men and women to Christ.

v) The Twelve: Final instructions

There are three main accounts, Matthew, Mark and Luke, of the final instructions given to the eleven apostles, all of which have slightly different aspects. John simply records Jesus as saying:

> "Peace be with you. *As the Father has sent me, even so I am sending you ... Receive the Holy Spirit ...* If you forgive the sins of any, they are forgiven them; if you withhold forgiveness from any, it is withheld." (John 20:21-23).

The difference between the Synoptists and John does, I believe, reflect not only when they were written but the purpose in writing. Matthew, Mark and Luke are more like histories, written well after the events they record. Luke (and Acts) in particular, were initially written for the benefit of an individual, Theophilus, whereas John has an urgent message for his readers (*while there is yet time*) 'Jesus is the Messiah ... believe!' (20:30,31).

John's brethren had rejected Jesus at the cross, and during the Acts Period were continuing to do so (John 1:11-13), but when John wrote his Gospel there was still time for their repentance and acceptance of Jesus as the Messiah. His 'history' reflects that urgency ("that you may believe"); it is ongoing. Hence he has no reason to record the Lord's instructions to the apostles.

As I have suggested, John's 'urgent' Gospel probably originally ended at 20:31; chapter 21 being added by him later (page 81). In chapter 21, apart from some references to the appearances of Jesus, the miracle (sign?) of the Draught of Fishes, and some observations concerning Peter and himself, his Gospel appears to end with his reason for writing at 20:31:

> Now Jesus did many other signs in the presence of the disciples, which are not written in this book; but these are written *so that you may believe that Jesus is the Messiah, the Son of God*, and that believing you may have life in his name. (20:30,31)

However, the other three Gospels and Acts do have accounts of 'The Great Commission':

> **Matthew 24:14:** Jesus prophesies: "This gospel of the kingdom

will be proclaimed throughout *the whole world* (*oikoumene*) as a testimony to all nations (*ethne*), and then the end will come."

Matthew 28:16,18-20: Jesus came and said to (the Eleven), "All authority in heaven and on earth has been given to me. Go therefore and *make disciples of all nations* (*ethne*), baptising them in the name of the Father and of the Son and of the Holy Spirit, teaching them to observe all that I have commanded you. And behold, I am with you always, to the end of the age (*aionos*)."

Mark 13:1-27: Jesus prophesies the close of the age and the coming of Son of Man in power and great glory.
vs. 10,11: "The Gospel must *first be proclaimed to* (*eis*) *all nations* (*ethne*)... *the Holy Spirit will speak through you* ... you will be hated of all men for my name's sake."

Mark 16:14-18: Jesus appeared to the Eleven ... and he said to them, "Go into all the world (*kosmos*) and proclaim the gospel to the whole creation (*ktisis*). Whoever believes and is baptised will be saved, but whoever does not believe will be condemned. And these signs will accompany those who believe: in my name they will cast out demons ... speak in new tongues ... pick up serpents with their hands ... if they drink any deadly poison, it will not hurt them; they will lay their hands on the sick, and they will recover ..." They went out and preached everywhere, while the Lord worked with them and confirmed the message by accompanying signs.

Luke 24:44-49: Jesus said to them ... "everything written about me in the Law of Moses and the Prophets and the Psalms must be fulfilled". Then he opened their minds to understand the Scriptures, and said to them, "Thus it is written, that the Messiah should suffer and on the third day rise from the dead, and that repentance and forgiveness of sins should be *proclaimed in his name to all nations* (*ethne*), beginning from Jerusalem. You are witnesses of these things. And behold, I am sending the promise of my Father upon you. But *stay* in the city *until you are clothed with power from on high*."

Acts 1:8: The Lord said to them, "*You will receive power when the Holy Spirit has come upon you*, and you will be my witnesses in Jerusalem and in all Judea and Samaria, and to the end of the earth."

Both Matthew and Luke refer to the apostles' 'commission' in the context of the "nations (*ethne*)"; the apostles are to make disciples of "the nations" (*ethne*), and to proclaim repentance and forgiveness of sins to them in Messiah's name. The Acts of the Apostles refers to a "witness" that is to be "to the end of the earth (*ge*)", which at first reading may seem to refer to a "witness" to the Gentiles, but see below. And "the end" will not come until, "the gospel of the kingdom has been proclaimed throughout "the whole world (*oikoumene*) as a testimony to all nations (*ethne*)".

Mark's account also records the Lord's commission to the apostles in terms of "*all nations (ethne)*" but speaks additionally of "all the world (*kosmos*)" into which the apostles must go, and "the whole creation (*ktisis*)" to whom "the gospel" is to be "proclaimed".

Whilst 'the nations' are of course made up of individuals, the emphasis here is on them *nationally*. As *nations* they had departed from the LORD, and as *nations*, when "the Son of man comes in his glory", they will be "gathered before him" for judgement (Matthew 25:31:32). But this was not expected to take place before Israel the nation was a redeemed people ("salvation is from the Jews" John 4:22) and it is quite evident from the Acts record that this never happened.

et us now proceed to the Acts Period and consider the witness of the apostles during that period, with particular reference to an expedient that was put into place to try and stir up a nation that continued to reject Jesus the Messiah and the message of salvation. That expedient was the introduction of the Gentiles into the equation.

The Holy Spirit and His Ministry

Chapter 11
The Holy Spirit during the Acts Period

A) Luke's record and the course of the Acts

Luke's record, *The Acts of the Apostles*, might well have been called, 'The Acts of the Holy Spirit'. His Gospel, his "former treatise", was "all that Jesus *began* both to do and teach" (Luke 1:1 *KJV*), and his second treatise was, what Jesus *continued* to do and teach through the Spirit-filled apostles. The Lord was keeping His promise to them, "I am going away and *I will come to you*", which He did through the Holy Spirit. Mark describing the Acts ministry wrote: "(the apostles) went forth, and preached everywhere, *the Lord working with them*" (Mark 16:20 *KJV*).

An understanding of what the Acts of the Apostles is about is the key to the whole of the New Testament. That understanding is not helped by referring to Pentecost as 'the birthday of the Church' and identifying it with "the church which is the body of Christ" in Ephesians 1:22,23 and Colossians 1:18.

The 'church' being called out at Pentecost was based upon Old Testament promises and prophesies concerning blessings on this earth. The 'church' spoken of in the two 'prison epistles', Ephesians and Colossians, was the subject of a 'mystery' not made known until revealed by Paul (Ephesians 3:3,6; Colossians 1:24-26), and whose blessings are "in the heavenly places" (Ephesians 1:3).

We could depict the course of the Acts Period like travelling along a road, not a new road, but a road already well established and going back to the very beginnings of the Lord's dealings with His people. That road had been travelled from the calling of Abraham out from the nations, through the whole of the Old Testament and Gospel Periods, and would continue until the 'road closed' sign appeared, which it did at the end of the Acts Period (Genesis 12 to Acts 28). At some time, still future to us, it will reopen until it reaches its goal: the Salvation of Israel and the Millennium Kingdom on earth.

In the meantime, God's people have been diverted on to another 'road', a road that leads to a heavenly destination, heavenly places with Christ at the right hand of God, where we await our appearance with Him (Ephesians 2:3-7; Colossians 3:1-4).

I will come back to the differences between these two callings of God in more detail later (see page 163). Also the author's book, *The Mystery of Ephesians* OBT.

i) References to The Holy Spirit in the Acts Period

There are some 54 references to the Holy Spirit (*pneuma*) in the Acts of the Apostles.[36] Here I can look at only a representative number that demonstrate how much the Holy Spirit figured in the lives of believers during the Acts Period. In addition to being *filled by* the Spirit (2:4; 7:55; 9:17) other references to the Holy Spirit's influence upon the lives of early ministers of the Gospel are:

- *Told* (*Go*) by the Spirit (11:12).
- *Led* (*and carried*) by the Spirit (8:39).
- *Forbidden* by the Spirit (16:6,7).
- *Warned* (*foretold*) by the Spirit (11:28; 21:11).
- *Constrained* by the Spirit (20:22).
- *Comforted* by the Spirit (9:31).

The Holy Spirit also *spoke through* the Old Testament prophets, as He did when Paul quoted Isaiah 6:9,10 in the Lord's judgement upon Israel (Acts 28:25-27). And there were those who *lied to* (Acts 5:3) and *resisted* (Acts 7:51) the Holy Spirit. But when we compare the situation during the Acts Period with our own today, there is a world of difference.

During the former, the Holy Spirit was very much in evidence outwardly in the lives of ministers of the Gospel and others, even to inflicting a judgement of death upon some who lied to Him (Ananias and Sapphira

Acts 5:1-11). Today the Holy Spirit is still very much with us, but working in a different way in relation to *our own calling and* 'hope'. I give here a selection of those occasions during the Acts Period that show the Holy Spirit at work in the lives of those living during that period:

ii) The Holy Spirit at work during the Acts Period

Acts 2:1-41: Peter and the Eleven in Jerusalem:

At the feast of Pentecost, filled with *the Holy Spirit,* they spoke with other tongues "as *the Spirit* gave them utterance" (v.4). Peter, speaking to "Men of Judea" (v.14) and those dwelling in Jerusalem, refers this phenomenon to Joel's prophecy with God's promise, "I will pour out *My Spirit* on all flesh" (v.17), and likens it to the circumstances of his day. He promises them that if they will repent and be baptised in the name of Jesus the Messiah, they will receive forgiveness of sins and the gift of *the Holy Spirit* (v. 38).

On this Day of Pentecost, Peter was using the "keys to the kingdom of heaven" (Matthew 16:19) to open the door to his own people, and many who received the word were added to their number that day (v.41).

[Later (Acts 10) he was to use those keys to open the door of salvation to the Gentiles.]

Acts 5:1-11: Ananias and Sapphira:

They were struck dead for trying to deceive Peter over a gift of money, since they were effectively "lying to *the Holy Spirit*".

Acts 6:8-7:60: Stephen stoned to death:

Having spoken with great wisdom and *the Spirit*, he is brought before the Sanhedrin (vs. 6:8-15), where after giving them a brief history of Israel, he accuses them, saying, "You stiff-necked people ... you always resist *the Holy Spirit*. As your fathers did, so do you" (7:51-53). In a fit of rage they came upon him, but he, "full of *the Holy Spirit*, gazed up into heaven and saw the glory of God, and Jesus standing at the right hand of God. And he said, 'Behold, I see the Son of Man standing at the right hand of God'". They rushed at him and dragged him outside, where they stoned him to death.

Acts 8:26-39: Philip (not the apostle):

An Ethiopian eunuch seated in his chariot was returning from worshipping in Jerusalem. *The Spirit* told Philip to join him. The man was querying to whom Isaiah 53 referred, and Philip explained that it referred to Jesus. Philip baptised him, and *"the Spirit of the Lord* carried Philip away". The eunuch left rejoicing.

Acts 9:1-22: Saul of Tarsus:

Having met and been called by the Lord and "filled with *the Holy Spirit*", Saul began his ministry in the synagogues of Damascus, proclaiming Jesus to be "the Son of God" and "proving that Jesus was the Messiah".

Acts 9:31: The Acts Church:

"The church throughout all Judea and Galilee and Samaria had peace and was being built up. And walking in the fear of the Lord and in the comfort of *the Holy Spirit* it multiplied."

Acts 10 & 11: Peter and the Gentile Cornelius:

Disturbed by a powerful vision from God and, as he reported later, at the bidding of *the Spirit* (11:12), Peter was persuaded to go to Caesarea and speak to the devout Gentile Cornelius and his company. As he spoke to them, "*the Holy Spirit* fell on all who heard the word" and they began to speak in tongues extolling God. The believing Gentiles were then "baptised in the name of Jesus the Messiah" (10:44-48). Peter came to recognise that God had chosen him to take "the word of the gospel" to the Gentiles (see Acts 15:7-9). Peter had used "the keys of the kingdom of heaven" (Matthew 16:19) a second time, and on this occasion to open the door to the Gentiles.

Acts 11:27-30: Agabus the Prophet:

Amongst some prophets who came down from Jerusalem to Antioch, was one named Agabus. He foretold "*by the Spirit*, that there would be a great famine over all the world". (That famine took place in the days of Claudius). So the disciples determined that they would send what relief they could. They did so "by the hand of Barnabas and Saul".

Acts 13:1-3: Barnabas and Saul:

The Holy Spirit said to the church in Antioch, "Set apart for me Barnabas and Saul for the work to which I have called them."

Acts 13:6-12: Saul also called Paul:

In Cyprus, Paul filled with *the Holy Spirit*, temporally blinds Elymas the magician, a Jewish false prophet who was seeking to turn the proconsul Sergius Paulus away from the faith. The proconsul "believed when he saw what had occurred, for he was astonished at the teaching of the Lord".

Acts 16:3,6,7-10: Paul and Timothy:

"Forbidden by *the Holy Spirit* to speak the word in Asia ... *the Spirit of Jesus* did not allow them to go into Bithynia", and consequently they went over to Macedonia.

Acts 20:22,23; 21:8-14: Paul's determination:

"Constrained by *the Spirit*" Paul determines to go to Jerusalem, even though he is warned by *the Holy Spirit* of the imprisonment and afflictions that await him there.

Acts 28:23-28: Paul in Rome:

After trying to convince the leaders of the Jews in Rome about Jesus from the Scriptures, "from morning till evening", and with no agreement amongst them, Paul pronounced judgement upon them, quoting the words of *the Holy Spirit* speaking through Isaiah the prophet (Isaiah 6:9.10). He began, "*The Holy Spirit* was right in saying to your fathers" ... and having quoted the Old Testament verses in full, he finished by saying, "Therefore let it be known to you that this salvation of God has been sent to the Gentiles; they will listen" (v.28). The door to "the kingdom of heaven on earth", opened with the keys by Peter in Acts 2, was closed. However, as one door closes another opens, and is waiting to be revealed.

Paul remains in Rome awaiting his audience with Caesar, and at some time during that confinement, he writes to various churches (Ephesians and Colossians for example) and reveals and expands on what "this salvation of God has been sent to the Gentiles" actually meant in practice

(Acts 28:30,31). This should become clearer when we look at those two 'prison epistles' and what Paul is saying there.

iii) The Holy Spirit and the individual believer in Acts

Although the Holy Spirit was very evident in the lives of believers at this time, this did not mean they had become faultless, having no doubts or even having no will of their own. They were not God's puppets, any more than we are today. John the Baptist (e.g.) was, "Filled with *the Holy Spirit*, even from his mother's womb", and yet later on during his ministry he began to doubt whether Jesus was the Messiah, in spite of all the evidence that demonstrated that He was (Matthew 11:2-6).

Paul and Barnabas had "a sharp disagreement" over Paul's unwillingness to take John Mark with them on a return visit to the brethren in those cities where they had proclaimed the word of the Lord. Paul was against it, since Mark had "withdrawn from them" on a previous occasion in Pamphylia (Acts 13:13). So Barnabas took Mark with him and sailed away, pursuing his own ministry independently of Paul (Acts 15:36-40).

The Corinthian church, blessed in abundance with the "gifts of the Spirit", was condemned by Paul because of their worldliness and divisions; he spoke of them as "still of the flesh" (1 Corinthians 3:1-4). And writing to the same church, Paul observed that, "the spirits of prophets *are subject to* prophets", which suggests that the prophets remained in control of their own lives, even if speaking the Word of God (1 Corinthians 14:32).

Then there was Paul's condemnation of Peter because of his hypocrisy at Antioch. Peter was eating with the Gentiles there, until a party arrived from Jerusalem. He then withdrew himself from their fellowship, allowing himself to be influenced by this "circumcision party" of Christian Jews (Galatians 2:11-14).

In all these cases it is clear that either through the weakness of the flesh, or fear of others, these were deviations from what we might expect to be a *Spirit-filled life*. But this observation must not be pressed too far. There are those who are prepared to believe that the Twelve, in their interpretation of "The Great Commission", misunderstood the Lord's teaching. This is known as 'apostolic mistakes'.

iv) 'Apostolic mistakes'

We don't hear it so much today, but in my early days as a Christian, there was talk of "apostolic mistakes" made by the Twelve and their "misunderstanding" of the Lord's teaching. Most notably I remember, that it was claimed that the Lord was not planning to set up a literal kingdom on earth, but a "spiritual kingdom in heaven"[37]. Hence by asking Him, "will you at this time restore the kingdom to Israel?" (Acts 1:6), they had completely misunderstood His ministry.

If there was any 'misunderstanding' here it is actually on the part of those who are confusing God's purpose for the Acts' church and its earthly 'hope' (Acts 26:6,7; 28:20) with "the Church which is the Body of Christ" and its heavenly 'hope' (Ephesians and Colossians). Underlying this confusion is the teaching that Pentecost was *the beginning* of the latter, rather than *a continuation* of Israel's 'hope' that rested upon the ministry and sacrifice of Jesus the Messiah, and which was "to confirm the promises given to the fathers" (Romans 15:8).

The 'hope' of the Acts Period was for an earthly kingdom and it hung in the balance *at that time*, since its fulfilment depended upon Israel's repentance (Acts 3:19-21). There was still an 'if' as to the response to the Lord's and the apostles' teaching when they posed their question to Him concerning the "restoration of the kingdom to Israel".

B) Pentecost: Why Pentecost?

Pentecost has been viewed in Christian teaching as 'the birthday of the Church'; the 'Church' generally understood as being made up of all Christians of whatever denomination that have trusted in Christ from that day forth—in short, "The Church which is the Body of Christ". Christian teaching on the subject generally acknowledges that Pentecost was a Jewish feast, but rarely asks the question 'Why Pentecost?' Should the question be asked, however, the answer will probably be something like; 'because so many people were gathered in one place at this feast, it was an ideal time to *spring Christianity upon the world*'.

But if we recognise that the Feast of Passover was 'typical' of the one great sacrifice of Christ—"Christ our Passover is sacrificed for us" (1 Corinthians 5:7 *KJV*)—why should Pentecost not also be 'typical', and also the other Jewish feasts?

In the plan and purpose of God, nothing is 'an accident of time and place'. "When *the fullness of time* had come, God sent forth his Son ..." (Galatians 4:4). "It is not for you to know *times or seasons that the Father has fixed* by his own authority" (Acts 1:7). Hence, the Day of Pentecost 'arrived' in due season and, as with every other part of God's dealings with man, that feast and its timing must have had some relevance in the 'seasons' of God. What was it then? In order to answer that question, we have to go back to the Old Testament and look at the inauguration of this feast in the time of Moses, and see it in the context of the other feasts to be kept by Israel in their 'seasons'.

i) Pentecost: Its history and significance

In the Jewish religious year there were three feasts in particular that were of the greatest importance:

> Three times a year all your males shall appear before the LORD your God at the place that he will choose: at the Feast of Unleavened Bread (Passover), at the Feast of Weeks (Pentecost), and at the Feast of Booths (Tabernacles). (Deuteronomy 16:16)

They came to be called "Pilgrim Feasts", because when Jerusalem was chosen by the Lord to be the place where He would meet with His people, many of the Jews were living at a distance from there and so had to make a 'pilgrimage' to keep these feasts (Deuteronomy 12:5). They were to be 'kept' by all mature males throughout the 'seasons' of Israel, and by the time the Lord walked this earth that 'place' had been well established as Jerusalem.

The great numbers of Jews in Jerusalem on the Day of Pentecost in Acts 2 were referred to as "devout men from every nation under heaven". They had come to keep the feast *in accordance with the word of the Lord*. The phenomenon of the apostles "speaking in other tongues (the tongues of the various nations) as *the Spirit gave them utterance*" so 'amazed' them all, that they asked "What does this mean?" Then "Peter, standing with the eleven, lifted up his voice and addressed them" ... in a language that all could understand, probably Greek[38]. He said, "Men of Judea and all who dwell in Jerusalem" (Acts 2:1-15).

Peter's answer put the phenomenon of the 'tongues' in context when he referred it back to the prophecy of Joel with its promise and warning to Israel "in the last days" (Acts 2:16-21).

ii) The prophecy of Joel

On the Day of Pentecost, Peter, "filled with the Holy Spirit" and addressing his own people, referred this phenomenon back to the prophecy of Joel—"This is what was uttered through the prophet Joel"— and he quoted it at length. Peter spoke to all in a language understood by all, probably Greek, the lingua franca in the Roman Empire at the time. The prophecy he quoted has two parts, the first relevant to all who heard his words at that time, and the second a warning of what was to come *before* the day of the Lord, that great and magnificent day spoken of more than once in the history of Israel (see page 110). I give it here at length: Joel 2:28-32 Acts 2:17-21):

God declares, "*I will pour out my Spirit on all flesh*, and
>your sons and your daughters shall prophesy,
>your young men shall see visions,
>your old men shall dream dreams,
>even on my male servants and female servants in those days,

I will pour out my Spirit, and they shall prophesy."

Peter continued his quotation:

>"*And I will*
>*show wonders* in the heavens above
>*signs* on the earth below,
>>blood and fire, and vapour of smoke:
>>the sun shall be turned to darkness
>>and the moon to blood,
>>*before* the day of the Lord comes,
>>the great and magnificent day.
>
>*And it shall come to pass that*
>>everyone who calls upon
>>the name of the Lord
>>shall be saved."

The first part of this quotation is not a universal promise for all Christians everywhere; the words, "all flesh" must be understood against the background of the terms, "the last days" (v.17) and "the Day of the Lord ... the great and magnificent day" (v.20). "All flesh" is explained by Joel as "your" sons and "your daughters"; i.e. Israel's sons and daughters. (As has been often observed, the use of the words 'all' and 'every', must always be understood within the context in which they are used and not necessarily applied universally.)

On the day of Pentecost, Peter was speaking in the same context as the Gospel call—"the kingdom of heaven *is at hand*"—and by quoting these words from Joel, suggests that this prophecy could have been fulfilled during his own generation. In Matthew 24, the Lord Himself had warned the disciples of the signs that were to immediately precede the close of the age and the return of the Son of Man to the earth. And those signs are similar to some of those in Joel's prophecy:

> "The sun will be darkened and the moon will not give its light, and the stars will fall from heaven, and the powers of the heavens will be shaken. Then will appear in heaven the sign of the Son of Man coming on the clouds of heaven with power and great glory." (Matthew 24:29,30)

Throughout the Acts Period there was an expectancy of the early return of the Lord to the earth (see note 24). If the prophecy of Joel was beginning to be fulfilled in regard to the pouring out of *God's Spirit* upon "all flesh" in Israel, then Peter's generation might have been living in "the last days" and "the Day of the Lord" could be upon them!

iii) The Day of the Lord

This expression, first used in Isaiah 2:12, is the first of twenty occurrences in the Old Testament, sixteen of which have *yom Jehovah* (LORD). In the New Testament it must be seen in contrast to "man's day", an expression Paul uses in 1 Corinthians 4:3 when he says to them, (lit.) "It is a very small thing to me that I am judged by you or by *man's day* (*anthropines hemeras*)", and which still reflects the present situation, "when man exalts himself, and bows God out of the world He has created" (*The Companion Bible*).

"The Day of the LORD" was anticipated by Israel as a future day of *Jehovah's visitation*. In the first reference to it Isaiah said:

> *The LORD of Hosts has a day* against all that is proud and lofty, against all that is lifted up—and it shall be brought low ... and the haughtiness of man shall be humbled, and the lofty pride of men

shall be brought low, and *the LORD alone shall be exalted in that day*. (cp. Isaiah 13:6,9-22)

And Paul, writing during the Acts Period, said (1 Thessalonians 5:2,3; cp. 2 Peter 3:10):

> "You are fully aware that *the day of the Lord* will come like a thief in the night. While people are saying, 'There is peace and security', then sudden destruction will come upon them."

This future day of judgement can be seen in Malachi's prophecy: "Who can endure the day of his coming, and who can stand when he appears" (Malachi 3:2) a passage that reflects John the Baptist's warning to the Pharisees and Sadducees; "who warned you to flee from the wrath to come?" (Matthew 3:7).

We must, therefore, see "the Gifts of the Spirit" during the Acts Period against the background of a people living in expectation of the Lord's return, and the fulfilment of Old Testament prophecies that would immediately precede that coming. These were the subject of Peter's speech on the Day of Pentecost, when he quoted Joel 2:28-32 in answer to the question, "What does this mean?", and in his next address spoke of "the time for restoring all the things about which God spoke by the mouth of his holy prophets long ago" (Acts 2:14-21; 3:18-21).

iv) Israel's feasts reflect their history in type

The feasts given to Israel to 'keep' are a kind of picture book setting forth God's purpose and His preparation of Israel for their place in world blessing. We Gentiles in the 21st century, whose 'hope' in the Church which is the Body of Christ is in the heavenly places, may learn from the way the Lord led and dealt with this nation, but here I must concentrate on the relationship of three feasts in particular and what they teach us of Israel's past and future.

In this study they are considered in the context of the Acts Period and the ministry of the Spirit-filled apostles during that period. During Acts, a believing 'remnant' of Israel tasted some of the blessings and power of the coming age on earth, an age which was anticipated during the Acts Period, and will be experienced during the Millennium (Hebrews 6:4,5).

The three feasts known as "the Pilgrim Feasts" may be set out as follows:

First Month:

The Feast of Unleavened Bread (15th-21st Abib, later called Nisan) followed **Passover** (14th) and commemorated the exodus from Egypt when the first Passover lamb was eaten and its blood was put on the sides and tops of the door frames of Israel's houses to protect the firstborn from the judgement of the LORD (Exodus 12). This was clearly recognised by Paul as foreshadowing the sacrifice of Jesus Christ as the Passover Lamb, and also The Feast of Unleavened bread that followed it:

> Cleanse out the old leaven that you may be a new lump. For **Christ, our Passover (lamb),** has been sacrificed. Let us therefore **celebrate the festival**, not with the old leaven ... but with **the unleavened bread** of sincerity and truth. (1 Corinthians 5:7,8)

Paul has set out the Old Testament festival (type) against the New Testament reality (anti-type).

Third Month:

The Feast of Weeks or Harvest (Pentecost) was held seven weeks after Passover. This feast was "the day of first fruits" Numbers 28:26) when Israel were to:

> Keep the Feast of Harvest, of the firstfruits of your labour, of what you sow in your field. (Exodus 23:16; 34:22)

If Christ's sacrifice is the anti-type of the Passover Lamb, then the Jewish Feast of Weeks answers to the anti-type of the Pentecost of Acts 2 that followed. Pentecost was a 'firstfruits'; a gathering, not of the complete harvest; that belongs to the end of the agricultural year, but a beginning— *a foretaste* of that full harvest to come. This 'foretaste' would represent the gathering of God's people during the Acts Period, the period in which Romans is set—the Pentecostal period, when "a remnant" of Israel was gathered (Romans 11:5,7,25)—"a kind of firstfruits of his creatures" (James 1:1,18).

The Holy Spirit and His Ministry

A gap of several months intervenes here:

This seems to answer to the undefined period (or 'season') during which "the hope of Israel" is in abeyance (Acts 28:20,25-28), a 'hope' that Paul had described to Agrippa as his, "hope in the promise made by God to our fathers, to which *our twelve tribes* hope to attain" (Acts 26:6,7).

During this season whilst Israel's 'hope' remains 'on hold', God revealed to Paul (initially) "the mystery" of a calling whose 'hope' is in "the heavenly places"—"The Church which is the Body of Christ" (Ephesians 3:2,6; 1:3,19-23). The nature and place of this "Church" is expanded later in this study (page 203).

Seventh Month:

The Feast of Tabernacles or Ingathering: The third 'pilgrim feast', that took place after a gap of several months, was held on 15th-21st Tishri. Preceded on the 10th by **The Day of Atonement**, a day of 'denial' on pain of being 'cut off' from Israel; it was the season when the fruits of the land (corn, grapes etc.) were gathered in—the full harvest (Leviticus 23:33-43; Deuteronomy 16:13-17). The full harvest of Israel is a future hope awaiting the return of the Messiah to His people Israel.

The Passover was associated with *Redemption* and Tabernacles was preceded by the great Day of *Atonement*; the first reminding us of Christ *dealing with sin* and the second with *the forgiveness of sins*. (The overall word that covers all that was accomplished by the Lord Jesus Christ for us is 'salvation'. For a detailed study of this in its various aspects, including 'redemption' and 'atonement', see the author's *Paul's Letter to the Romans* pp. 68-86 OBT.)[39]

v) Pentecost in the context of the New Testament

The Old Testament sacrifice of the Passover lamb was *symbolic*; *a type* of the sacrifice of "the Lamb of God who takes away the sin of the world" (John 1:29). The Feast of Pentecost, standing at the head of the Acts Period, should be understood in the same way. It was a feast of "firstfruits", when the firstfruits of God's people were being gathered; Paul described these believing Jews in Romans 11 as "a remnant", those who alone had responded to the Gospel (vs.1-7).

They were eventually joined by a company of believing Gentiles who were called "to make Israel jealous" (vs. 11,13,14). James said of these Gentiles when referring back to Peter's visit to Cornelius: "God first visited the Gentiles, *to take from them a people for his name*" (Acts 15:13-17).

Paul presented this Jew/Gentile coming together *at this time* as being like an Olive Tree; the Gentiles were "wild olive shoots ... grafted, *contrary to nature";* Jewish believers were "the natural branches" (vs.17,24). This difference reflected the privilege and priority of the Jew as Paul noted elsewhere in this epistle (Romans 1:16; 2:9,10; 3:1,2; 9:3-5).

Writing during this period in Israel's history when a 'firstfruits' were being gathered, the writer of Hebrews said of his believing Jewish brethren that they had:

> *Tasted* the heavenly gift, and have *shared in the Holy Spirit*, and have *tasted* the goodness of the word of God and *the powers* (*dunamis*, miracles) of the age to come. (6:4,5)

The Jewish believers during the Acts Period were experiencing just 'a taste' of the blessings and power of the age to come at the return of the Messiah, which was believed to be imminent. In that context Pentecost, standing at the head of the Acts Period, must influence our understanding of the ministry of the Holy Spirit and the actions and teaching of the apostles at that time.

Chapter 12
Gifts of the Spirit during the Gospel and Acts Period

I have already observed that, whilst the LORD "changes not" (Malachi 3:6) and "Jesus Christ is the same yesterday today and for ever" (Hebrews 13:8), so is it with the Holy Spirit. He "changes not" but His ministry is likely to be different towards a people whose hope lies in blessings upon the earth in accordance with promises made to Abraham (Genesis 12:1-3: Acts 3:25) and those whose blessings are "in the heavenly places" (Ephesians 1:3; 2:6). And what we read in the Acts Period, and those epistles that were written at that time, since they minister to people whose 'hope' was on earth, cannot be taken *carte blanche* to apply to us today whose 'hope' is in the heavenly places.

A) Power and authority given to the apostles pre-Pentecost

Before we look at the list of His 'gifts' to believers in 1 Corinthians 12, we should remember that the Lord's disciples, and not just the Twelve, were given the ability to heal and cast out demons before ever the Holy Spirit descended upon the apostles at Pentecost:

> Jesus called *the twelve* together and gave them power and authority over all demons and to cure diseases, and he sent them out to proclaim the kingdom of God and to heal. (Luke 9:1,2)

> After this the Lord appointed *seventy-two others* and sent them on ahead of him, two by two, into every town and place where he himself was about to go ... "Whenever you enter a town and they receive you ... Heal the sick in it and say to them, 'the

kingdom of God has come near to you'" ... The seventy-two returned with joy saying, "Lord, even the demons are subject to us in your name". (Luke 10:1,5-9,17)

The ability to do some 'miracles' was nothing new to the disciples, but their experience at Pentecost, when "they were filled with (or by) the Holy Spirit" and were able "to speak in other tongues" was something new (Acts 2:4). Paul did, however, make an enigmatic connection between the 'tongues' in 1 Corinthians 14:21,22 and the "strange lips" and "foreign tongue" (Isaiah 28:11) with which "the LORD will speak to this people" (Ephraim, Isaiah 28:1,3).

B) Other Tongues at Pentecost

When the day of Pentecost arrived, the Twelve apostles[40] were all ...

> ... filled with (or by) the Holy Spirit and began to speak in other tongues as the Spirit gave them utterance. (Acts 1:26; 2:1,4)

The *NIV* has, "as the Spirit enabled them". The apostles spoke in the native languages of the Jews and proselytes "from every nation under heaven", proclaiming "the mighty works of God" (Acts 2:5-12). All were bewildered by this phenomenon and asked what it meant. Peter and the Eleven were to explain in a language understandable to all.

I used to visualise this scene as twelve gatherings, according to nation, listening to the particular apostle who was preaching the gospel in their own native tongue—twelve apostles, twelve gatherings, twelve languages. But I do not consider this is how it was, or that it was the reason for the "other tongues".

When Peter stood up with the Eleven, he spoke to the whole assembly, not just one group, and it is likely that he did so, either in Greek, the *lingua franca* spoken throughout the Roman world, or, less likely, Aramaic, the language of Judea.[41] I have already referred to Joel's prophecy on page 109 where it is quoted at length.

The Holy Spirit and His Ministry

C) Tongues following Pentecost: Acts Period

i) Romans and Corinthians

Some commentators are inclined to treat the gift of tongues in Romans 12:6-8 and 1 Corinthians 12 &14 as being somewhat different to that given on the Day of Pentecost. For example, Leon Morris thinks that the main difference is:

> In Acts 2 the characteristic is *intelligibility*, whereas in Romans and Corinthians ... the characteristic is *unintelligibility* (no one understands him 1 Corinthians 14:2) ... The gift here is not part of the Church's evangelistic programme (as in Acts 2), but one exercised among believers.

He states that at Pentecost the 'tongues' were understood because they were in the language (*dialektos*) of the hearers. In contrast, the gift of tongues spoken of by Paul in his epistles, was not understood without interpretation, being in no known language.

Whether or not it is correct to make this 'difference' depends, I believe, whether or not the 'gift of tongues' possessed by the churches made up of Jews and Gentiles, is a (partial) fulfilment of Joel's prophecy quoted by Peter on the Day of Pentecost. That prophecy was originally set in the context of Zion, Judah and Jerusalem and the Land of Israel (Joel 1:2; 2:1; 3:1) and Peter when quoting it, addressed it to, "Men of Judea and all who dwell in Jerusalem" (Acts 2:14-16).

So in consideration of this exclusively Jewish connection, we might at first conclude that Gentiles were not in view in Joel's prophecy. However, *at that time*, during the Acts Period (when Romans and Corinthians were written), believing Gentiles were considered as "wild shoots grafted into the Olive Tree of Israel" and "shared in the nourishing root of the Olive Tree" (Romans 11:13-21). It may be that we can include Gentile believers as *sharing* in the "spiritual gifts" of 1 Corinthians 12 & 14. Before we come to consider these lists of spiritual gifts referred to by Paul, here are a few observations on 'tongues' specifically.

ii) Tongues: Purpose and place

'Tongues', sometimes referred to as 'Glossolalia', in accordance with the

Lord's words to the disciples in Mark 16:16,17 was one of the 'signs' that would "accompany those who believed". This was seen in practice in Acts 10:45,46, when the Holy Spirit fell on Cornelius and his company, the evidence being that they were "speaking in tongues and extolling God" (Acts 10:45,46).

What was spoken in the 'other tongues' at Pentecost was associated with the glorification and praise of "the mighty works of God". It was also in the experience of the Gentiles spoken of above (Acts 2:11; 10:46).

They were "spoken to God ... uttering mysteries in the Spirit" (1 Corinthians 14:2).

They were unintelligible, unless interpreted, and unless there was someone present to interpret, those speaking in tongues "should keep silent in church and speak to themselves and to God" (1 Corinthians 14:2,13,27,28).

Their abundance caused problems in the Corinthian church, so much so that Paul wrote at length in his first epistle to put them into perspective especially in relation to prophecy (1 Corinthians 14).

Paul concluded that, although he spoke in tongues more than all the Corinthians, he said he would, "rather speak five words with my mind in order to instruct others, than ten thousand words in a tongue" (1 Corinthians 14:18,19).

In terms of priority, tongues took second place to prophecy, for "the one who speaks in a tongue builds up himself, but the one who prophesies builds up the church" (1 Corinthians 14:4,5).

When used in assemblies, this 'gift of the Spirit' should be for the "building up" of the church and so that "all things should be done decently and in order" (1 Corinthians 14:26,40).

I have left out of this list, Paul's enigmatic reference to a passage in "the Law" concerning the Lord's coming judgement of Isaiah's generation and the Assyrian language. He quotes it to his Jewish brethren in Corinth to demonstrate another reason for 'tongues'.

iii) Tongues are a sign for unbelievers

Paul makes a connection between Isaiah 28:11,12 and 1 Corinthians 14:20-25 in respect of 'tongues' in his own generation, contrasting it with prophecy:

> In your thinking be mature. In the Law it is written, "By people of strange tongues and by the lips of foreigners will I speak to this people (Ephraim Isaiah 28:1), and even then they will not listen to me, says the Lord." Thus tongues *are a sign not for believers but for unbelievers*, while prophecy is a sign not for unbelievers but for believers. If, therefore, the whole church comes together and all speak in tongues, and outsiders or unbelievers enter, will they not say you are out of your minds? But if all prophesy, and an unbeliever or outsider enters, he is convicted by all, he is called to account by all, the secrets of his heart are disclosed, and so, falling on his face, he will worship God and declare that God is really among you.

Paul's connection between speaking in tongues and Isaiah's prophecy has led to a number of explanations.[42] I do not pretend to know which, if any, are correct. I can only make a few observations, and then, only insofar that "tongues" are *a gift of the Holy Spirit*.

By quoting "the Law" Paul refers to the whole of the Hebrew Bible (cp. Romans 3:19; John 10:34). He evidently has in mind the Jews in the Corinthian church; it would probably mean nothing to the Gentiles there.[43] He reminds Jews in the Corinthian church of a time in their history, when Ephraim was condemned for its "drunkenness" (Isaiah 28:1,7,8); a time when the LORD's judgement would fall upon them and they would be faced with a people who spoke the Assyrian language, a "people of strange lips and with a foreign tongue" (see also 33:19). The LORD would "speak to this people" (Ephraim), but in the unintelligible tongue of the Assyrians. This phenomenon had long been threatened from the days of Moses upon those who were disobedient and who did not keep His commandments:

> If you will not obey the voice of the LORD your God or be careful to do all his commandments and his statutes ... all these curses shall come upon you ... The LORD will bring a nation against you from far away ... *a nation whose language you do not*

The Holy Spirit and His Ministry

> *understand.* (Deuteronomy 28:15, 49)

"Tongues" as "*a sign ... for unbelievers*", served perhaps, "as a sign *of judgement* upon those who are unbelievers".

> Speaking in tongues does not open up access into *the mysteries of God* (14:2) for the unbeliever, but actually bars this. (Anthony C. Thiselton *Commentary on 1 Corinthians*)

The unbeliever hears only unintelligible speech that leads them to think that the speakers are "out of their minds" (14:23). This is not dissimilar to the reaction of those on the Day of Pentecost who mocked those who spoke in "other tongues", accusing them of being "filled with new wine" (Acts 2:13). And, it is not without significance that Paul in Ephesians 5:18 contrasts getting drunk with wine with being "filled with the Spirit". It suggests that, to outward appearances, the result might look the same (more on Ephesians 5:18 later page 203).

iv) Prophecy rather than tongues

Paul's attitude to tongues was that, although he spoke in tongues more than all the Corinthians, he said, "I would rather speak five words with my mind in order to instruct others, than ten thousand words in a tongue" (1 Corinthians 14:18,19). He rated the intelligible speech of prophecy above speaking in tongues.

Apart from instructing believers, "prophecy *is a sign* not for unbelievers but *for believers*" (14:22)—although there was always the possibility that should "an unbeliever or outsider enter, he is convicted by all, he is called to account by all, the secrets of his heart are disclosed, and so, falling on his face, he will worship God and declare that God is really among you" (14:24,25). Prophecy "speaks to people for their upbuilding and encouragement and consolation" (14:3,4), and "the one who prophesies is greater than the one who speaks in tongues, unless someone interprets, so that the church may be built up" (14:5).

v) Gifts of the Spirit during Acts

In both Romans and 1 Corinthians Paul likens believers during the Acts Period to members of the human body in respect of the 'gifts' of God given to them (Romans 12:4-6; 1 Corinthians 12:1,7,12,27). In Romans he refers to those gifts as being "according to the measure of faith" and "the grace given" (vs.3,6). In 1 Corinthians they are described as "spiritual gifts" (12:1).

I take it that the similarities between these two passages suggests that in both cases the 'gifts' are 'assigned' to believers by the Holy Spirit—'Gifts of the Spirit' (*charismata*). I set them out together for comparison in the order they appear in the *ESV* (they vary in some versions).

| Romans 12:6-8 | 1 Corinthians 12:8-10 |
Gifts according to grace/faith	Gifts of the Spirit
Prophecy, in proportion to faith	Utterance of wisdom
Service	Utterance of knowledge
Teaching	Faith
Exhortation	Gifts of healing
Generosity	Working of miracles
Leadership	Prophecy
Acts of mercy	Ability to distinguish between spirits
Interpretation of tongues	Various kinds of tongues

In addition, Paul gives a list of 'appointments in the church' in 1 Corinthians 12:28-31:

> God has appointed in the church first apostles, second prophets, third teachers, then miracles, then gifts of healing, helping (others), administrating and various kinds of tongues ...

He goes on to say, "earnestly desire the higher gifts".

The first three 'appointments' seem to be of prime importance, emphasising the importance of **the word of God** over all the other gifts. The same priority of the Word of God is associated with the promise of the Holy Spirit in John's Gospel. Jesus said of Him:

> "He will teach you all things and bring to your remembrance all that I have said to you ... I still have many things to say to you, but you cannot bear them now. When *the Spirit of truth comes*, he will guide you into all truth ... he will declare to you the things

that are to come." (John 14:26; 16:12,13)

A similar list of 'gifts' appears in Ephesians 4:11 (with significant omissions) given to the Church which is the Body of Christ. I will look at, and compare these with the above when we come to consider that calling (page 221). One of the key thoughts underlying the giving of these gifts during the Acts Period is expressed in 1 Corinthians 12:11:

> All these (gifts) are empowered by *one and the same Spirit,* who apportions to each one individually as he wills.

They are the work of the same Spirit (*pneuma*) referred to twelve times in 1 Corinthians 12: 3-13. They appear to fall into three categories:

a) Wisdom, knowledge and a special faith (1 Corinthians 12:8).

Faith is not that initial faith of a person when he/she becomes a believer, but is seen here as something more. Wisdom and knowledge were special gifts such as the LORD gave to Solomon (1 Kings 4:29-34). In Romans 12:3 the apostle said, "think with sober judgement ... according to *the measure of faith* that God has assigned".

Faith is something that can be measured. To the Canaanite woman the Lord said, "O woman, *great* is your faith" and to the disciples, "O you of *little faith*" (Matthew 15:28; 16:8). It would seem that great faith was also a "gift of the Spirit" at this time; perhaps Paul had this in mind when he spoke of "all faith, so as to remove mountains" (1 Corinthians 13:2; cp. Matthew 17:20).

b) Healing and working of miracles (1 Corinthians 12:9,10, 28,29).

It required a 'special faith' to perform these. Healing was probably distinguished from miracles as referring to curing different kinds of sickness. It is sometimes associated with prayer, as when James, writing to the Jewish Dispersion said,

> Is anyone among you sick? Let him call for the elders of the church, and let them pray over him, anointing him with oil in the name of the Lord. And *the prayer of faith will save the one who is sick, and the Lord will raise him up.* (James 5:14,15)

Miracles would, however, include 'healing', the basic meaning of the Greek (*dunamis*) being "power", as in Acts 1:8 when the Lord promised the apostles, "You will receive *power* when the Holy Spirit has come upon you."

c) Prophecy, the ability to distinguish between spirits and interpretation of tongues (v.10).

All have underlying them the thought of clear, truthful and understandable teaching for the building up of the individual and the church. Prophecy does not necessarily mean forecasting the future, but "speaks to people for their upbuilding and encouragement and consolation" (1 Corinthians 14:3,4). But it does not exclude insight and revelation, and certainly includes the Holy Spirit speaking through prophets the word of God to the people, as in Old Testament times. The ability to distinguish between spirits (1 Corinthians 12:10) is reminiscent of 1 John 4:1-3:

> Beloved, do not believe every spirit, but test the spirits to see whether they are from God, for many false prophets have gone out into the world. *By this you know the Spirit of God*: every spirit that confesses that Jesus Christ has come in the flesh is from God, and every spirit that does not confess Jesus is not from God. This is the spirit of the Antichrist, which you heard was coming and now is in the world already.

John warned his readers of false prophets and the spirit of Antichrist. These false prophets deny **i)** that Jesus has come in the flesh, and/or **ii)** maintain that Jesus is not from God. So John gave his readers two criteria upon which to form a judgement, both of which impinge upon the nature and being of Jesus Christ.

One of the 'gifts of the Spirit' in 1 Corinthians 12 is "to distinguish between spirits" (v. 10). This reminds us that just because a person was speaking 'by a spirit', he/she was not necessarily 'speaking by the Holy Spirit'. As John wrote, "*test the spirits to see whether they are from God.*" Hence there was a need in the church for someone with the ability "to *distinguish (diakrisis)* between spirits".

This Greek word for 'distinguish' is used only twice more in the New Testament. In Romans 14:1 the *KJV* has rendered it "disputations"; the

ESV has "quarrel over opinions" and *The New Greek-English Interlinear New Testament* gives "(with a view) to passing judgement". The third reference is Hebrews 5:14 where it is used of those described as "mature", who "have their powers of discernment trained by constant practice to *distinguish* good from evil" (*ESV*). This last reference takes us back to the Garden of Eden where our (*immature*) first parents were forbidden to eat from "the tree of the knowledge of good and evil" on pain of death (Genesis 2:16,17).

Applying these thoughts to the 'gift' of being able to "distinguish between spirits", shows that even here we cannot omit the human factor. When Paul was speaking of a number of prophets prophesying in the same assembly, not only was he concerned that they should speak one at a time, but that others should be allowed to "weigh (*diakrino*) what is said." The *KJV* has "judge" here. Thiselton suggests "sift" and gives a suggestion that it means:

> To distinguish between (i) prophetic speech which is God-given and coheres with the gospel of Christ and the pastoral situation and (ii) speech which is merely self-generated rhetoric reflecting the speaker's disguised self-interests, self-deceptions or errors, albeit under the guise of supposed prophecy. (*Commentary on 1 Corinthians* 14:29)

With respect to 'Interpretation of tongues', if tongues were spoken at all in the assembly, there must be one present to interpret them, otherwise, "if there is no one to interpret, let each of them (those speaking in tongues) keep silent in church and speak to themselves and to God" (1 Corinthians 14:27,28).

There is an important observation that is rarely observed by those who believe that 'speaking in tongues' is still relevant for today. During the Acts Period the Corinthian church possessed not only this gift but *all these gifts of the Spirit* mentioned above *in abundance* (14:26 to "each one"), even though they were a church split by divisions (1 Corinthians 1:10-13) and described by Paul as "people of the flesh" (3:1).

They were not given these 'gifts' because they were better Christians than others, or had greater faith than others. Their privilege was to experience the work of the Holy Spirit giving them a foretaste of the coming age, a foretaste of "the powers of the coming age" (Hebrews 6:4,5).

There are some in our present age who say that if only we were faithful and holy enough, we could possess all these gifts today, but is that true? I come to this later when we look at the later epistles of Paul.

Chapter 13
The Holy Spirit in the non-Pauline Acts Epistles

A) The dating of all the New Testament epistles

There has been little or no agreement amongst commentators and scholars, either in the past or now, as to when each individual epistle was actually written, but they all agree that they do not appear in our Bibles in date order. There is, however, a general consensus of opinion about which were written during the Acts Period, and which were written after it. For those who make no distinction between the two 'callings' and 'hopes' in the New Testament, their time of writing is not of great importance, but for those who do, it is vital.

It has remained a puzzle to many Christians as to why Luke never mentioned in his history, that some of the apostles wrote epistles to the communities that sprang up during the Acts Period, in particular Paul who had a close association with Luke. But it goes without saying that whatever appears in those letters, must have been specifically relevant to that period and the 'hope' of those who lived in it.

Also, before we start applying what was being taught at that time to ourselves, we must understand what that teaching was and what it meant to those to whom it was first addressed. This is particularly important with regard to the Holy Spirit's ministry during the Acts Period, in contrast to His post-Acts ministry. Here I set out the epistles written *during* the history of the Acts of the Apostles, and will consider the rest later.

The following epistles were, I believe, written during the Acts Period, and sent to individual churches, regions, and even to individuals. They fall into two categories.

> **Epistles by ministers to the circumcision;**
> **Letters to the Jews of the Acts Period**
> Hebrews, James, 1 & 2 Peter, 1 & 2 & 3 John, Jude, Revelation

> **Epistles by Paul, minster to the uncircumcision;**
> **Letters to the Jews and Gentiles of the Acts Period**
> Galatians, 1 & 2 Corinthians, 1 & 2 Thessalonians, Romans

I originally intended to set out in full every reference to *pneuma*, when referring to "the Holy Spirit", in each and every New Testament epistle. However, having in mind the amount of space that would take, and would add little to what has already been said so far, I include here just those references that I trust will put the Holy Spirit's ministry in those epistles into context.

B) Epistles to the circumcision: PETER and JAMES

It seems strange in view of all the evidence against it, that the epistles of Peter and James (together with John and Jude) should have been called "the catholic epistles" by the early Church Fathers. Given that 'catholic' means universal, the addressees of their epistles hardly fit that description—they are *specific* in their destinations, having been addressed to The Dispersion of Israel (1 Peter 1:1; 2 Peter 3:1; James 1:1). Hence their content must be considered within the 'hope' of the Acts Period; "the hope of Israel" expressed in terms of "the twelve tribes of Israel" (Acts 26:6,7; 28:20; James 1:1) and the Holy Spirit's ministry at that time.

James uses the word *pneuma* twice (2:26; 4:5) neither referring to the Holy Spirit.

Peter refers to the Holy Spirit five times in his two epistles (1 Peter 1:2,11,12; 4:4; 2 Peter 1:21 *ESV*). Assuming that "the Spirit of Christ" is in essence the same as "the Holy Spirit", Peter reiterates in his second epistle what he had said in his first. There he is affirming that the Hebrew Scriptures were "God breathed" (cp. Paul in 2 Timothy 3:16):

> Concerning this salvation, *the prophets* who prophesied about the grace that was to be yours searched and enquired carefully, enquiring what person or time *the Spirit of Christ in them* was indicating when he predicted the sufferings of Christ and the subsequent glories. It was revealed to them that they were serving not themselves but you, in the things that have now been announced to you through those who preached the good news to you by *the Holy Spirit* sent from heaven, things into which the angels long to look. (1 Peter 1:10-12)

> No prophecy was ever produced by the will of man, but men spoke from God as they were *carried along by the Holy Spirit*. (2 Peter 1:21; The *KJV* has "moved by the Holy Spirit"; the *NEB* "impelled by the Holy Spirit".)

Two main conclusions emerge from these verses;

> **a)** That the ministry by the Holy Spirit to the circumcision during the Acts Period was based upon promises and prophecies made by the Old Testament prophets carried along (or impelled) by *the Holy Spirit*, and

> **b)** That the ministry of Peter and James, (and John and Jude), was just as much the teaching of that same *Holy Spirit* that came upon the apostles on the Day of Pentecost.

The epistles to the circumcision must be read in that light. They all expected the Lord to return to the earth shortly (Acts 1:11; James 5:8), restore the kingdom to Israel (Acts 1:6) and fulfil the prophecies associated with that return. In the meantime, *The Holy Spirit* was at work in those to whom these epistles were addressed, who were:

- The Twelve Tribes in the Dispersion ... (James 1:1)
- Elect exiles of the dispersion... foreknown by God, who have been sanctified in or by (*en*) *the Spirit*, (resulting) in (*eis*) their obedience to Jesus Christ and sprinkling with His blood. (1 Peter 1:1-2)

These verses set the scene and provide the context in which the Holy Spirit's ministry to the circumcision is to be understood. These epistles were not written to mixed churches of Jews and Gentiles, but to Peter's own people who, at that time, had a special place in the purpose of God, and as such were separated (sanctified) by God to bring that purpose about, according to ancient promises and prophecy spoken by men who were "carried along by the Holy Spirit". And Peter draws their attention to one of their responsibilities in particular. They were called to be:

A kingdom of priests and a holy nation

Jehovah had separated ancient Israel from the nations and promised:

> "If you will obey my voice and keep my covenant, you shall be my treasured possession among all peoples, for all the earth is mine, and you shall be to me *a kingdom of priests and a holy nation.*" (Exodus 19:5,6)

Peter addressed his own "born again" brethren living at that time, in the same terms; at present exiled in the Dispersion but *sanctified by the Spirit* and chosen as part of a holy nation separated to the Lord as a priesthood:

> "You are a chosen race, *a royal priesthood, a holy nation*, a people for his own possession." (1 Peter 1:23; 2:9)

Faithful Jews living during the Acts Period, were "a chosen race", trusting in Jesus as their Messiah. They were already considered by Peter to be part of "a royal priesthood, a holy nation"—*God's chosen people.* They were ready to fulfil their place in the purpose of God that would bring worldwide blessing, based upon the "the promises given to the Fathers" (Romans 15:8,9)—so fulfilling the ancient promises given to Abraham (Genesis 12:1-3) and Moses (Exodus 19:5,6).

God chose them to "proclaim the excellences of him who called (them) out of darkness into light", and they were urged to keep their conduct honourable among the Gentiles. Paul referred to this "elect company" (not necessarily living in the places referred to by Peter), when he wrote concerning those of his own people "foreknown by God":

> At the present time there is *a remnant chosen by grace,* not on the basis of works ... (so that although) Israel failed to obtain what it was seeking, *the elect* obtained it, but the rest were hardened. (Roman 11:5-7)

From one perspective, the Acts Period is a record of the failure of Israel *as a nation*, "a disobedient and contrary people" (Romans 11:21), most of whom failed to recognise their Messiah. But there was "a remnant" that had "obeyed the gospel" (Romans 10:16). Peter, James, John and Jude wrote to that elect company to urge them to be "doers of the word" (James 1:22), to be "obedient to the truth" (1 Peter 1:22), to "keep God's commandments" (1 John 1:3), and to continue "building themselves up in the faith" (Jude 20) and being "patient until the coming of the Lord" which was "at hand" (James 5:7-9).

C) The epistle of JUDE

I have put this short epistle next due to its similarity to 2 Peter. It is thought to have been written by Jude, the brother of James (the Lord's brother, in which case he was the brother of Jesus, *Strong's Concordance*). Jude has two references to *the Holy Spirit* (*ESV*). Verses 17-21:

> Remember the predictions of the apostles of our Lord Jesus Christ … they said to you, "In the last time there will be scoffers, following their own ungodly passions." It is these that cause divisions, worldly people, devoid of *the Spirit*. But you, beloved, building yourselves up in your most holy faith and praying in *the Holy Spirit*, keep yourselves in the love of God, waiting for the mercy of our Lord Jesus Christ that leads to eternal life.

E.W. Bullinger's comments in *The Giver and His Gifts* are apposite here. He takes the first reference to *pneuma* to refer to "the new nature" which these "natural men" (*psuchikoi*) do not have, since it is the gift of the Holy Spirit. The second reference which reads literally, "praying in (the) Holy Spirit" (*en pneumati hagio*), he refers to "the power from on high", which describes the gift of the Holy Spirit promised to the apostles in Luke 24:49; Acts 1:8.

In Jude's epistle, these "worldly people … devoid of the Spirit" are set over against those who both have, and who *pray in, the Holy Spirit*. Jude has several Old Testament examples of people "devoid of the Spirit" who serve as examples and warnings to his own generation.

Jude looks back to the days of Enoch, whose prediction had a 'fulfilment' in the Great Flood of Noah's days, but which Jude sees as also having relevance to his own generation:

> Behold, the Lord comes with ten thousands of his holy ones, to execute judgement on all and to convict all the ungodly of all their deeds of ungodliness ... (vs. 14,15; cp. Mark 8:38)

Jude, like other writers of the New Testament epistles written during the Acts Period, believes he is living in "the last time", and sees the return of the Lord in terms of judgement, just as in the days of Noah. Hence he urges his brethren to live, "praying in the Holy Spirit" (v.20).

D) The three epistles of JOHN

These epistles require special mention, since they particularly stress the negative usage of *pneuma*, with specific mention of "the *spirit* of Antichrist", over against the positive ministry of "the Holy Spirit".

The second and third are personal; 2 John is addressed to "the elect lady" and 3 John to "the beloved Gaius". In these short epistles of John, the warning about being deceived is repeated (2 John 7-11) and there is reference to "wicked nonsense" (3 John 9-11), but there is no reference to the Holy Spirit.

John's first epistle, which has thirteen references to *pneuma*, has a strong 'warning' element in it. The apostle's concern is that his readers should discern between "the spirits". Are they from God, or are they "false prophets"? He gives 'an acid test' whereby they can "test the spirits to see whether they are from God" (1 John 4:2,3):

> By this you know *the Spirit of God*: every spirit that confesses that Jesus Christ has come in the flesh is from God, and every *spirit* that does not confess Jesus, is not from God, this is the *spirit* of Antichrist.

The false prophets denied the humanity of Jesus. John R.W. Stott *Tyndale Commentaries* wrote *in loco:*

> The fundamental Christian doctrine which *can never be compromised* (my italics) concerns the divine-human person of Jesus the Son of God.

The appearance of this false doctrine in John's day was an indication that it was "the last hour" (1 John 2:18), and places this epistle alongside those other epistles that belong to the Acts 'hope' and the early return of the Messiah (1 John 2:28; 3:2; see note 24). Elsewhere in John's first epistle we have:

> You have been anointed by *the Holy One*, and you have all knowledge. (1 John 2:20)

The *NIV* has the alternative translation, "all of you know the truth", and in view of what follows I am inclined to think that this is better. The apostle is not here speaking of "all knowledge", but knowledge in respect of Jesus Christ specifically. The liars deny "Jesus is the Christ"; they "deny the Father and the Son"; John's 'anointed' readers know and believe otherwise (1 John 2:21-23).

The connection of 'anointing' with the Spirit of God and His gifts was seen first in the Old Testament. It is seen in its fullness in Christ, the Lord's "Anointed One" (Acts 4:27; 10:38). Here in John, *the Holy One's* 'anointing' abides in and protects the believer from being deceived (1 John 2:26.27).

A requirement and evidence of a Spirit-filled life for John's brethren is brought out in 1 John 3:24:

> Whoever keeps his commandments abides in God, and God (Greek 'He') in him. And by this we know that he abides in us, by *the Spirit* whom he has given us.

Whether or not *pneuma* here should be a small 's' and refers to the new nature (Bullinger *in loco*), it is the abiding of the Holy Spirit in the believer that leads him/her to "keep His commandments". This had special reference to John's brethren who had the Law, but its interpretation is just as relevant to us today as it was to John's brethren— the greatest of which is, "love one another" (1 John 3:11,23,24; John 13:34).

i) A warning for readers of the KJV:

In most editions I have come across, the *King James Version of the New Testament* (1611) has the words in verses 7,8: "... in heaven, the Father the Word and the Holy Ghost: and these three are one. And there are three that bear witness in earth ..." But, much as we might like to use them as a plain statement of the Trinity, this is an unreliable source for such a proof.

The Revised Version (1881) omitted these words on the grounds that they did not appear in all the best texts. Also (as far as I know) all modern versions omit them. (Some Concordances list these words, without a warning, which may give rise to the belief that they are genuine.)

ii) John's Epistle v John's Gospel

Both written by the apostle John, his first epistle should be read in conjunction with his Gospel. In the Gospel we have the appeal and the evidence that "Jesus *is* the Messiah" (20:30,31); in the Epistle, there is a warning about the Antichrist who *denies* that Jesus is the expected Messiah, and so "denies the Father and the Son". John adds the test of truth, "everyone who believes that Jesus is the Messiah has been born of God" (1 John 5:1).

E) The Holy Spirit in the epistle to the HEBREWS

With the exception of Paul's epistle to the Romans, the epistle to the Hebrews reveals the situation in the Christian community during the latter part of the Acts Period more so than any other New Testament epistle. The "Great Salvation" of the peoples on earth, promised by the LORD to Abraham (Genesis 12:1-3) and made possible by the once-for-all sacrifice by Jesus Christ, "to put away sin by the sacrifice of himself" (Hebrews 9:26-28) had been made. Now the author of this epistle writes to his brethren, urging them to fulfill the LORD's promise to Abraham, for they had been given the privilege of proclaiming this 'salvation' to the Gentiles and teaching the Gentiles the Law of God. He urged them to embrace this 'salvation' and that responsibility with the warning:

> How shall we escape if we neglect such a great salvation? It was declared at first by the Lord, and it was attested to us by those who heard, while God also bore witness by signs and wonders and various miracles and by *gifts* of *the Holy Spirit* distributed according to his will. (Hebrews 2:3,4)

i) Who wrote Hebrews and to whom was it written?

There is no agreement amongst scholars and commentators as to who actually wrote this epistle, and several names have been suggested. I would not discount that it could have been written by Paul in spite of the unpopularity of that view. However, there can be no doubt that it is rightly named as having been written to Jews.

> According to the earliest evidence the epistle was addressed to 'Hebrews' ... The title properly describes 'the people from beyond the river Euphrates', and is the national name of the race having regard to the divine call. (B.F. Westcott *The Epistle to the Hebrews*).

Although Gentiles today might learn much from it, to describe Hebrews as having been written to 'Christians in general' (i.e. to include Gentiles) is clearly not logical and it could never have had that original destination. It makes reference to the Law of Moses, Israel's sacrificial system and the history of that nation particularly during the era of Moses; that would have meant nothing to the average Gentile at the time of writing.

The content suggests to me that it belongs to the Acts Period, but specifically which 'Hebrews' it was originally written to and where, is impossible to ascertain. Whoever they were, their 'status' suggests he was writing to immature Jewish believers. He says of those he writes to, that "by this time you ought to be teachers", but they "need milk, not solid food. For everyone who lives on milk is unskilled in the word of righteousness", and he urges them to "go on to maturity" (Hebrews 5:11-6:6).

ii) References to the Holy Spirit in Hebrews

There are twelve references to *pneuma* in Hebrews; in the *KJV* and *ESV*, seven of them refer to the Holy Spirit having a capital 'S'. They are 2:4; 3:7: 6:4; 9:8; 9:14; 10:15 and 10:29.

I have already referred to the first of these: "How shall we escape if we neglect such a great salvation?", that goes on to refer to "*gifts* of *the Holy Spirit* distributed according to his will" (Hebrews 2:3,4). This puts this epistle clearly within the Acts Period, as in 1 Corinthians with its abundance of 'spiritual gifts', and referred to in Hebrews 6:5 as, "the powers of the age to come". Compare Luke 24:49; Acts 1:8.

iii) The Holy Spirit spoke through the O.T. prophets

> As *the Holy Spirit* says, "Today, if you hear his voice, do not harden your hearts as in the rebellion" (in the days of Moses in the wilderness). (Hebrews 3:7)

Citing Psalm 95:7-11 as being the words of *the Holy Spirit* at that time, the writer reminds his readers of the rebellion of Israel under Moses and the consequences of their disobedience in incurring God's wrath.

Referring to the words of the LORD in the Old Testament as being those of 'the Holy Spirit' was quite common in New Testament times. In Hebrews 10:15 the Holy Spirit is said to "bear witness" to the New Covenant made by the LORD with "the house of Israel and the house of Judah" (Jeremiah 31:31; Hebrews 8:8-10) when He said:

> "I will put my law within them, and I will write it on their hearts ... I will forgive their iniquity, and I will remember their sin no more." (Jeremiah 31:33,34; Hebrews 10:15-17)

Acts 28:25 is another example, where Paul refers to the prophecy of Isaiah as being what the Holy Spirit said to the fathers of Israel, quoting Isaiah 6:9,10. These examples confirm the claim that the Old Testament Scriptures are "God breathed", just as much as the New Testament (2 Timothy 3:16). In Hebrews 10:15,16, the Holy Spirit "bears witness" to the "single offering" of Messiah that enables the LORD to say of Israel under the New Covenant: "I will remember their sins and their lawless deeds no more" (Hebrews 10:15-17; Jeremiah 31:31-34).

iv) Sharing in the Holy Spirit

In Hebrews 6:4,5 the readers are reminded that they have

> *Tasted* the heavenly gift and *shared in the Holy Spirit,* and have *tasted* the goodness of the word of God and *the powers* of the age to come.

The Acts Period was a time when a 'firstfruits' of God's people was being called. The gifts of the Holy Spirit, which He "apportions to each one individually as he wills" (1 Corinthians 12:11), were the powers of a coming age which we generally refer to as the Millennium. They were exhibited in the signs, wonders and various miracles that were taking place every day during the Acts Period, *a taste* of "the powers of the age to come". In this way they "shared in the Holy Spirit" and He worked through them to effect His ministry during the Acts Period.

v) Redemption and the blood of Christ

The next two references to the Holy Spirit, Hebrews 9:8 and 9:14 take us into the temple and the Holy Places, where the redemption and atonement of God's people were 'signified' in type and shadow. In reality they were fulfilled in the one sacrifice of Messiah, once and for all (9:26b-28). The writer describes the 'earthly' actions performed in an 'earthly tabernacle' under the Mosaic Law and the Old Covenant as "symbolic for the present age", and being "the copy of the heavenly things" and "copies of the true things" (9:9,23,24).

Under the Old Covenant with Israel, the High Priest went once a year into the Most Holy Place on the Day of Atonement (*Yom Kippur*):

> Not without taking blood, which he offers for himself and for the unintentional sins of the people. By this *the Holy Spirit* indicates (signified) that the way into the holy places is not yet opened as long as the first section is still standing (which is symbolic for the present age). (Hebrews 9:7-9)

The whole ritual of *Yom Kippur* is prefaced here by the vital element, "Not without taking blood", and the point is made that when the High Priest entered the holy places every year, it is "with blood not his own". In contrast, in the 'true' tabernacle, "heaven itself", Christ did not enter with "the blood of goats and bulls" but "by means of his own blood, thus securing an eternal redemption" (9:11,12,24).

The ministry of *the Holy Spirit* indicated that the Old Testament ritual that took place on that one day during Israel's year (The Day of Atonement) was 'symbolic' for those living at that time. That symbolism looked forward to the "once for all" entrance of the Messiah into the Most Holy Place, who "offered himself without blemish to God through *the eternal Spirit*" (9:14). As Dr. Bullinger argues, this epithet is one and the same as 'the Holy Spirit'. He wrote:

> It was *by means of* the energy of the Holy Spirit that Christ's

> spotless human nature was formed (Luke 1:35), and could be 'offered to God' on our behalf. (*Word Studies on the Holy Spirit*)

The writer's argument here is of course contained within the parameters of the Mosaic Law and directed towards those who were under it. They were in covenant relationship to the Lord under the Old Covenant. Not only so, but the New Covenant was made with them also—"the house of Israel and the house of Judah"—referred to earlier (Hebrews 8:8). In the next reference to the Holy Spirit in Hebrews, the "single offering" of Messiah is related to that covenant and borne witness to by Him.

vi) The Two Covenants: Old and New

> By a single offering he (Messiah) has perfected for all time those who are sanctified.
>> And the Holy Spirit also bears witness to us, for after saying,
>
> "This is the covenant that I will make with them after those days, declares the Lord: I will put my laws on their hearts, and write them on their minds",

then he adds,

> "I will remember their sins and their lawlessness no more." (Hebrews 10:15-17)

The Old Covenant of Law given to Israel and implicitly contained within the Ten Commandments—"God spoke all these words, saying, I am the LORD your God ..." (Exodus 20:1)—was *the word of Jehovah*, and, just as Jesus said to His disciples, "The words that I have spoken to you are *spirit (pneuma)* and life" (John 6:63), so it was with the words of Jehovah. As E.W. Bullinger wrote:

> *Pneuma* is necessary to life; and it quickens and gives life to the Old Covenant, which is a dead letter without it. (On 2 Corinthians 3:6 *Word Studies on the Holy Spirit*).

Bullinger here points out the important truth that the Holy Spirit "gives life to the Old Covenant" not just the New. And as he noted, "The scope of this whole passage (2 Corinthians 3:6-18) is to show that the Old Covenant, *apart from Christ*, is like a dead body." Compare James 2:26,

"The body apart from the spirit (*pneuma*) is dead".

The Ten Commandments were "written with *the finger* of God" (Exodus 31:18), an expression the Messiah used of His own ministry when casting out demons: "it is by *the finger of God* that I cast out demons" (Luke 11:20). But in Matthew's version this reads, "it is by *the Spirit of God* that I cast out demons" (Matthew 12:28). Jesus evidently took "*the Spirit of God*" to be the same as "*the finger* of God". And as the Messiah said to His disciples:

> It is *the Spirit* that gives life ... *the words* that I have spoken to you are *spirit* and life. (John 6:63)

Here we have yet again the connection between "word(s)" and "spirit" (see page 33).

Paul's contrast in 2 Corinthians 3:6 between the two Covenants, would naturally mean much more to a Jew than a Gentile who knew little or nothing of the Old Testament. And keeping that in mind, we must not lose track of the 'thrust' of the Acts Period that was still primarily concerned with *preparing Israel* for their duty and responsibility for world blessing according to the promises made to the fathers. In the passage that follows, 2 Corinthians 3:7-16, Paul compares the "glory" associated with Moses who received the Old Covenant, with the "even more glory" of the New Covenant. So we have:

Old Covenant:

"Carved in letters on stone ... that kills ... the ministry of death ... the ministry of condemnation ... coming to an end." And in Hebrews 8:13: "In speaking of a New Covenant, he makes *the first one obsolete. And what is becoming obsolete and growing old is ready to vanish away.*"

New Covenant:

"Not of the letter but of *the Spirit* ... gives life ... the ministry of *the Spirit* ... the ministry of righteousness ... *is permanent.*" And Paul concludes:

> Now if the ministry of death, carved in letters on stone, came with such glory that the Israelites could not gaze at Moses' face

> because of its glory, which was being brought to an end, will not *the ministry of the Spirit* have even more glory? (2 Corinthians 3:7-8)

Hebrews 8:13 sums up the situation that existed when 2 Corinthians and Hebrews were written. The Old Covenant of Law was *becoming* obsolete, but *had not yet become so*; it was *ready* to pass away, but the situation was *not yet right*. That situation remained throughout the Acts Period pending the repentance of Israel as a nation (Acts 3:19-21). For more on The New Covenant see Michael Penny's *The New Covenant! Who is it with? When is it for?* (OBT).

vii) The Lord will judge His people

The last reference to the Holy Spirit in Hebrews is 10:29. The writer, after warning his readers not to "go on sinning deliberately after receiving the knowledge of the truth", speaks of "a fearful expectation of judgement and a fury of fire that will consume the adversaries". After reminding them that "Anyone who has set aside the Law of Moses dies without mercy on the evidence of two or three witnesses", he goes on:

> How much worse punishment, do you think, will be deserved by the one who has spurned the Son of God, and has profaned the blood of the covenant, by which he was sanctified, and has *outraged the Spirit of grace*. (Hebrews 10: 26-29)

Instead of 'outraged', Dr. Bullinger has suggested, "insulted the *pneuma* of grace", and refers this to the rejection of the Messiah by the Jews who had, "trodden underfoot the Son of God, and counted the blood of the covenant (wherewith He was sanctified) an unholy thing. They had thus *insulted the Holy Spirit*, the author and giver of all grace, by Whose power and gift the blessings and grace of this New Covenant had been brought to them" (*Word Studies on the Holy Spirit* in loco). 'Insulting the Holy Spirit' is reminiscent of the Lord's warning concerning the 'blasphemy' of the Holy Spirit which "will not be forgiven, either in this age or in the age to come" (Matthew 12:32).

These verses, however, must be kept in context; they do not here include unbelieving Gentiles but are a warning that the Lord does not only bless His people (Israel), but will also, "judge his people"; a "fearful thing to fall into the hands of the living God" (Hebrews 10:30,31). And by "his people" is meant those Hebrews who can look back into their past and compare such judgement with the Lord's judgement upon the Moses generation (Hebrews 10:28).

All this is written in the context of the expectation of the early return of the Lord to the earth at this time, as most of the other epistles written during this Acts Period state (see note 24). Hebrews 10:37,38:

> Yet a little while,
> and the coming one will come
> and will not delay,
> but my righteous one shall live by faith,
> and if he shrinks back,
> my soul has no pleasure in him.

However, the writer of Hebrews concludes this warning with a touch of comfort: "But we are not of those who shrink back and are destroyed, but of those who have faith and preserve their souls" (Hebrews 10:39). And he then turns their attention to many of the Old Testament men and women who are examples of acting by faith and had "the assurance of things hoped for, the conviction of things not seen" (Hebrews 11:1).

F) The Book of THE REVELATION OF JESUS CHRIST

I make no attempt here to consider the many different interpretations of this enigmatic book. In my book *Apocalypse* OBT, I made some observations that would in my view help in understanding its contents, and that led me to place the writing and expectancy of that 'revelation' within the Acts Period. Not only is the emphasis upon the early return of Jesus the Messiah, but John is told that the things he has seen "must soon take place" (Revelation 1:7; 22:6,12,20). But just as the Acts 'hope' of the early expectancy of the Lord's return never happened *at that time*, so much of what John records in Revelation belongs to a time still yet future even to ourselves. However, the purpose of this study is concerned with what is said of *the Holy Spirit* in this book.

References to the Holy Spirit in Revelation

There are 23 references to *pneuma* in Revelation; eight, (possibly nine if we include 11:11 *"the Spirit* of life from God" *KJV*), that refer to the Holy Spirit Himself. Seven are in the repeated warning given to all seven churches to which the book is addressed:

> "He who has an ear, let him hear what *the Spirit* says to the churches." (2:7,11,17, 29; 3:6,13,22)

These were seven *actual* churches existing at the time, who are addressed by location. John (the apostle I believe) is told to write what he sees in a book (Revelation 1:11) and send it to the seven churches. Each church should read not only the section addressed to them, but also "what the Spirit says to the [other] churches". Each letter was relevant to a particular church's own situation which praised and warned those in them about their conduct, and each closed with words which were linked to a promise for faithfulness to God:

> "To the one who conquers I will grant to eat of the tree of life which is in the paradise of God ... I will give you the crown of life ... a new name written on a white stone ... the morning star ... etc."

In the absence of the Messiah, and as promised by the Lord to the disciples following His own departure (John 14:25,26; 16:12-14), these words are addressed to the churches through John *by the Holy Spirit*. However, the expression "He who has an ear" may indicate that the words written are addressed to a wider audience than is at first suggested (compare Revelation 22:18):

> I warn *everyone who hears* the words of the prophecy of this book: if anyone adds to them, God will add to him the plagues described in this book, and if anyone takes away from the words of the book of this prophecy, God will take away his share in the tree of life and in the holy city, which are described in this book.

The two other references in Revelation are:

> I heard a voice from heaven saying, "Write this: blessed are the dead who die in the Lord from now on." "Blessed indeed", says *the Spirit*, "that they may rest from their labours, for their deeds follow them!" (Revelation 14:13)

This promise from heaven (the voice of God?) is confirmed on earth by *the Holy Spirit.*

> *The Spirit* and the Bride say, "Come." And let the one who hears say "Come." And let the one who is thirsty come; let the one who desires take the water of life without price. (Revelation 22:17)

This verse is linked back to the angel testifying to John "about these things for the churches" (v.16), and looks to when paradise is restored (Revelation 2:7). Then "the water of life" will flow from the throne of God in the New Jerusalem, the centre of the new earth at that time (Revelation 21:6; 22:1). The invitation of *the Spirit* and the Bride here may be to the nations, who walk in the light of the glory of God and bring their glory into it (Revelation 21:22-26).

Chapter 14
The Holy Spirit in the Pauline Acts Epistles (Part 1)

1 & 2 Thessalonians and 1 & 2 Corinthians

Luke's history of the apostle Paul in The Acts of the Apostles, whilst it is not a straight line from 'A' to 'B', does proceed from East to West and from Asia[44] (as a Continent) to Europe; from Jerusalem to Rome. Paul's (extant) epistles written during this period, six in all, fall into three main areas of activity:

> i) The churches of South Galatia (Iconium, Lystra and Derbe).
> ii) Greece (Corinth).
> iii) Macedonia (Thessalonica and Philippi)[45].

Not all agree on the order or exact dates of writing these epistles. I am taking them here in the order given by J.B Lightfoot in *Biblical Essays* and J.A.T Robinson in *Redating the New Testament*. In this study it is important to remember that these six epistles belong to the Acts Period and therefore must be read in the light of the 'hope' of that period—"the hope of Israel" (Acts 26:6,7; 28:20).

We might also consider that since they appear to have been written over a period of almost ten years, Paul, in common with every Christian growing in the knowledge and love of God and "strengthened with power *in the Spirit*" (Ephesians 3:14-19), might himself have a better knowledge of *the Holy Spirit* than at the beginning of his ministry in Acts 9. This is borne out by the Lord's words to him at his conversion, "I have appeared to you for this purpose, to appoint you as a servant and witness to the things in which you have seen me and *to those in which I will appear to you*" (Acts 26:16). And later he claimed to have received many revelations (2 Corinthians 12:7).

Paul's letter to the Romans, "more of a treatise than an epistle" (Lighfoot), with its exposition of every aspect of the Christian faith, including its enlightenment of the plan of God for Jew and Gentile, is an example of the knowledge Paul had of the 'deeper' things of God some three years before the end of the Acts Period.

A) Macedonia: The Epistles to the THESSALONIANS

Paul's first visit to Macedonia was described by J.B. Lightfoot as "the dawn of a new era in the development of the Christian Church" (*Biblical Essays*). In modern day terms, it was a move from the continent of Asia to the continent of Europe. Thessalonica was the capital of Roman Macedonia. The Acts record seems to show that Paul had no immediate plans to go there, because he went there initially as a result of *the Holy Spirit* forbidding him and Silas to continue their ministry in Asia, and then, because "*the Spirit of Jesus*", did not allow them to go to Bithinia (Acts 16:6-8).

Paul had a vision of "a man of Macedonia urging him to 'Come over and help us'" and he concluded by this that God had called him to preach the gospel to the Macedonians (Acts 16:9,10). And so, crossing the narrow sea that separated Asia from Europe, Paul and his companions eventually reached Philippi, also a Roman colony.

Spending some time there, and being accused of "disturbing our city", they were arrested and kept in prison overnight. Having been released they left and eventually arrived in Thessalonica. It was probably at this time that the foundations were laid of "the church of the Thessalonians", in spite of the apostles' persecution there (Acts 17:1-9). This persecution may be what Paul was referring to in 1 Thessalonians 1:6, "you received the word in much affliction" but "with *the joy of the Holy Spirit*".

The Holy Spirit in Thessalonians

There are five references to *pneuma* in 1 Thessalonians (1:5,6; 4:8; 5:19,23 and three in the second epistle (2:2,8,13). The KJV has a capital 'S' in all but 1 Thessalonians 5:23 and 2 Thessalonians 2:2,8. The *ESV* concurs with the exception that in the second epistle it translates *pneuma* as "breath" in 2:8.

THESSALONIANS: FIRST EPISTLE

> Our gospel *came to you* not only in word, but also in power and in *the Holy Spirit* and with full conviction. You know what kind of men we proved to be for your sake ... You became imitators of us and of the Lord ... You received the word in much affliction, with *the joy of the Holy Spirit* ... You became an example to all the believers in Macedonia and in Achaia ... your faith in God has gone forth everywhere, so that we need not say anything. (1 Thessalonians 1:5-8)

Paul praises the Thessalonians; they had become "imitators" of both himself and his companions, as well as the Lord. So much so in fact, that they were examples to all the believers in those parts—in fact "everywhere". Hence, they needed no testimony from Paul; *their lives spoke for themselves*!

All this sprang from the ministry of *the Holy Spirit* through the apostles, that had "turned (them) to God from idols to serve the living and true God" (v9). The Thessalonians were reminded that the gospel that was preached to them came with "power from on high", but their conviction and faithfulness had led to "much affliction". However, with that persecution came also, "*the joy (kara) of the Holy Spirit*".

In these early days, and at times in every generation, being a Christian was (and can be) accompanied by persecution, but as James remarked: "*Count it all joy (kara)*, my brethren, when you meet trials of various kinds, for you know the testing of your faith produces steadfastness". Such steadfastness would lead to them being "perfect and complete, lacking nothing" (James 1:2-4).

Joy (*kara*) is used elsewhere in this first epistle in 2:19,20 where the apostle says of the Thessalonians, "What is our hope or *joy* or crown of boasting before our Lord Jesus at his coming? Is it not you? *For you* are our glory and *joy*." Paul visualises presenting the Thessalonians before the Lord as his own joy, and that of Silvanus and Timothy, associated with him in his ministry (1 Thessalonians 1:1).

> **1 Thessalonians 4:8:** "God has not called us for impurity, but in holiness. Therefore whoever disregards this, disregards not man but God, who gives *his Holy Spirit*."

> **1 Thessalonians 5:19:** "Do not quench *the Spirit*. Do not despise prophecies, but test everything; hold fast that which is good. Abstain from every form of evil."

Two warnings here, both relevant to our own calling, as well as the Acts Period, and both concerned with an *attitude* towards the Holy Spirit; disregarding Him and quenching Him. In both cases, and in spite of the *KJV* and *ESV* using a capital 'S', I believe that Bullinger argues convincingly that in these references, 'gift(s)' *from* the Holy Spirit Himself are meant. The warning "Do not despise prophecies", certainly suggests this in 1 Thessalonians 5:19.

"Disregard" (*atheteo*) is elsewhere translated (*KJV*) of 'rejecting' the Messiah (John 12:48), 'will bring to nothing' (1 Corinthians 1:19), 'frustrate' (Galatians 2:21) and 'despised' (Hebrews 10:28), which gives a fair idea of its meaning. Here we are told that to disregard God's gifts through the ministry of the Holy Spirit is not to disregard man, but to disregard God.

"Quench" (*sbennumi*) is used elsewhere of putting out 'smoking flax', lamps or fire (Matthew 12:20; 25:8; Mark 9:44). It is used most importantly in Ephesians 6:16: "In all circumstances take up the shield of faith, with which you can *extinguish* all the flaming darts of the evil one."

In 1 Thessalonians 5:19, the gifts of the Holy Spirit can be *extinguished* either in ourselves or in others; an example of the latter is to "despise prophecies". Compare Joshua's attempt to get Moses to stop Eldad and Medad, upon whom the Spirit had rested, from prophesying, which Moses refused to do (Numbers 11:26-29).

THESSALONIANS: SECOND EPISTLE:

The Holy Spirit Himself is referred to only once in Paul's second epistle:

> "We ought always to give thanks to God for you, brethren beloved by the Lord, because God chose you as the firstfruits to be saved, through *sanctification by the Spirit* and belief in the truth." (2 Thessalonians 2:13)

Here it is clearly *the Holy Spirit* and His work of sanctification that is meant. Peter refers to this aspect of the Holy Spirit's work in the believer in 1 Peter 1:2, when he addresses those scattered, dispersed Jews. They were the "elect ... according to the foreknowledge of *God the Father*, in the *sanctification of the Spirit*, for obedience to *Jesus Christ*"; a Divine Trinity all associated with the calling, separation and obedience of the believer to the One Saviour and "the sprinkling of his blood".

Sanctification of God's people

The Lord commanded Israel:

> "I am the Lord your God, *consecrate yourselves* therefore, and *be holy, for I am holy* ... I am the Lord who brought you up out of the land of Egypt to be your God. You shall therefore *be holy, for I am holy*." (Leviticus 11:44)

Holiness is required of a redeemed people. In Israel's case they were *delivered* from the land of Egypt. In this command there are three reasons, therefore, why they should be holy:

i) because He is the Lord *their God*,
ii) because *He had redeemed them* and
iii) because *He is holy*.

They were not only to be holy as individuals but as a nation among the nations. And that called for obedience:

Chosen and redeemed by the Lord, this was to be their place and responsibility "among all peoples". This was an expansion of that original promise given to Abraham in Genesis 12:1-3. But neither the Moses generation, nor any generation of Israel since, has ever been in a position to be used by the Lord to bring this promise to its fulfilment, and that includes the generation when Thessalonians was written, the Acts generation. Peter, speaking to that generation dispersed among the Gentiles in (what is now) Turkey, reminded them that they were "a chosen race, a royal priesthood, *a holy nation*" (1 Peter 1:1; 2:9). And therefore:

> As he who called you is holy, *you (must) also be holy* in all your conduct, since it is written "*You shall be holy, for I am holy*". (1 Peter 1:15,16)

Looked at as individuals, however, believers, both Jew and Gentile, were called to holiness. And that call is just as relevant today as it was during Acts. So what is sanctification and holiness? Andrew Bonar wrote in his *Commentary on Leviticus*:

> Holiness is the Lord's design and aim. He longs to have His creature freed from all uncleanliness, and made holy. He seeks to hear on earth no longer the cry of wickedness and woe, but the blissful cry that seraph utters to seraph, "Holy, holy, holy". (See Isaiah 6:1-3)

There are many words that we associate with holiness and that represent different aspects of it: sanctification, consecration, purity, hallowing, reverence, piety, devotion, dedication etc. In the Scriptures, sanctification and holiness are mainly represented by the Hebrew *qodash/qadosh* and the Greek *hagios/heiros*. From these words are derived temple (with its Holy place and Holiest of all), priest(hood), and 'saint' (holy person). Paul addressed the Roman believers as "loved by God and called to be saints" (*hagios* 1:7). (For more on "saints" see the author's *Christians: Their Message and Their Witness* OBT.)

The fundamental meaning of *hagios* is "separation and, so to speak, consecration and devotion to the service of Deity" (Trench *Synonyms*). In the New Testament the individual believer is called upon to be **in** the world but not **of** the world, and as the Lord prayed to His Father concerning His disciples:

> "They are not of the world, just as I am not of the world. *Sanctify* (*hagiazo*) them in the truth, your word is truth. As you have sent me into the world, so I have sent them into the world. And for

their sake I *sanctify* (*hagiazo*) myself, that they also may be *sanctified* (*hagiazo*) in truth." (John 17:16-19)

In everyday living, a life consecrated to God; separated from, but not in isolation (in the world but not of the world, not conformed to this world Romans 12:2); dedication (presenting yourselves as living sacrifices, your logical service Romans 12:1) and devotion (loving your neighbour as yourself; Romans 13:8-10). And the goal of sanctification is "eternal (*aionios*) life", not just in the future as a gift of God, but here and now as an experience (Romans 6:22,23).

B) Greece: The Epistles to the CORINTHIANS

Corinth was a Roman colony and its inhabitants were very cosmopolitan, being made up of Romans, Greeks, and a mixture from other nations; in particular Jews, who built a synagogue there (Acts 18:4). It was situated at the junction of two trade routes, East/West and North/South, and had a sea port at Cenchrea which made it a very prosperous city. But in common with other trading cities it had a reputation for sexual immorality, corruption and religious differences, and this is reflected in some of the things Paul refers to in his first epistle especially.

Paul, who was initially somewhat apprehensive about going there (1 Corinthians 2:3), after being opposed and reviled by the Jews, turned to the Gentiles. He may have been thinking of 'wrapping up' his ministry there, but the Lord spoke to him one night in a vision and said,

> "Do not be afraid, but go on speaking and do not be silent, for I am with you, and no one will attack you to harm you, for *I have many in this city who are my people.*" (Acts 18:9-10)

And so Paul remained there for eighteen months, "teaching the word of God among them" (Acts 18:11).

i) The Holy Spirit in Corinthians

- There are 41 occurrences of *pneuma* in 1 Corinthians and the *KJV* uses a capital 'S' in translation on 21 occasions.
- There are 17 occurrences of *pneuma* in 2 Corinthians and the *KJV* uses a capital 'S' in translation on 8 occasions.

In 1 Corinthians, however, *the disposition* of the occurrences of *pneuma* is that out of the total of 41, as many as 21 are found in just two of its chapters, twelve and fourteen. And those chapters are concerned with "spiritual gifts" which the Corinthian church seems to have possessed in abundance. I have already touched upon these 'gifts' see (page 121) and so will be brief here. Perhaps the most important 'fact' that has to be emphasised, especially today, is that these "gifts of the Spirit" were possessed by a church of which the apostle wrote:

> I, brethren, could not address you as *spiritual people*, but as people of the flesh, as infants in Christ ... For while there is jealousy and strife among you, are you not of the flesh and behaving only in a human way (i.e. 'according to human inclinations'). (1 Corinthians 3:1-3)

Paul then went on to relate how this had led to divisions among them, for they were saying, "I follow Paul"; another, "I follow Apollos", and hence their thinking was merely human (see also 1:11-13). Yet this church possessed many "gifts of the Spirit", enumerated in 1 Corinthians 12:4-11, especially prominent being "various kinds of tongues" and "the interpretation of tongues".

Some believe Christians should possess these today, but should they? I have heard it claimed that if only Christians were more 'spiritual', had 'greater faith' and lived 'more holy lives', these gifts could be ours today, but is that so? Are we missing them through lack of faith? The Corinthian church as presented in Paul's letter does not show any evidence of great faith, holy lives or of being very 'spiritual', in fact quite the contrary. To understand why they possessed these gifts and why we today should not expect to, they must be seen in their right context. Those gifts belong to the purpose of God for the Acts Period, where the context was:

- The conviction that the Lord would come to "restore the kingdom to Israel" (Acts 1:6).
- The 'hope' of the twelve tribes (Acts 26:6,7), which was that they would be settled in The Promised Land as prophesied in Ezekiel chapters 47 & 48.
- The fulfilment of the ancient promise to Abraham that the blessing of all the peoples of the earth would come via Abraham's seed (Genesis 12:1-3; Acts 3:25,26).
- The expectancy of the early return of the Lord to the place where

His feet had last touched the earth before His ascension—The Mount of Olives —"in the same way as he went into heaven" (Acts 1:9-12; Zechariah 14:4).

The gifts of the Spirit in 1 Corinthians 12 were never promised to a company of Christians whose 'hope' and 'blessings' are in "the heavenly places" far above all and "seated with Christ" (Ephesians 1:3; 2:5-8). This should become clearer when we consider the ministry of *the Holy Spirit* in the Ephesian epistle.

ii) The Holy Spirit and the Word of God in Corinthians

I have already touched upon the connection between the Holy Spirit and the Word of God (page 33), here in Corinthians Paul is claiming that his "message" is *a demonstration of the Holy Spirit's power*. If this is a figure of speech, *hendiadys* (where two words are used but one thing is meant), then it refers to "the powerful gift of Divine wisdom", as distinct from "the (weak) wisdom of men." In our own calling, whereas the "gifts of the Spirit" of the Acts Period are missing, the power of the Holy Spirit through the Word of God is just as relevant without them. I will come to this when we compare Ephesians 5:18 with Colossians 3:16 (page 202).

CORINTHIANS: FIRST EPISTLE:

The events that prompted Paul to write this letter, was a letter he had received from the Corinthian church which required a reply (1 Corinthians 7:1), but also, and more worrying, was news that he had received quite independently concerning the conduct of many of the believers in Corinth (1 Corinthians 1:11). To refer to this at length is not within the remit of this study, but only insofar that it impinges on the ministry of the Holy Spirit in that church.

Paul wrote at the beginning of his first epistle to the Corinthians:

> "*My speech and my message* were not in plausible words of wisdom, but *in demonstration of the Spirit and of power*, (in order that *hina*) your faith might not rest in the wisdom of men but in *the power of God*." (1 Corinthians 2:4)

Were I asked what I believed to be the most important 'fact' about *the Holy Spirit's ministry today* (and probably in every age and calling), I would refer to this quotation, and to what follows in verses 6-16:

> "These things God has *revealed to us through the Spirit*. For *the Spirit searches everything*, even the depths of God ... the natural person does not accept t*he things of the Spirit of God* ... he is not able to understand them because *they are spiritually discerned* ... But we have the mind of Christ." (1 Corinthians 2:10-16)

i) The depths of God and the mind of Christ

> "It is written, 'What no eye has seen, nor ear heard, nor the heart of man imagined, what God has prepared for those who love him'—these things God has *revealed to us through the Spirit*. For *the Spirit searches* everything, *even the depths of God.*" (1 Corinthians 2:9,10)

The 'role' of the Holy Spirit is not like someone looking for information in a book. "He penetrates *all things*. There is nothing beyond his knowledge" (Leon Morris *Tyndale Commentaries in loco*). "The depths of God" is reflected in "the thoughts of God" (1 Corinthians 2:11). In verses 11-16, the Spirit's insight into the mind of God is contrasted by an analogy drawn from the nature of 'man' and man's 'mind'.

Nobody can really know what another individual is thinking, in *their spirit*, but themselves. And none "can comprehend the thoughts of God except *the Spirit of God*" (1 Corinthians 2:11). To the "natural person" the things of the Spirit of God are "folly to him", but the believer "has the mind of Christ" (2:15,16).

This claim, "we have the mind of Christ", does not imply that every Christian can understand all Christ's thoughts, even given the Lord's claim in John 15:15—"all that I have heard from my Father I have made known to you". His words on that occasion were spoken by the Lord to His apostles, and would include only what they *needed to know* to effect their coming mission, not all that He was thinking.

In the Old Testament, Isaiah 40:13 refers to *the mind of Jehovah* when it says, "Who has measured (or directed) the Spirit of the LORD." Paul cites this in Romans 11:34 as "Who has known *the mind of the Lord*, or who has been his counsellor?" In Paul's estimation "the mind of the Lord" was equivalent to "the Spirit of the Lord". The Holy Spirit conveys to the believer something of the "mind of the Lord"; I say 'something of' for I believe that the giving of the spirit *by measure* will condition this 'something' according as we "*let* the word of Christ dwell in you richly ... in all wisdom" (cp. John 3:34; Colossians 3:16).

In Philippians 2:5 *KJV*, Paul said to his readers, "*Let* this mind be in you, which was also in Christ Jesus." Here Christians were being urged to 'imitate' Christ's humility when He made the salvation of man possible—*think like Him* (Philippians 2:6-8). This involved a conscious effort on the part of the believer, much in the same way as Paul was to write later, "*Let* the word of Christ dwell in you richly" (Colossians 3:16) and, as we shall see later (page 202), that is equivalent to saying, "*Be* filled with the Spirit" (Ephesians 5:18).

ii) The Holy Spirit in relation to the 'old self' and 'the new self'

Paul introduces the concept of two 'personalities' within the believer; the old 'natural' one and the new 'spiritual' one.

> "**Now** we have received not the spirit of the world, but *the Spirit who is from God*, that we might understand the things freely given us by God. And we impart this in words not taught by human wisdom but *taught by the Spirit*, interpreting spiritual truths to *those who are spiritual*." (1 Corinthians 2:12,13)

Dr. Bullinger (*The Giver and His Gifts*) refers the Greek *pneuma* here to 'the new nature'. In verse 12 he describes "the *pneuma which is from God*" as "the new nature which is set in contrast with the natural man, and the rest of the world". Peter in his second epistle (1:4) spoke of "the divine nature", which answers to "the new nature" referred to by Bullinger, and to Paul's "new man (self)". It is in contrast to "the old man (self)" (Romans 6:6: Ephesians 4:22-24).

The old creation:

The "Spirit of God" is first introduced in the Scriptures in relation to the present Creation. "*The Spirit of God* was hovering over the face of the waters. And God said ..." (Genesis 1:2,3). When He came to make 'man' God said:

> "Let **US** make man in the likeness of **OUR** image ... male and female he created them."[46]

Some see a suggestion, or even a 'proof' of, the Trinity, in the plurals, 'us' and 'them'. Without either believing or rejecting this, put in human terms, the Spirit of God is *the agent* through which the will of God is effected. And this is further demonstrated when the 'man', whose existence began as a series of 'body parts', had God *breathe* "into his nostrils *the breath of life* and the man *became a living creature*" (Genesis 2:7; 1 Corinthians 15:45).

We can visualise this man Adam and his wife Eve as being physically perfect. They were able to think and communicate, and each had a conscience. But they were not mature, having had no experience of life, and certainly had no knowledge of good and evil (Genesis 2:17; 3:5-7). (The creation of "the tree of the knowledge of good and evil", was surely not simply to 'test' the couples' obedience but, in time, when they had 'matured', they would need to have that 'knowledge'.)

The writer of Hebrews referred to 'discerning good and evil', when he wrote in his epistle:

> Solid food is for *the mature*, for those who have their powers of discernment *trained by constant practice* to *discern good and evil*. (Hebrews 5:14)

Experience is built up over time by constant practice. That is true of believers and unbelievers.

The record of 'the fall' that made man 'a sinner' is well known, and its consequences were spelled out by Paul in Romans 5:2-21—"death spread to all men" (v.12). Paul enlarges upon this 'condition' that afflicts humanity in Romans 6:6 when he refers to it by the term "our old man" (*KJV*) or "our old self" (*ESV*).

In 1 Corinthians 2:14 he referred to the same when he wrote, "*the natural man* does not accept the things of the Spirit of God for they are folly to him". He draws a contrast between the "the old self", derived from Adam and his sin, and which, together with death, is the lot of all mankind, and "the new self" implanted by *the Spirit of God* and which leads to eternal life. (I cannot here go into the 'warring' that goes on in the believer between these two, the 'natural' and that implanted by the Spirit of God. Paul deals with it at length in relation to the law in Romans 6:7-25 and the author has included it in his *Paul's Letter to the Romans* OBT, pages 88-92.)

The new creation:

The transformation from the first to the second 'condition' is spelt out in several ways in the Scriptures; by the Lord Himself, by Peter and by Paul.

> **John 3:3-8:** "You must be born again ... born from above ... *born of the Spirit* ... that which is born of the flesh (the old self) is flesh, that which is born of the Spirit (the new self) is spirit."
>
> **2 Peter 1:3,4:** "*His divine power* has granted us all things that pertain to life and godliness ... precious and very great promises, so that through them you may become *partakers of the divine nature* (the new self), having escaped the corruption that is in the world because of sinful desires (characteristic of the old self)."
>
> **1 Corinthians 5:17:** "If anyone is *in Christ*, he is a *new* creation. The *old* has passed away; behold, *the new* has come."
>
> **1 Corinthians 15:45:** "The first man Adam became a living being (*psyche*); the last Adam became a life-giving spirit (*pneuma*)."

In brief: When the first 'man', 'a living being', sinned, 'the old self' was the result, but when Adam's descendants are touched by the 'life-giving Spirit', 'the new self' is created and opposes 'the old self' in a battle for the heart and mind. That battle between the two natures in the child of God[47] is developed in Romans 7:7-25, where Paul relates his own experience, ending with:

> I do not do the good I want, but the evil I do not want is what I keep on doing ... I delight in the law of God, in my inner being, but I see in my members another law waging war against the law of my mind and making me captive to the law of sin that dwells in my members. (Romans 7:19,22,23)
>
> Wretched man that I am! Who will deliver me from this body of

death? Thanks be to God through Jesus Christ our Lord! So then, I myself serve the law of God with my mind, but with my flesh I serve the law of sin. (Romans 7:24,25)

iii) God's Spirit in God's temple

The concept of Christians as a temple indwelt by the Holy Spirit is common to both God's earthly purpose during Acts, and in The Church which is the Body of Christ, post-Acts. Hence it appears here in 1 Corinthians 3:17; 6:19 and 2 Corinthians 6:16, and post-Acts in Ephesians 2:22. The difference is that in 1 Corinthians Paul applies the figure to *the individual's human body*, but in Ephesians to the saints *as a corporate body*, which "grows into a holy temple in the Lord ... a dwelling place for God in the Spirit" (Ephesians 2:21,22).

The Ephesian concept will be considered in its own place, but in 1 Corinthians it is introduced to remind the Corinthians, "you are not your own, for you were bought with a price. So glorify God in your body" (1 Corinthians 6:19,20). Joining their bodies in "one flesh" with prostitutes, dishonoured the Lord, since "the body was not meant for sexual immorality, but for the Lord, and the Lord for the body" (1 Corinthians 6:15-20).

1 Corinthians 3 begins by drawing attention to the divisions in the Corinthian church, the factions that said, "I am of Paul, I am of Apollos" (3:1-9). The two apostles were but "fellow workers" working for the same cause; the Corinthians were "God's field, God's building" *indwelt by the Holy Spirit*, a holy temple. Those building upon its foundation would suffer loss, if their "works" did not stand the test of fire. However, they would still be saved—"but only as through fire" (1 Corinthians 3:12-15).

So then, if anyone defiled this temple, presumably by their way of life, "God will destroy him". An example of this was when Paul, calling for judgement upon the man who committed incest with his father's wife, instructed that he should be "delivered to Satan for the destruction of the flesh, so that his spirit may be saved in the day of the Lord" (1 Corinthians 5:1-5; and compare this with the judgement upon Ananias and Sapphira in Acts 5:1-10).

iv) Washed, sanctified, justified: The Name and the Spirit of God

The apostle, looking back to the immoral practices of some of the Corinthians, said,

> And such were some of you. But you were washed, you were sanctified, you were justified in the name of the Lord Jesus Christ and by *the Spirit of our God*. (1 Corinthians 6:11)

There is more than a hint of the Trinity in this last reference; nothing less than the sacrifice and resurrection of the Lord Jesus Christ, washing, sanctifying and justifying the sinner, and *the power of the Spirit of God*, were necessary for them to inherit the kingdom of God (1 Corinthians 6:10).

The Name of Jesus Christ:

This 'Name' was at the very centre of the gospel message preached by the apostles during the Acts Period, and is still very relevant today:

> There is salvation in no one else, for there is *no other name* under heaven given among men by which we must be saved. (Acts 4:12; cp. 2:38; 3:6; 9:21 etc.)

The 'name' denoted authority, hence the Council had asked Peter and John concerning the healing of the lame man, "*By what power* or *by what name* did you do this?" (Acts 4:7). For the Jews, 'Jesus' was the 'Name' of the Messiah. Later, looking ahead to Saul's mission, the risen Jesus says to Ananias, concerning Saul and his ministry, that he is "to *carry my name* before the Gentiles" (Acts 9:15).

That 'Name' is just as important to the Church which is the Body of Christ, as it was during the Acts Period—'Jesus' is *the Name* upon which the whole purpose of God, earthly and heavenly, comes to fruition. It was *in that name* that all the Miracles, Wonders and Signs were done by the apostles. In Acts, it began in Jerusalem when Peter (together with John) said to the man lame from birth:

> "Look at us." And he fixed his attention on them, expecting to receive something from them. But Peter said, "I have no silver

and gold, but what I do have I give to you. *In the name of Jesus Christ of Nazareth*, rise up and walk" ... he began to walk ... entered the temple with them ... all who saw him were filled with wonder and amazement. (Acts 3:1-10)

The importance of "the name" was seen when the apostles were brought before the council in Jerusalem concerning the healing of the lame beggar; they were asked, "*by what name* did you do this?" (Acts 4:7) and Peter, "*filled with the Holy Spirit*" answered, "by *the name* of Jesus Christ of Nazareth, whom you crucified ... this man is standing before you well"; the Name and the Holy Spirit (Acts 4:7-10). Even opposition to the apostles was expressed in terms of the charge that they must not "speak in *the name* of Jesus" (Acts 4:17,18; 5:40).

Today, we may not be able to produce the miracles, wonders and signs that were so prevalent during the Acts Period associated with that name, but we are called upon to approach God the Father in our prayers of thankfulness, "*in the name* of our Lord Jesus Christ", as a result of being "*filled by the Spirit*" (Ephesians 5:18-20).

v) Our judgement and the Spirit of God

Paul evidently trying to answer one of the many questions that he had been asked by the Corinthians said:

> A wife is bound to her husband as long as he lives. But if her husband dies, she is free to be married to whom she wishes, only in the Lord. Yet in my judgement she is happier if she remains as she is. And I think that I too have *the Spirit of God*. (1 Corinthians 7:39,40)

To understand his answer, which may seem hard and intrusive to us today, we must recall the situation at the time. There was a very real expectancy that the last days immediately preceding the coming of Christ were upon them (see notes 23 and 24). Paul had already made a similar judgement earlier in this chapter based upon what he referred to as "the present distress" and "the appointed time has grown very short" (1 Corinthians 7:25,26,29). With the imminence of Christ's return and the terrible prelude to it a possibility, Paul gives his judgement, but suggests it is also the judgement of *the Spirit of God*—"I think that **I too** have *the Spirit of God*."

Moffatt's translation of 1 Corinthians 7:40 is apposite:

> "However, she is happier if she remains as she is; that is my opinion—and I suppose I have the Spirit of God as well as other people!"

Paul is not giving his judgement here as the grand apostle whose word must be obeyed, but seeing himself like others who also have "the Spirit of God". Here human opinion is operating within the exigency of the current situation; even the Spirit of God has not laid down a 'hard and fast' rule; the widow makes her own choice whether to remain a widow or remarry, with one proviso, he must be a Christian.

This leads me to ask how anyone today who claims to be 'a new self' can be sure that their own judgement (or opinion) is right in relation to "the Spirit of God"? There must be a thousand and one situations that may arise where we might be called upon to make a decision, but for which, as Christians, we have no *specific* answer from the Scriptures. In other words, we are left *to interpret* what the Bible says in forming our own judgement. Can we, like Paul, when making such judgements or giving our opinion, say, "I think that *I too have the Spirit of God*"?

In my past as a young Christian, I met a number of people who were often claiming that something they had done or spoken was initiated by God; the favourite comment was, "I was led by the Lord". At first, I found this disturbing because I never felt that I could make that claim. Later, when I knew a bit more about what the Scriptures teach, I did try to balance any decision I had to make against the Word of God.

Two good examples during the Acts Period where man's 'judgement' and the Holy Spirit's leading come together with different final results are:

Acts 15:1-21:

The Jerusalem Council, made up of "the apostles and elders" of the Acts Period 'Church', met together to decide whether it was necessary for Gentile believers to be circumcised in order to be saved, as some asserted. After some discussion, testimonies from Peter, Barnabas and Paul, James, after quoting from the Hebrew Scriptures, gave his judgement based on the general testimony of the assembly:

> "We should not trouble those of the Gentiles who turn to God, but to write to them ..." (Acts 15:19-20)

And he wrote that *"It seemed good to the Holy Spirit and to us* to lay on you no greater burden than these requirements" (Acts 15:28), which he named as abstention from:

> i) what has been sacrificed to idols,
> ii) and from blood,
> iii) and from what has been strangled,
> iv) and from sexual immorality. (Acts 15:29)

Here the Holy Spirit *authenticates the decision* of James and the assembly that circumcision was not necessary, but that a way of life was required from them coincident with Jewish standards.

Acts 16:4-10:

Paul and Silas had been going through Syria and Cilicia with Timothy, (after his split with Barnabas, Acts 15:36-39):

> As they went on their way through the cities, they delivered to them for observance the decisions that had been reached by the apostles and elders who were in Jerusalem. So the churches were strengthened in the faith, and they increased in numbers daily. And they went through the region of Phrygia and Galatia, *having been forbidden by the Holy Spirit* to speak the word in Asia. And when they had come up to Mysia they attempted to go into Bithynia, but *the Spirit of Jesus did not allow them.* (Acts 16:4-7)

As a result of this, Paul received a vision in the night and heard "a man of Macedonia" ... saying, "Come over to Macedonia and help us", and *so the apostles "concluded that God had called us* to preach the gospel to them" (Acts 16:9-10). And so Paul's missionary journey moved from Asia to Europe, from East to West, which was not part of his immediate plans. Here the Holy Spirit, "the Spirit of Jesus", *opposes* the plans of the apostles.

In the first reference He *authenticates a decision*; in the second He *overturns an intention*. But what of today? Can we claim to have been influenced by the Holy Spirit? I will come to this later when we consider His ministry associated with "the Church which is the Body of Christ" (page 203). For now, we can do no better than notice that James made his decision at the Council in Jerusalem based upon the Scriptures, *the God-breathed Scriptures* (2 Timothy 3:16), and follow his example, as Paul wrote:

> Walk in love, as Christ loved us and gave himself up for us, a fragrant offering and sacrifice to God. (Ephesians 5:2)

Paul interprets "walk in love" in the following verses (Ephesians 5:3-20), where he lists *things to avoid and things to embrace*. However, in situations not covered by Scripture we are left to interpret this ourselves. This, where it is not obvious, brings us back to our conscience.

vi) One Spirit, many gifts, a warning and a goal: (1 Corinthians 12-14)

The references to *pneuma* in 1 Corinthians chapters 12 & 14 are largely concerned with the Holy Spirit's gifts to the Corinthian church and the reason why they have been given. Paul begins with a cautionary warning that not all 'spirits' are from God; a warning that needs to be heeded in meetings where "spiritual gifts" like those listed in Corinthians are claimed to be relevant for today.

> No one speaking in *the Spirit of God* ever says, "Jesus is accursed!" and no one can say "Jesus is Lord" except in *the Holy Spirit* ... there are varieties of gifts, but *the same Spirit* ... *the same Lord* ... *the same God* who empowers them all in everyone. (1 Corinthians 12:3,4)

Paul is not referring here to ordinary speech, but "various kinds of tongues", and hence there is a need for another of these 'gifts of the Spirit'; "the ability to distinguish between spirits" (v.10). There may be other 'gifts', but it is the Triune God who "empowers them all in everyone".

> To each is given the manifestation of the Spirit *for the common good* ... the utterance of wisdom ... knowledge ... faith ... gifts of healing ... working of miracles ... prophecy ... tongues ... interpretation of tongues ... *the same Spirit*, who apportions to

> each individually as he wills. (1 Corinthians 12:7-11)

Note particularly that all these 'gifts' were given "for the common good" and according to "*the will of the Holy Spirit*"; not left for the individual to choose what he wanted! Later in 1 Corinthians 14:5,12 he states that 'speaking in tongues' was for "building up the church". and hence must be interpreted for, "if with your tongue you utter speech that is not intelligible, how will anyone know what is said? For you will be speaking into the air" (1 Corinthians 14:9).

> As the (human) body is one and has many members, and all the members of the body, though many, are one body, so it is with Christ. For in *one Spirit* we were all baptised into one body—Jews or Greeks, slaves or free—and all were made to drink of one Spirit. (1 Corinthians 12:12-14)

"Made to drink of one Spirit" is probably better "all in one Spirit were given to drink". Paul takes "the Spirit as the element 'in' which they were baptised" (Leon Morris *Tyndale Commentaries*). The connection between the Holy Spirit and living water was considered on page 78 and see the author's *Baptisms in Scripture* OBT for the various baptisms referred to in the Scriptures.

Paul's reference to the human 'body', as an analogy to describe the different 'gifts' in the Corinthian church, has led to the mistaken belief that 'the body of Christ' alluded to here and referred to in 1 Corinthians 2:27 and Romans 12:5, is one and the same as that referred to in Ephesians 1:22,23; 4:12; Colossians18; 2:24). But is it?

vii) The 'Body of Christ': During the Acts and post-Acts Periods

I give here reasons why I believe that "the church which is the Body of Christ", referred to in the Ephesian and Colossian epistles, belongs to a dispensation that was not revealed until *after* Acts 28:28, and must, therefore, be distinguished from the 'church' being called out *during* the Acts Period.

That Acts 'church' looked to the fulfilment of "the hope of Israel" (Acts 28:20), a 'hope' that Paul expanded to Agrippa as:

> "My hope in the promise made by God to our fathers, to which our twelve tribes hope to attain, as they earnestly worship night and day. And for this hope I am accused by Jews, O king." (Acts 26:6,7)

This 'hope' was expected to be fulfilled within the lifetime of Paul and the Christian 'church' at that time (see note 22). It was an earthly hope based on the LORD's promises to Abraham and "the promises given to the fathers" (Genesis 12:1-3; Romans 4:17,18; 15:8,9). The Acts Period was a dispensation under which, in God's purpose, the Jew came first, not just in time but in relation to that purpose.

The Jew had *priority* over the Gentile in many ways and *by birth had all the privileges*; the covenants and the promises listed in Romans 9:3-5. They were the "natural branches" in the olive tree of Romans 11, in contrast to the Gentiles who were but "wild shoots", grafted in "contrary to nature" (Romans 11:17, 24). But this 'status' does not reflect the situation in "the Body of Christ" spoken of in Ephesians and Colossians, and there are important differences that show that this cannot be so.

The scriptural meaning of the term "***The*** body of Christ" must be clearly defined and distinguished from similar terms used by Paul *before Acts 28:28* (Romans & 1 Corinthians), when "the hope of Israel" was in view (Acts 28:20), and his usage *after that time* (Ephesians & Colossians). The two earlier epistles belong to the Acts (kingdom) period, but the two prison epistles to The Post Acts Period, to the Dispensation of the mystery revealed after Israel's 'hope' had gone into abeyance. Compare these references (*literal* renderings):

Prior to Acts 28:28.

Paul wrote:

> For as in one body we have many members, and all the members have not the same function, so we the many are *one body in Christ* and each one members of one another. And having differing gifts according to the grace given us ... prophecy ... ministry ... exhortation ... etc. (Romans 12:4-8)

> Now you are *a body of Christ*, and members in part. And God placed some in the church, firstly apostles, secondly prophets,

> thirdly teachers, then works of power (miracles), then gifts of healing ... tongues etc. (1 Corinthians 12:27,28)

In this second passage, there is no definite article before 'body' in the Greek original. It has been supplied by the translators in the *NIV* and other versions; it is '**a** body'; not '**the** body'. Also, in these two references above, the 'body of Christ' is introduced *as an illustration based on the human body* that has many different parts. It illustrates in the church of the Acts Period there were differing gifts of the spirit (1 Corinthians 12:1-4), gifts that are evidently not with us today. Every member of this 'body' was necessary for the growth of the church, even though some members seemed less important than others (1 Corinthians 12:22-24). Within this 'body', with its many parts, Paul likens some to a foot, a hand, an ear, an eye (12:14-17), but in particular he makes the significant comment:

> The eye is not able to say to the hand 'I have no need of you'; or again **the head** to the feet, 'I have no need of you'. (1 Corinthians 12:21)

The 'head' of the body spoken of in Romans and 1 Corinthians, is just one of its members; **it does not represent Christ**, whereas in "The Body of Christ" in Ephesians and Colossians, **the Head is Christ** (Ephesians 1:22,23; Colossians 1:18). And the 'gifts' given to this post-Acts 'church', do not include (as they did in the Acts 'church') healing, miracles, tongues etc., but are listed as 'apostles, prophets, evangelists, pastors and teachers' (Ephesians 4:11-13).

The conception of "a body of Christ", as used in Romans and 1 Corinthians, is of a human body, of which one of its members could be likened to the 'head'. But when we cross the boundary between it and the 'church which is the body of Christ' of Ephesians and Colossians, the 'Head' is Christ Himself.

Post-Acts 28:28.

"The Body of Christ" is **a title** of the church spoken of in Ephesians and Colossians, and its 'Head' is Christ Himself. Of Him it is written:

> God put all things under his (Christ's) feet and gave him *as head* over all things to the church, which is his body, the fullness of him who fills all in all. (Ephesians 1:22,23)

A further aspect of this distinction is that Christ, as "head over all things", has been given "to the church which is his body". That 'church' and its relationship to its members is *not* described elsewhere as that between a bridegroom and a bride. That relationship belongs to Israel's 'hope' as set out in the closing chapters of Revelation. For more on this see *The Wife the Bride and the Body,* OBT by Charles Ozanne.

In 1 Corinthians 14 there are references to *pneuma* in verses 2,12,14,15,16 & 32. The whole chapter is concerned with prophecy and the gift of tongues, especially in the light of keeping orderly worship in the church of the Acts Period, when those gifts were displayed in those present.

CORINTHIANS: SECOND EPISTLE

i) The Holy Spirit in relation to 'anointing' and 'sealing'

It is necessary to emphasise *the difference between* the ministry of the Holy Spirit during the Acts Period, and that which followed when the 'hope' of that period went into abeyance. This is especially important in respect of 'the gifts of the Spirit' as set out in the Corinthian epistles. But it is equally important to remember that some aspects of the Holy Spirit's ministry are *common to both* periods; the need and provision of salvation for the individual is the most obvious example, but there are others. And this (recognising certain nuances) is so in the first reference to *the Spirit* in the second of the Corinthian epistles.

> It is God who establishes us with you in Christ, and has *anointed us*, and who has also *put his seal on us*, and who has *given us his Spirit* in our hearts as *a guarantee*. (2 Corinthians 1:22; see also 5:5)

These words were written by Paul during the Acts Period when "the hope of Israel" was still 'live' (Acts 28:20). But compare them with what he wrote post-Acts, in regard to those whose 'hope' lies within "the Church which is the Body of Christ":

> In him you also, when you heard the word of truth, the gospel of your salvation, and believed in him, were *sealed with the promised Holy Spirit*, who is *the guarantee* (margin 'down payment') of our inheritance until we acquire possession of it, to the praise of his glory ... *the Holy Spirit* of God, by whom *you were sealed for* the day of redemption. (Ephesians 1:13,14 & 4:30)

In Corinthians the Holy Spirit's 'seal' is a *guarantee* that God has 'anointed' Paul, Silvanus and Timothy for their ministry, a testimony *inwardly* to themselves and *outwardly* to the Corinthians, together with whom they are "established in Christ" (2 Corinthians 1:18,19).

In Ephesians the Holy Spirit *is Himself the guarantee* of the individual's inheritance, kept for the day of redemption. The Ephesian passage is considered later in its own place.

ii) A letter from Christ written with *the Spirit of the living God*

> You show that you are a letter from Christ delivered by us, written not with ink but with *the Spirit of the living God*, not on tablets of stone but on tablets of human hearts. (2 Corinthians 3:3)

Considering the hard things that Paul has had to say of some of those in the Corinthian church, this is a 'breath of fresh air'. Paul likens the Corinthians to "a letter from Christ" that he and his compatriots had delivered. Their lives *speak of Him*, but not in words written in ink or on tablets of stone, but by "*the Spirit of the living God*" on human hearts. If Paul needed a letter of recommendation, it was here:

> You yourselves are our letter of recommendation, written on your (margin) hearts, to be known and read by all. (2 Corinthians 3:2)

> A living letter dictated by Christ, but enscribed by Paul through the apostolic ministry of gospel proclamation ... *carried out by the Spirit* of the living God ... *empowered by the Spirit* of God so that *any changes wrought* in the lives of his hearers *were effected by the Spirit*. (Colin Kruse *Tyndale Commentaries in loco*)

This "letter ... written on human hearts" was in every way the work of *the Holy Spirit* and a testimony to His power to change 'the lives of his hearers'. Paul's 'apostolic ministry' is referred to here in 2 Corinthians 3:6-8 and later the extent of it during the Acts Period is recorded in Romans 15:17-19:

> By *the power of the Spirit of God*—so that from Jerusalem and all the way round to Illyricum I have fulfilled the ministry of the Gospel of Christ.

The reference to "tablets of stone" in 2 Corinthians 3:3 lead Paul, as a minister of a new covenant, to contrast the Old with the New Covenant and the Holy Spirit's ministry in both.

iii) Old Covenant letter v. New Covenant *Spirit*

> God has made us competent to be ministers of a new covenant, not of the letter but *of the Spirit*. For the letter kills, but *the Spirit gives life* ... will not *the ministry of the Spirit* have even more glory. (2 Corinthians 3:6-8)

I look at the contrast between the two covenants, Old and New, in the Hebrews epistle below. Here I will simply remind the reader how great that contrast between the two was as related by Paul in 2 Corinthians 3:6-18, which can be summed up in the case of the New Covenant in the phrase, "even more glory". The basic facts are:

Old Covenant:

> "Carved in letters on stone ... kills ... the ministry of death ... the ministry of condemnation ... coming to an end." (2 Corinthians 3:4-9)

It was in operation during the Acts Period, as Hebrews states (8:13), and as the actions of the apostles during the Acts Period show (cp. Acts 3:1; 15:21; 20:16; 21:20-26; 24:11):

> In speaking of a New Covenant, he makes the first one obsolete. And what is becoming obsolete and growing old is ready to vanish away. (Hebrews 8:13)

Hebrew sums up the situation that existed when 2 Corinthians was written. The Old Covenant of Law was *becoming* obsolete, but *had not yet done so*; it was *ready* to pass away, but the situation was *not yet right* for it to do so. That situation remained throughout the Acts Period, pending the repentance of Israel as a nation (Acts 3:19-21).

New Covenant:

> A new Covenant, not of the letter but of *the Spirit* ... gives life ... the ministry of *the Spirit* ... the ministry of righteousness ... is permanent. (2 Corinthians 3:6-11)

(To fully appreciate the import of the apostle's comparison in what follows, read the passage of Scripture he is referring to in the Old Testament history of Israel recorded in Exodus 34:29-35. This event would almost certainly be well known to the Jews in Corinth, but unlikely to have been so to the Gentiles there.) Paul reasons:

> Now if the ministry of death, carved in letters on stone, came with *such glory* that the Israelites could not gaze at Moses' face because of *its glory*, which was being brought to an end, will not *the ministry of the Spirit* have *even more glory*? For if *there was glory* in the ministry of condemnation, the ministry of righteousness must *far exceed it in glory.* (2 Corinthians 3:7-9)

As to 'glory', Paul here compares the differences between the two covenants. In 2 Corinthians 3:17 he sees as part of the 'glory' of the New Covenant *of the Spirit* as, not only 'life', but 'freedom':

> Now the Lord is the Spirit, and where *the Spirit of the Lord is, there is freedom*. And we all with unveiled face, beholding the glory of the Lord, are being transformed into the same image *from one degree of glory to another.* For this comes from the Lord who is the Spirit. (2 Corinthians 3:17,18)

And later in the epistle he compares the present status of the believer as "this light momentary affliction", with the "an *eternal weight of glory beyond all comparison*" (2 Corinthians 4:17).

Glory:

The meaning of 'glory' as used in the Scriptures is a subject in itself, so I will be brief here. In 2 Corinthians chapter 3 it is the translation of the Greek *doxa* that has the underlying meaning, 'dignity, honour, magnify, praise'. In 2 Corinthians 4:17,18, Paul links this *eternal weight of glory* with "things that are (at present) unseen" and "eternal", and which await the believer in the coming age.

The context in which the word *doxa* is used here suggests that the 'glory', although unseen at that time, would be something *that would be seen* in the age to come. When this was written, the Jews of the Acts Period looked forward to the 'age' to come, to a hope of a kingdom upon this earth, "the hope of Israel" (Acts 28:20). But this 'glory' has its 'equivalent' in our own calling today in "the Church which is the Body of Christ" (see Ephesians).

In 2 Corinthians 3:18, the apostle speaks of "from one degree of glory to another", a change that also describes what happens when 'the glory' associated with the Old Covenant is replaced by 'the glory' brought in by the New Covenant in 'the age to come'.

It is important to point out that there is a difference between 'being saved' and a consequent 'faithful life' which should follow, but does not necessarily do so. In Paul's second and last (extant) letter to Timothy, in a context of suffering for the Lord's sake, he is at pains to point this out. He writes:

> I endure everything for the sake of the elect, that they also may obtain the salvation that is in Christ Jesus *with eternal glory*. The saying is trustworthy, for,
>
> **a:** If we *died* with him, we will also *live* with him;
> **b:** if we *endure*, we will *also reign* with him;
> **b:** If we *deny him*, he will also *deny us*;
> **a:** if we are faithless, he *remains faithful*—for he *cannot deny* himself.

Here, in 2 Timothy 2:10-13, 'glory' (*doxa*) is associated with 'endurance' and 'faithfulness'. Paul makes a difference between, "the salvation that is in Christ Jesus" (for all believers) and "eternal glory" (for the faithful who 'endure').

a:*a*: As to the first, the 'salvation' of the believer is *secure* because "he (Jesus Christ) remains faithful" and "he (Jesus Christ) cannot deny himself". (For an exposition of salvation in relation to the believer's security see   Sylvia Penny's booklet *Salvation: Safe and Secure* OBT.

b:*b*: But in regard to the second, "if we deny him" (Jesus Christ) by failing to live a life worthy of Him and are "faithless", He will "deny us" the privilege of reigning with Him. Reigning is *over and above* living as can be seen in 2 Timothy 2:10-13 (above).

Identification:

To 'die with him' and to 'live with him' is an accomplished fact in the believer, as Paul explains in Romans 5:12-21, and is part of the believer's 'identification' with Christ. (See the author's *Paul's Letter to the Romans* OBT, pages 68 to 86, for more on 'identification' in relation to 'salvation'[48].)

But in chapter 6 of Romans, Paul turns these facts into practical living: "So you must *consider yourselves* dead to sin and alive to God in Christ Jesus" (v.11). The word translated "consider" is here *logizomai*, the same word Paul used when he wrote, "Abraham believed God, and it was *counted* to him as righteousness" (Romans 4:3 and throughout that chapter).

Identification with Christ in the everyday life of the believer is seen in Romans 6 and 8 in five steps:

- Crucified with Him (6:6).
- Dead with Him (6:8).
- Buried with Him (6:4).
- Quickened with Him (8:11 *KJV*).
- Raised with Him (6:5).

These five aspects of the believer's status in Christ were true of all believers during the Acts Period, and hence relevant to the apostles' teaching at that time. After the Acts Period they are still relevant for the Church, the Body of Christ, but there are two further aspects: "*raised up with Him* to be *seated with Him* in the heavenly places"; a sevenfold unity

(Ephesians 2:6).

iv) The Spirit of the Lord: 'Freedom' and degrees of 'glory'

Now the Lord is (or means) *the Spirit*, and where t*he Spirit of the Lord* is, there is freedom ... we all ... are being transformed ... from one degree of glory to another. For this comes from the Lord who is *the Spirit.* (2 Corinthians 3:17,18)

These difficult verses have occasioned a number of interpretations which seem to say that 'the Lord (Christ) *is the same as* the Holy Spirit'. In this respect see the juxtaposition in Romans 8:9,10 between the phrases, "The Spirit of God dwells in you" and "Christ is in you". In Romans these are generally taken to mean the same thing, even though there may be nuances of meaning between the two statements. We must remember we are looking here at the 'mystery of the Godhead'.

I cannot give here the various interpretations that have been put upon this verse, but I give what (in my view) is the best interpretation I have come across (R. H. Strachan *Moffatt's New Testament Commentaries in loco*):

"The Lord" is Christ ... "The Lord means the Spirit" identifies Jesus and the Spirit, at least in the experience of men ... In the experience of men, the power of God, of the exalted Christ, and the Spirit are identical ... wherever the Spirit of the Lord is, there is open freedom, not enforced, but free acceptance of the will of God. (John 8:31-36)

In the passage in John, the Lord speaking to the Jews is comparing 'freedom' with 'slavery', with the underlying implication that, even though they are "offspring of Abraham", they are not 'free' in the real sense of 'freedom'. So He said to them, "If the Son sets you free, you will be *free indeed.*" This truth Jesus had seen with His Father, but they were doing what they had heard from their father, the devil, which was to seek to kill Him (John 8:44).

For "one degree of glory to another" (2 Corinthians 3:18) see page 169.

v) A Doxology: The fellowship of the Holy Spirit

The grace of the Lord Jesus Christ and the love of God and *the fellowship of the Holy Spirit* be with you. (2 Corinthians 13:14)

These were Paul's final words to the Corinthians in his second letter, in which, following his first letter to them, he had tried to sort out all their problems and having at times had to rebuke them. These words, at the end of 2 Corinthians, involved all three 'persons' of the Trinity. Whilst this doxology can be considered in respect of each of its three parts, we can expand it:

> It is through *the grace* of God demonstrated in *the Person and sacrifice* of Jesus Christ, that *the love* of God is expressed toward mankind, and *new life* is experienced through *the fellowship* of the Holy Spirit.

At the beginning of his first epistle to the Corinthians, Paul had promised them that Jesus Christ would:

> Sustain you to the end, guiltless in the day of our Lord Jesus Christ. God is faithful, by whom you were *called into the fellowship of his Son*, Jesus Christ our Lord. (1 Corinthians 1:8,9)

And John wrote, "Indeed *our fellowship* (Greek *koinonia*) is with the Father and with his Son Jesus Christ" (1 John 1:3).

Coming back to 2 Corinthians 13:14, the *KJV* has translated *koinonia*, "communion", as it has also in 1 Corinthians 10:16 (twice); and 2 Corinthians 6:14. In 2 Corinthians 9:13 (*KJV*) it is used of the "distribution" of food etc., by the Corinthians to the saints and all men.

In its noun form *koinonos*, it is variously translated, "partakers" (Matthew 23:30; 1 Corinthians 10:18; 2 Corinthians1:7; 1 Peter 5:1; 2 Peter 1:4); "partners" (Luke 5:10; 2 Corinthians 8:23; Philemon 17); and "companions" (Hebrews 10:33). The underlying meaning in all of these *KJV* renderings is, 'sharing with somebody else' and hence 'identifying oneself with them'. Here are a few examples of its usage:

- James and John ... were *partners* with Simon (Peter). (Luke 5:10)
- The people of Israel who ate the sacrifices (made at the altar) were *participants* in the altar. (1 Corinthians 10:18)
- The Hebrew believers became *companions* of them that were afflicted. (Hebrews 10:33)

The most wonderful example of the usage of the word *koinonos* in the New Testament is undoubtedly where Peter, referring to his dispersed brethren, wrote:

> (God's) divine power has granted to us all things that pertain to life and godliness, through the knowledge of him who called us to his own glory and excellence, by which he has granted to us his precious and very great promises, so that through them you may become *partakers* of the divine nature. (2 Peter 1:3,4)

This was written to a company of believing Jews during the Acts Period, and as such cannot therefore be applied automatically to ourselves today. But as we will see when we look at what Paul has written concerning our own calling, even though it may be expressed in different terms, it is just as true for us as it was for Peter's brethren.

Chapter 15.
The Holy Spirit in the Pauline Acts Epistles (Part 2)

Galatians; Romans

We come now to the two great epistles upon which the great Reformers built the Protestant faith. Each epistle could well have as its title; "The righteous shall live by faith" (Romans 1:17; Galatians 3:11). Cited from Habakkuk 2:4, this quotation occurs also in Hebrews 10:38, a verse that leads us straight into 'the gallery of faith' in Hebrews 11; men and women, drawn from many parts of the Hebrew Scriptures, set before Hebrew believers during the Acts Period as examples of those who lived and died by faith. The writer's object was to urge his readers, that whatever they were suffering for their faith at present, something better awaited them in the future when:

> Yet a little while, and the coming one will come and will not delay ... my righteous one shall live by faith. (Hebrews 10:37,38)

The belief that the Second Coming of the Lord was imminent when these three epistles were written has been noted before, and this must be kept in mind in any interpretation of the Holy Spirit's ministry at that time.

A) The Epistle to the GALATIANS

i) Paul Entrusted with the Gospel to the uncircumcised

Whilst this was probably not the first (extant) epistle that Paul wrote, it does provide us with an expansion of the ministry to which the apostle Paul was first called and entrusted with at his conversion. The Lord had said of him: "He is a chosen instrument of mine *to carry my name before the Gentiles and kings and the children of Israel*" (Acts 9:15). I emphasise the last of these three aspects of his ministry, because it is easy to forget that, even as an "apostle to the Gentiles" (Romans 11:13), his first priority was to his own people, the Jews. And his actions and words during the Acts Period testify to that:

> Paul and Barnabas said *to the Jews* in Pisidian Antioch, "It was necessary that the word of God be s*poken first to you* ... for so the Lord has commanded us saying, '*I have made you a light for the Gentiles, that you may bring salvation to the ends of the earth*'" (Acts 13:46,47).

> Paul to the Romans: "I am eager to preach the gospel to you ... for it is the power of God for salvation to everyone who believes, *to the Jew first* and also to the Greek" (Romans 1:15,16).

And in Luke's record of Paul's ministry throughout the Acts Period, whenever he visited a new venue he always went first to the Jewish synagogue there, "as was his custom" (Acts 17:2; see also 9:20; 13:5,14; 14:1; 17:10; 18:4,19:8).

Paul also taught that, at that time, when salvation came to the Gentiles it was "to make Israel jealous", and hence he *magnified* his apostleship to the Gentiles "in order somehow *to make my fellow Jews jealous, and thus save some of them*" (Romans 11:11-14).

ii) Paul's authority in relation to the apostles of the circumcision

Galatians begins and is occupied mainly in the first two chapters, with Paul establishing both his own authority as an independent apostle from the Twelve, "not from men nor through man, but through Jesus Christ and God the Father" (1:1), and claiming that the gospel he preached was "not man's gospel" but was "received through a revelation of Jesus Christ" (1:11,12).

In chapter 2 Paul describes the conversation that he had when he visited the apostles in Jerusalem, and the difference between their ministries and his; between Peter, James (the Lord's brother) and John on the one hand, and that of Paul and Barnabas (and later with such as Silas and Timothy) on the other. It was agreed between the two parties:

> When James and Cephas (Peter) and John ... perceived the grace that was given to me, they gave the right hand of fellowship to Barnabas and me, that we should go to the Gentiles and they to the circumcised. (Galatians 2:9)

The main thrust of the epistle to the Galatians revolves round the need or otherwise to circumcise Gentile converts to Christ. In that respect it stands alongside the decision made by the apostles and elders at the Jerusalem Council who met to consider this question (Acts 15). Both the Council and Paul were strongly against such a need, but the problem still remained at least amongst the Galatians (3:1-3; 5:1-4).

iii) The Holy Spirit (*pneuma*) in Galatians

There are eighteen occurrences of *pneuma* in the epistle, and according to the *KJV's* use of the capital 'S', the majority of them refer to the Holy Spirit Himself. Dr. Bullinger, however, refers some of these occurrences (3:2,3; 5:16-18; 6:1,8) to "the new nature". However, we interpret them, all except one (6:18 the believer's own *spirit*) refer back to the Holy Spirit and His gifts to the believer; He is the one who "supplies *the spirit* to you (Galatians) and works miracles among you" (Galatians 3:3-5).

iv) Receiving the Holy Spirit

Paul wrote to the Galatians:

> O foolish Galatians! Who has bewitched you? ... Did *you receive the Spirit* by works of the law or by hearing with faith? (Galatians 3:2)

> If you are *led by the Spirit*, you are not under the law. (Galatians 5:18)

> In Christ Jesus the blessing of Abraham might come to the Gentiles, so that *we might receive the promise of the Spirit* through faith (Galatians 3:14)

In these cases, *the spirit* already received and *the spirit* promised, are by hearing with faith, quite apart from any merit from keeping the law (3:2; and they are the 'gift' of *the Holy Spirit* who leads them. Verses 3:2,5 should be read in the context of verse 14: "He (the Holy Spirit) *who supplies* the spirit to you ... works miracles among you." The reference to "miracles" as one of the 'gifts of the Spirit', places this epistle within the Acts Period, with its many evidential miracles.

The *ESV* translation of *epichoregeon*, "(who) *supplies* the Spirit to you" in Galatians 3:5, seems rather a mundane rendering of the Holy Spirit's 'gift'. The *KJV* has "ministers to" which is probably less accurate, but more in keeping with our concept of the Holy Spirit's ministry. The word is used in 2 Peter 1:11 where the *ESV* speaks of, "an entrance into the eternal kingdom of our Lord and Saviour Jesus Christ ... will be richly *provided* for you". But perhaps the most enlightening context in which this word is found is 2 Peter 1:5 *KJV*:

> "That by these (precious promises v.4) you might be *partakers of the divine nature* having escaped the   corruption that is in the world through lust. And besides this, giving all diligence, a*dd* (*epichoregeon*) to your faith virtue; and to virtue knowledge; and to knowledge temperance ..."

Here, we have the idea of "adding" more to something that is already possessed. This does not mean that a second experience of the Holy Spirit is necessary for salvation, for as Paul assured the Ephesian believers, "***when you heard*** the word of truth, the gospel of your salvation, ***and believed in him, (you) were*** sealed with the promised Holy Spirit" (Ephesians 1:1,13). What it does teach, however, is that there is a difference between *the work of the Holy Spirit* in creating "a new self" within the believer - "putting on the new self" (Ephesians 4:24) - and being "***filled** with the Spirit*" (Ephesians 5:18).

v) The curse of the law and the promise to Abraham

Paul's arguments in Galatians 3:10-14 are logical but not always easy to follow. The *crucifixion* of Christ had satisfied the Law's demand that anyone breaking the law should be "put to death" and their body "hanged on a tree" —"a hanged man is cursed by God" (Deuteronomy 21:23). (In the New Testament 'crucifixion' of one's body and 'hanging on a tree' are one and the same, see Acts 5:30; 10:39; 1 Peter 2:24.)

All mankind is involved in the sin of Adam, but *the death* of Christ in our place has satisfied the demands of God, so that we might live (Romans 5:12-21). But in the case of the Jews, who were given the Law of Moses and had declared, "All that the LORD has spoken we will do" (Exodus 19:8), this introduced another factor.

> Cursed be anyone who does not confirm the words of this law by doing them. (Deuteronomy 27:26)

This is interpreted by Paul in Galatians 3:10 as,

> Cursed is everyone who does not abide by all things written in the Book of the Law, and do them.

Paul's argument in Galatians 3 is that for the Jew, in addition to Christ's death to give salvation to them, (as it was also for the Gentile see Romans 1:16), it was necessary to pay the price of *a broken law*, which was crucifixion (hanging on a tree). Hence Paul wrote to his Jewish brethren:

> Christ redeemed us from the curse of the law by *becoming a curse for us*—'Cursed is everyone who is hanged on a tree'—so that in Christ Jesus *the blessing of Abraham* might come to the Gentiles, so that we might receive *the promised Spirit* through faith. (Galatians 3:13,14)

Keeping strictly to the Acts Period, during which Galatians was written, God's purpose for the earth was intended to be fulfilled through the seed of Abraham, the Jews:

> The LORD said to Abram ... "I will make of you *a great nation*, and I will bless you and make your name great, so that you will be a blessing ... and *in you all the families of the earth shall be blessed*." (Genesis 12:1-3)

This ancient promise was being worked out during the Acts Period, as far as it could be through a nation, many of whom were rejecting their Messiah. Everything was ready on God's part; Jesus had paid the price for sin, and dealt with the curse of a broken law that had stood in the way of the promise being fulfilled. All was ready for the promise given to Abraham to become a reality, bringing blessing to both Jew and Gentile. And it began to do so.

But in the Galatian church(es), believers who had begun by receiving *the Holy Spirit* by faith, were now attempting to become perfect (mature) by "works of the law", "by the flesh" (Galatians 3:2,3). The great truth of the Lord's words to Nicodemus was being ignored— "That which is born of the flesh is flesh, and that which is born of the Spirit, is spirit" (John 3:6). "Flesh cannot be converted or changed into spirit" (Bullinger *in loco*).

This 'flesh versus spirit' argument is taken up later in the epistle:

> The desires of the flesh are against *the Spirit*, and the desires of *the Spirit* are against the flesh, for these are opposed to each other, to keep you from doing the things you want to do. (Galatians 5:17)

Here we have the 'two natures in the child of God' being in conflict; the old man versus the new man. (See further 'The old self and the new self' page 153). In this verse *pneuma* should be with a small 's' in both cases.

However, whilst it may seem disrespectful to speak of *the Holy Spirit* as having 'desires', Paul is observing, as he did to Timothy, that "*the Holy Spirit dwells within us*" (2 Timothy 1:14; cp. Romans 8:9). Hence it is He, the Holy Spirit, upholding the will (desires) of God, and who stands against the will (desires) of sinful man.

It is not completely clear what was the exact nature of the Galatians' foolishness here. But Bullinger goes on to suggest that they were "seeking to improve the flesh by mortifying it".[49] They were ignoring the status of the believer that Paul wrote of in Romans 6:6,11; "Our old self was *crucified with him* (Christ) ... so you must consider yourselves *dead to sin* and alive to God in Christ Jesus." If they had been *justified by faith*, why were they now seeking to be *sanctified by works*? (See Michael Penny's *Galatians: Interpretation and Application* OBT for more on this epistle.)

vi) No longer a slave but a son ... crying Abba! Father!

Paul sets out the position of the Galatians in relation to Father, Son and Spirit:

> Because you are sons, God has sent *the Spirit of his Son* into our

> hearts, crying, Abba! Father! (Galatians 4:6)

> All who are *led by the Spirit of God* are the sons of God. For you did not receive the spirit of slavery to fall back into fear, but you have *received the Spirit of adoption as sons*, by whom we cry, "Abba! Father!" (Romans 8:14,15)

The status of the believer is that of a son to a father, not a slave to a master, and hence believers are, "children of God ... heirs of God and fellow heirs with Christ" (Romans 8:16,17). The proof of this is *"the Spirit of his Son"* in their hearts and that they were *"led by the Spirit of God"*.

vii) The fruit of the Spirit

There is every reason to believe that the Galatians, like the Corinthians, possessed some, if not all, of the 'gifts of the Spirit', since they were part of the witness of *the Holy Spirit* during the Acts Period. But here we have 'the fruit of the Spirit', just as important in the Church which is the Body of Christ today as it was during the Acts Period (see Colossians 3:12-17).

> The *fruit of the Spirit* is love, joy, peace, patience, kindness, goodness, faithfulness, gentleness, self-control: against such things there is no law ... If we *live by the Spirit*, let us also *walk by the Spirit* ... the one who sows to his own flesh will from the flesh reap corruption, but the one who *sows to the Spirit will from the Spirit reap* eternal life. (Galatians 5:22,25;6:8)

Here the 'works' of the believer are looked at in terms of 'sowing seed'. It is part of the natural progression ... living by the Spirit ... walking by the Spirit ... sowing to the Spirit. *Moffatt's version* has instead of 'the fruit of the Spirit', *"the harvest* of the Spirit" which draws attention to the *end result* of the believer's 'works'; what have they achieved?

Moffatt also translates: "there is no law against those *who practise* such things". The apostle contrasts this 'practice' with that of those whom the Galatians should avoid: "sexual immorality or greed, or is an idolater, revelry, drunkard or swindler" (Galatians 5:19-21).

For an exposition of the various 'fruits of the Spirit', see *The Fruit of the Spirit* edited by Michael Penny (OBT).

B) The Epistle to the ROMANS

Probably the greatest of Paul's Acts epistles is Romans. It encompasses every aspect of the Christian life and hope, from the means to salvation to the work of the Holy Spirit in the heart and mind of the believer. Although it is almost certainly the last (extant) epistle that he wrote before his arrest and confinement in Rome, it was given 'pride of place' by those who brought together the New Testament, and appears in our Bibles as the first of all the New Testament epistles. It was written some three years before he arrived in Rome.[50] See the author's *Paul's Letter to the Romans: Background and Introduction* OBT for an analysis of this epistle.

i) The Holy Spirit (*pneuma*) in Romans

In the *KJV* there are 36 occurrences of *pneuma* in Romans of which 23 occur in chapter eight. Out of the total of the 36, 26 have been translated by the *KJV* with a capital 'S' "Spirit", suggesting that the Holy Spirit is meant. However, there are cases where only the context can determine this, and even then not all are agreed. Taking E.W. Bullinger's book, *The Giver and His Gifts* as a standard work on this subject, and the *ESV*, I will consider here only those references that I feel throw light on *the Holy Spirit's ministry*, particularly as it relates to us today.

ii) The Holy Spirit and the love of God

> Through him we have also obtained access by faith into this grace in which we stand, and we rejoice in hope of the glory of God. More than that, we rejoice in our sufferings, knowing that;
>> suffering produces endurance, and
>> endurance produces character, and
>> character produces hope, and
>> hope does not put us to shame, because
>
> God's love has been poured into our hearts through *the Holy Spirit* who has been given to us. (Romans 5:2-5)

Here we have the story of the life of a believer, going through the different 'stages' that lead to the ultimate experience of God's love being poured into their heart through the ministry of the Holy Spirit. It begins with our access by 'faith' into a position of 'grace' and 'hope'. That is our *status* before God, which nothing and nobody can take away from us.

But, "more than that", it is possible/probable, that we might have to 'suffer' for our beliefs, as the Roman believers seem to have been experiencing. However, 'endurance' under those circumstances builds 'character' and produces 'hope'; hence we are not 'put to shame' before God, because we have the 'love of God' that is 'poured into our hearts' and witnessed to through 'the Holy Spirit who has been given to us'.

Elsewhere, 'love' is the first of the fruits of the Spirit (Galatians 5:22), and there it is the response to God's love. John wrote, "We love him, because he first loved us" (1 John 4:19 *KJV*). The *ESV* here, following the main texts, omits the word 'him', which expands John's meaning to 'we love' (not just God, but all)—'love' is the 'driving force' in the Christian life, or should be, in all believers.

John put 'love' into perspective in 1 John 4:10 (*Moffatt version*) when he wrote "Love lies in this, not in our love for God but in his love for us—in the sending of his Son to be the propitiation for our sins".

iii) No condemnation ... no separation from God's love in Christ

Romans 8 is bounded by the two facts that those who believe in Christ should never forget:

- There is therefore now no condemnation for those who are in Christ Jesus. (8:1)
- I am sure that (nothing), in all creation, will be able to separate us from the love of God in Christ Jesus our Lord. (8:38,39)

Between these two 'facts' that set out *the confidence* the believer should have of their status in Christ, Paul expands on the life in the Spirit that should characterise all who grasp the truth of the above statements.

iv) Life in the Spirit

Romans chapter 8 contains a veritable plethora of references to the Holy Spirit and His ministry (*pneuma*); I have listed them in note[51]. However, Bullinger's observations on the use of *pneuma* in this chapter are apposite: "Few chapters have suffered more from the loose renderings of *pneuma* than this: for not until we come to verse 16 is the Holy Spirit himself mentioned" (*The Giver and His Gifts*). Listing the earlier verses in chapter 8 that Bullinger does not think refer to *the Holy Spirit himself* we have:

> **Romans 8:2,4,5,6**: The law of the *pneuma* of life ... us who walk according to the *pneuma* ... those who live according to the *pneuma* set their minds on the things of the *pneuma* ... to set the mind on the *pneuma* is life ...
>
> **Romans 8:9-11:** You are in the *pneuma* if the *pneuma* of God dwells in you ... anyone who does not have the *pneuma* of Christ does not belong to him ... if Christ is in you the *pneuma* is life because of righteousness ... if the *pneuma* of him who raised Jesus from the dead dwells in you, he who raised Christ Jesus from the dead will also give life to your mortal bodies through his *pneuma* who dwells in you ...
>
> **Romans 8:13-15:** If you live by the *pneuma* you put to death the deeds of the body, you will live ... all who are led by the *pneuma* of God are sons of God ... you did not receive the *pneuma* of slavery ... you have received the *pneuma* of adoption as sons by whom we cry, "Abba! Father!"

It would require a great deal of space to attempt to explain these various aspects of the Holy Spirit's ministry in any detail; the most I can do here is to note the following.

v) Paul and the laws of life

Paul, the Jew, looked upon every aspect of life as related to and controlled by laws; from the laws of nature (cp. Romans 2:14) to "the law of commandments expressed in ordinances" (Ephesians 2:15). Here in Romans he speaks of "the law of sin and death" that came upon all men through the sin of Adam (Romans 5:12-21) and is seen at work in "the old self". But thanks be to God, there is "the law of the *pneuma* of life in Christ Jesus", that has delivered us from that law of sin and death. Believers can now look upon themselves as being 'in the spirit' rather than 'in the flesh' since "the spirit of God" dwells in them. Now they are "a new self", and have a new nature (see page 155).

But there is a practical and responsible side to this indwelling of the *pneuma* of God. The coming of *the Holy Spirit* into our lives by no means makes us sinless. The "old self" can still be active as I have already noted. The 'battle' between the two natures in the child of God is developed in Romans 7:7-25, where Paul relates his own experience, and which I repeat here:

> I do not do the good I want, but the evil I do not want is what I keep on doing ... I delight in the law of God, in my inner being, but I see in my members another law waging war against the law of my mind and making me captive to the law of sin that dwells in my members.
> Wretched man that I am! Who will deliver me from this body of death?
> Thanks be to God through Jesus Christ our Lord! So then, I myself serve the law of God with my mind, but with my flesh I serve the law of sin. (Romans 7:19-25)

Hence, in chapter eight, the believer is urged to **walk** according to the *pneuma*; **set his/her mind on** the things of the *pneuma*, for just as setting one's mind on the things of the flesh is death, so setting the mind on the things of the *pneuma* is life. The Christian must endeavour to **live** by the *pneuma*. More on this when we get to Ephesians.

vi) Heirs of God ... fellow heirs with Christ

> *The Spirit* himself bears witness with *our spirit* that we are children of God, and if children then heirs—heirs of God and fellow heirs with Christ, provided we suffer with him in order that we may also be glorified with him. (Roman 8:16)

We now see "*the Spirit himself*" in His 'role' as *a witness* to believers. (Compare this with the conscience that 'bears witness' in Gentiles who, although they did not have the Law, yet "*the work* of the law was written on their hearts", Romans 2:15). The Holy Spirit witnesses to the believer's status before God as:

- a child of God
- an heir of God and,
- "*provided we suffer with him*", a fellow heir with Christ, leading to being "glorified with him".

I read this promise as making a distinction between: **a)** salvation and **b)** the reward for faithfulness. I draw attention to this 'fact of life' for the believer on page 187, but it is so often misunderstood that I introduce it here. Paul drew attention to this distinction in his second letter to Timothy, where he appears to be quoting a well-known saying, possibly an early hymn or Creed (2 Timothy 2:10-13):

> I endure everything for the sake of the elect, that they also may obtain the salvation that is in Christ Jesus with eternal glory.
> The saying is trustworthy, **for**:
>   **i)** If we have died with him, we will
>   also live with him;
>   **ii)** if we endure, we will
>   also reign with him;
>   **ii)** if we deny him,
>   he will also deny us;
>   **i)** if we are faithless
>   he remains faithful—
> **for** he cannot deny himself.

a) Salvation:

Once saved, always saved. (See Sylvia Penny's book *Salvation: Safe and Secure*, OBT, for more on this.)

Salvation is made possible by *being identified* with Christ through faith in His death and resurrection. It is by grace and will not be taken away, even if the believer subsequently becomes "faithless".

b) Reigning with Christ:

In addition to salvation, for those who "*suffer with him*", those "*who endure*" and are not "faithless", there is a reward; they "*will also reign with him*". They will become "a fellow heir with Christ" (Romans 8:16).

However, if believers do not endure and deny Christ (ii), even being "faithless" (i), He will deny them the reward of reigning with Him, but salvation is still safe and secure; the Lord will never deny such to any believer.

vii) The groaning creation and the waiting with patience

> The whole creation has been groaning together in the pains of childbirth until now. And not only the creation, but we ourselves, who have *the firstfruits of the Spirit*, groan inwardly as we wait eagerly for the adoption as sons, the redemption of our bodies ... we wait for it with patience. (Romans 8:22-25)

The apostle moves from the present life, and looks back to the burden that was placed upon all men because of the disobedience of Adam and the cursing of the earth for man's sake. This disobedience affected not only mankind but all creation (Genesis 3:17-19); this situation had produced a "groaning" creation.

But it is not a creation without hope, especially for those who are part of it and who have "the firstfruits of the Spirit". They await eagerly for their adoption as sons of God; they are already so, 'then and there', *de jure* (Romans 8:14-16) and will be *de facto,* when they experience "the redemption of our bodies" (Romans 8:23).

However, that was still in the future. As I have observed (see note 24), believers at this time were living in hope of the imminent return of Christ and the realisation of "the hope of Israel". As such, they were a kind of "firstfruits" of God's redeemed people and they had *"the firstfruits of the Spirit"*. But they were living through a time described by Paul to those in Corinth as a "present crisis" (1 Corinthians 7:26), and to those in Lystra (where he was stoned) he said it is "through *many tribulations* we must enter the kingdom of God" (Acts 14:19-22).

Paul described the suffering and the pain at that time as, "groaning together in the pains of childbirth", just like a woman about to give birth before the joy of the baby's arrival was realised. The Roman Christians were waiting for the age to come when even the creation would be "set free from its bondage to corruption and obtain the freedom of the glory of the children of God"; Paul urged them to "wait for it with patience".

viii) The Holy Spirit and the prayer of the believer

The situation in which Paul and the Roman believers found themselves, their present "weakness", brought to mind what "to pray for as we ought", but yet again the Spirit of God is there to help.

> Likewise, *the Spirit* helps us in our weakness. For we do not know what to pray for as we ought, but *the Spirit himself* intercedes for us with groanings too deep for words. And he who searches hearts knows what is *the mind of the Spirit*, because *the Spirit* intercedes for the saints according to the will of God. (Romans 8:26-27)

The Holy Spirit was introduced to the first disciples of Jesus as, the *Parakletos*, "Helper" (John 14:16 etc.). In Romans 8:26 the word "help" (*sunantilambanomai*) is used only here and Luke 10:40, where Martha asks the Lord to get Mary to *help* her in her "much serving". This usage points to its literal meaning as, "joins in to help ... assists in supporting".[52] Just as Martha was not asking Jesus for Mary to 'take over' from her, but 'help her', so the Holy Spirit *works together with* our "weakness". He does not take over the believer; they are still involved, however 'weak' they may be; they do not become automatons!

There is also the intercessory nature of the Holy Spirit's ministry. For a Jew, "He who searches the hearts", was Jehovah ("the LORD", 1 Chronicles 28:9; Proverbs 15:11) and He "knows the mind of the Spirit", who in turn "intercedes for the saints according to the will of God". Here again is another action of the Triune God in the blessing of mankind.

ix) Paul's conscience and anguish of heart for his brethren

(See page 30 for the connection between the Holy Spirit and man's conscience.)

> I am speaking the truth in Christ—I am not lying; my conscience bears me witness in *the Holy Spirit*—that I have great sorrow and unceasing anguish in my heart ... for the sake of my brethren, my kinsman according to the flesh. They are Israelites and to them belong the adoption, the glory, the covenants, the giving of the law, the worship, and the promises. To them belong the patriarchs, and from their race, according to the flesh, is the Christ, who is God over all. (Romans 9:1-5)

Paul brings together his own conscience, which he appealed to on several other occasions (Acts 23:1; 24:16; 2 Timothy 1:3), and *the Holy Spirit's witness*, to the truth of what he is about to affirm. As elsewhere, that witness is before his own brethren, and as such he is an example of all who believe in Christ and seek to follow Him. The difference between *the Holy Spirit's ministry,* and *testimony* to the believer and the *conscience built into humanity* at large, may be expressed so:

> **All humanity:** "Their conscience bears witness, and their conflicting thoughts accuse or even excuse them." (Romans 2:15)
>
> **The believer:** Using Paul as an example: "My conscience bears me witness *in the Holy Spirit*." (Romans 9:10)

I have heard it suggested that this 'difference' between the two is that *the Holy Spirit* takes the conscience "to a new and higher level", from which I assume is meant a higher moral standard. Certainly, Paul called upon *the Spirit's witness* here to his truthfulness, when he claimed that "I am speaking the truth in Christ—I am not lying."

x) Paul's 'priestly service' to the Gentiles

> I (Paul) ... a minister of Christ Jesus to the Gentiles in *the priestly service* of the Gospel of God, so that the offering of the Gentiles may be acceptable, *sanctified by the Holy Spirit*. In Christ Jesus, then, I have reason to be proud of my work for God. (Romans 15:16)

Underlying the reference here to "sanctified by the Holy Spirit", are the circumstances occasioned by the status of the uncircumcised Gentile during the Acts Period. (For a detailed consideration of the meaning of 'sanctification' see the author's *Paul's Letter to the Romans: Background and Introduction*.)

Here in Romans 15:16, Paul describes his ministry to the Gentiles as "priestly", and he sees himself as a channel through which the "offering of the Gentiles" becomes acceptable, because that offering, and they who give it, are "*sanctified by the Holy Spirit*". The whole of this passage should be read from 15:8-19 to clarify the position that the 'saved' Gentiles of the Acts Period held at that time. Paul was at pains to show that *at that time* the Gentiles were included in "the hope of Israel" (Acts 28:20). He quotes at length four Old Testament passages as proof of this. Romans 15:9-12:

- I will praise you among *the Gentiles*, and sing to your name.

(verse 9; Psalm 18:49)
- Rejoice, O *Gentiles*, with his people. (verse 10; Deuteronomy 32:43)[53]
- Praise the Lord, all *you Gentiles*, and let all the people extol him. (verse 11; Psalm 117:1)
- The root of Jesse will come, even he arises to rule *the Gentiles*; in him will *the Gentiles* hope. (verse 12; Isaiah 11:10)

Believing Gentiles *at that time* were acceptable within "the hope of Israel" and, like Israel of old who were called by the LORD as a 'sanctified' people, so these Gentiles were "sanctified by the Holy Spirit".

In Romans 15:18,19, Paul enlarges on this position and says:

> I will not venture to speak of anything except what Christ has accomplished through me to bring Gentiles to obedience—by word and deed, by the power of signs and wonders, by *the power of the Spirit of God*—so that from Jerusalem and all the way round to Illyricum I have fulfilled the ministry of the gospel of Christ ...

Paul acknowledges that his ministry among the Gentiles in particular, had been the work of *"the power of the Spirit of God"*. The expression, "words and deeds", was a particularly Jewish way of referring to the ministry of such as Moses (Acts 7:22) and was also used of the Lord's earthly ministry (Luke 24:19). Both the ministry of Moses (Exodus 7:3), and that of the Lord (Acts 2:22), were accompanied by "signs and wonders". They were also "the signs of a true apostle" (2 Corinthians 12:12).

With Romans, written some three years before Paul's two-year confinement in Rome, we have the last of the apostle's writings before the events of Acts 28:25-28. For what followed we first turn to the record of Luke.

Chapter 16.
One door closes; another door opens

A) The Holy Spirit in Luke's history in THE ACTS OF THE APOSTLES

The Acts of the Apostles is the only reliable history we have of the ministry of the apostles during the period covered by the thirty five years or so from the resurrection of the Messiah, to the two years confinement in Rome. When the New Testament was coming together as a series of writings, this book was the only history of that period that was considered 'authentic' and so became part of the Holy Scriptures. It relates the labours of the apostles and others, who had preached the Gospel to the Jews, in Judea, Samaria and Galilee, and even amongst the Dispersion throughout the Roman Empire. It also relates the introduction of the Gospel to the Gentiles.

The references to the Holy Spirit and His ministry in this book are so numerous that it has been dubbed, 'The Acts of the Holy Spirit'. Taken as a complete history, however, it might also be considered to be a record of *the rejection* by the Jewish nation of Jesus as their Messiah. And that record is bounded by the actions of the Holy Spirit in Jerusalem and Rome.

At Pentecost the Holy Spirit came upon the apostles and they called the nation to repentance from sins and acceptance of Jesus as, "both Lord and Messiah" (Acts 2:36-38). And after some thirty-five years, during which they largely withstood the apostles' testimony, and continued to reject Jesus, the Holy Spirit pronounced judgement upon the nation and "the hope of Israel" went into abeyance (Acts 28:20,25-28).

Luke's history has generally been seen in Christian circles as the beginnings of the Christian Church that today is mostly made up of

Gentile Christians. But that is not only too simplified an interpretation, but actually inaccurate. Looking at it as a complete history in its own right, rather than seeing it as a 'building up' of a community, it records the 'rejection' by the Jewish nation of Jesus as their Messiah, which remains to this day, but will be 'reversed' at some future day at the second coming of the Messiah. So what now, after Acts 28:25-28?

B) Impasse: Israel rejected and Paul turns to the Gentiles

An 'impasse' is a position from which progress is no longer possible. Such a position became a reality between Paul's writing of Romans and the epistles he wrote during his two year confinement in Rome. The hope of the Acts Period was "the hope of Israel" (Acts 28:20), defined more specifically by Paul to Agrippa as, "the promise made by God to our fathers, to which our twelve tribes hope to attain" (Acts 26:6,7). That hope had been expressed in the words of the apostles who asked Jesus just prior to His ascension, "Lord, will you at this time *restore the kingdom to Israel*?" (Acts 1:6). He gave them neither a 'Yes' nor a 'No' answer, but by the end of the Acts Period it became evident that the answer was 'No'; this was not the time—the door had closed, *the Holy Spirit* had closed it!

Against all the testimony of the apostles, the prophetic evidence of the Scriptures, and the Miracles, Wonders and Signs "that God did through him in their midst", they mostly encountered only deaf ears, blind eyes and minds that refused to understand. So it is no surprise that by the end of the Acts Period God's 'patience' had finally run out—Israel's 'hope' (Acts 26:6,7; 28:20) was sent into abeyance to await another day. **Impasse!**

Things had come to a head when Paul arrived in Rome and called together the leaders of the Jews. Having appointed him a day they came to his lodging in great numbers, and "from morning till evening he expounded to them, testifying to the kingdom of God and trying to convince them about Jesus both from the law of Moses and from the Prophets" (Acts 28:23). But there was no agreement among them and as they left Paul made a parting statement by quoting a passage from Isaiah 6:9,10. Relevant in Isaiah's day, but Paul now applied it as a judgement upon his own generation.

"Go to this people and say,
>'You will indeed hear but never understand,
>and you will indeed see but never perceive.
>For this people's heart has grown dull,
>and with their ears they can barely hear,
>and their eyes they have closed,
>lest they should see with their eyes
>and hear with their ears
>and understand with their heart
>and turn,
>and I would heal them.'

Therefore let it be known to you that,
>this salvation of God has been sent to the Gentiles;
>they will listen." (Acts 28:26-28 *ESV*)

The door had closed on Israel's 'hope'. In a few short years this judgement was confirmed by the destruction of Jerusalem and the end of institutional temple worship. And it has remained that way to this day, to await God's time for the re-commencement of "the hope of Israel" with some future generation.

BUT another door was opening.

Luke evidently refers to this in Acts but gives us no details. He simply records that Paul remained confined in Rome for two years and:

>Welcomed all who came to him, proclaiming the kingdom of God and teaching about the Lord Jesus Christ with all boldness and without hindrance. (Acts 28:30,31)

At first sight this might seem like a pretty general statement of what Paul had been teaching anyway, but when we read the letters he wrote during this confinement, in particular Ephesians and Colossians, we soon come to realise that the calling he now reveals plumbs depths that go beyond anything he had taught up until then to both Jews and Gentiles.

The implications of the closing verses in Acts 28 are great, leading as they do to the setting aside of one aspect of the purpose of God and the revelation of another. God's purpose using Israel to bring blessing to the peoples of the earth was now, for the time being, in abeyance. His purpose, quite independent of Israel, and concerning the heavenly places, was now to be revealed, and the blessings there are all spiritual (Ephesians 1:3).

Whilst Luke makes no mention of any epistles written by Paul (or others), either during the Acts Period or whilst Paul was under house arrest in Rome for two years, it has been generally agreed among commentators that during this latter period Paul wrote at least four epistles, copies of which have survived. They are:

> Ephesians, Philippians, Colossians and Philemon – during the two-year imprisonment – followed later by 1 & 2 Timothy and Titus.

C) The 'Prison epistles' of Paul

i) Paul's letter to PHILEMON

Of the four epistles that are generally agreed to belong to Paul's two years under house arrest in Rome (Acts 28:30,31), Philemon is a short letter concerning the reconciliation of a runaway slave, Onesimus, to his master, Philemon. Its one reference to *pneuma* (verse 25) occurs in Paul's closing benediction: "The grace of the Lord Jesus Christ be with your *spirit*."

Written at the same time as Colossians, this letter was carried back to Philemon together with that epistle (Colossians 4:9). Onesimus had apparently stolen something from his master, but after meeting Paul in Rome, he became to him "a beloved brother", and Paul urged Philemon to take him back as such (vs. 17,18). We may see here the work of *the Holy Spirit* overseeing the 'conversion' of Onesimus, and the Christian faith in action.

ii) The Holy Spirit in PHILIPPIANS

Of the three longer epistles, I have considered Philippians first, because there are two views as to when it was written and from where; Caesarea or Rome. For those who acknowledge the differences between Paul's epistles written during the Acts Period, and those epistles written post-Acts, this is obviously important. If written from Caesarea then it was written during the Acts Period when "the hope of Israel" was 'live', and so it must be seen as ministering to that calling. On the other hand, if written from Rome during Paul's confinement, and following the rejection and judgement upon Israel, then it can be read as relevant *in every way* for us today.

J.B. Lightfoot, *Epistle to the Philippians*, has referred to a number of expositors who hold the Caesarean view, and concluded, "I cannot attach any weight to them", and hence he argues strongly for the view that the epistle was written from Rome. And this is the general consensus, which I have assumed in this study. It was written from Rome during the two years of Acts 28:30,31.

It should be noticed, however, that Philippians is mainly concerned with practice rather than doctrine, and much is applicable to either period. As an example, one passage that is equally relevant for all callings, is the wonderful 'portrait' of the Lord Jesus Christ (chapter 2) from His voluntary humiliation to His eventual glorification.

There are five references to *pneuma* in the epistle; (*ESV*) 1:19,27; 2:1; 3:3 and 4:23 (a doxology).

iii) The Spirit of Jesus Christ and Paul's deliverance

Paul wrote with a view to his immediate future:

> I know that through your prayers and the help of *the Spirit of Jesus Christ* this will turn out for my deliverance, as is my eager expectation and hope that I will not be at all ashamed, but that with full courage. Now as always Christ will be honoured in my body, whether by life or by death. For to me to live is Christ, and to die is gain. (Philippians 1:19-21)

The expression "the Spirit of Jesus" occurs in Acts 16:7 (*NRSV*, following texts) where Paul and Silas "attempted to go into Bithynia but the *Spirit of Jesus* did not allow them". Elsewhere, Paul wrote, "Anyone who does not have the *Spirit of Christ* does not belong to him" (Romans 8:9), and in Galatians 4:6, "Because you are sons, God has sent *the Spirit of his Son* into our hearts crying, 'Abba! Father!'"

J. B. Lightfoot (*Epistle to the Philippians*) translates the phrase "help of the Spirit" as "bountiful supply of the Spirit". He links the two clauses together; "the supply of the Spirit is the answer to their prayers". This brings us back to the concept that the Holy Spirit "*gives by measure*" to some but "*without measure*" to the Messiah. I draw attention again to

Macgregor's comment on John 3:34:

> The words 'not by measure' (*KJV*) mean ... beyond the measure experienced by all who are sent by God ... for each of His messengers God has given a measure of His Spirit *proportionate to his task*, and that this is surpassingly true of Christ.

But why "the Spirit of Jesus Christ"? Why did Paul not write, "*the Holy Spirit*"? Lightfoot evidently considered them one and the same when he posed the question, "Is the Spirit the giver or the gift?" And he added, "the language of the original suggests no limitation, that it will bear both meanings equally well, and that therefore any such restriction is arbitrary. The Spirit of Jesus is both the giver and the gift" (*in loco*).

The word used here to describe Paul's 'deliverance' is *soterian*, salvation. Paul is not doubting that he is 'saved', nor is he relating it to his personal safety at that time. Paul is asking for prayer so that he "will not be ashamed, but that with full courage now as always Christ will be honoured in my body, whether by life or death" (Philippians 1:20). This desire fits well with what we know of Paul, but what of believers generally? Whatever calling we belong to we all need "a bountiful supply of the *Spirit of Jesus*". We need to be "filled by *the Spirit*" (Ephesians 5:18), if we are to follow Paul in his desire that "Christ will be honoured in my body".

iv) Standing firm in one spirit

Paul urges the Philippians to "stand firm in one spirit", literally, "hold your ground" (Philippians 1:27). This is a call to unity in battle—"striving side by side for the faith of the Gospel". This call underlies all five references to *pneuma* in this epistle, as regards Paul's own present circumstances and that of the Philippians.

> Let your manner of life be worthy of the gospel of Christ, so that whether I come and see you or am absent, I may hear of you that you are *standing fast in one spirit*, with one mind *striving side by side for the faith* of the gospel. (Philippians 1:27)

The "standing" and the "striving" are two aspects of Paul's call to the Philippians, in a context in which the apostle speaks of 'opponents', 'suffering' and 'conflict' (Philippians 1:28-30). The Philippians manner of life must be "worthy of the gospel of Christ." Paul's urges them, "conduct your citizenship (*politeuesthe*) worthily of the gospel of Christ", (a literal translation, see margin). He returns to this metaphor in Philippians 3:20,21:

> Our citizenship (*politeuma*) is in heaven (lit. '*the* heavens'), and from it we await a Saviour, the Lord Jesus Christ, who will transform our lowly body (lit. 'body of humiliation') to be like his glorious body, by the power that enables him even to subject all things to himself.

Writing to believers living in Philippi, a Roman colony and a leading city in Macedonia, and not forgetting Paul's pride in being a Roman citizen (Acts 16:12,37,38), his reference to 'citizenship' would 'strike a chord' with the Philippians. Their current citizenship was in Philippi, in an environment of conflict and suffering, and up against opponents. This they bore in bodies of humiliation, but their true citizenship was in heaven. From there they awaited the Saviour, who by His power to subject all things to Himself, would transform their bodies into bodies like His body, bodies suited to a "citizenship in heaven".

The Holy Spirit is not named here, but His work in the believer is spoken of elsewhere in terms of being "clothed with *power* from on high" (Luke 24:49; Acts 1:4). Paul assures them that the same 'power', "*the Spirit of Jesus Christ*", that will one day "transform our lowly bodies" was already available to them in their present circumstances—"the bountiful supply of *the Spirit of Jesus Christ*" of which he had already spoken (Philippians 1:19).

In Philippians 2:1 Paul's call to unity, "standing firm in *one spirit*" (Philippians 1:27) continues. Citing the grounds from which it springs, he poses a condition:

> **"If there is any encouragement in Christ**,
> > any comfort from love,
> > any *participation in the Spirit*,
> > any affection
> > and sympathy,
>
> **complete my joy by**
> > being of the same mind,
> > having the same love

being of full accord and of one mind."

'Comfort' here, is better rendered 'incentive' (Lightfoot), demonstrated by 'affection' and 'sympathy.' 'Participation' (*KJV* 'fellowship') *in the Spirit* leads to being of "the same mind having the same love". The Spirit's work here is communal, not just individual, where each one is looking beyond themselves to "the interests of others" (Philippians 2:4). Paul's joy will be complete when he hears that all are of "the same mind".

He then defines this 'mindfulness' by referring to the greatest and humblest mind of all, that of Christ Jesus, as an example for them to follow—"Have this mind among yourselves, which is yours in Christ Jesus"; He is the supreme example (Philippians 2:6-11). If unfamiliar with this great testimony to the Lord Jesus Christ, a testimony even to His Deity, please take a moment to read that passage.

v) The (true) circumcision worship by the Spirit of God

Paul warns the Philippians about an old problem that seems to have been raising its head again, if indeed it ever went away: the place of circumcision in the life of the believer, especially the Gentile. Ostensibly this had been solved at the Jerusalem Council (Acts 15) and Paul's teaching on the subject in Galatians and Romans.

> Look out for the dogs, look out for the evildoers, look out for those who mutilate the flesh. For we are the circumcision, who worship by *the Spirit of God* (or 'worship *God in spirit*' as in some texts) and glory in Christ Jesus and put no confidence in the flesh. (Philippians 3:2,3)

Circumcision is a subject by itself and largely beyond the remit of this study, however here are some observations. (See *The Sabbath and Circumcision* by Charles Ozanne OBT for more on this.) In the New Testament, circumcision is mentioned in three contexts:

1) Status:

"What advantage has the Jew? Or *what is the value of circumcision? Much in every way*. To begin with, the Jews were entrusted with the oracles of God ... To them belong the adoption, the glory, the covenants, the giving of the law, the worship, and the promises. To them belong the patriarchs, and from their race, according to the flesh, is the Christ" (Romans 3:1,2; 9:4,5).

During the Acts Period the Jew was not only 'first' (Romans 1:16; 2:9,10) but had all the privileges listed above. In Romans 11, in the figure of the olive tree, the Jew is likened to 'the holy branches' and the Gentile to 'a wild olive shoot' (verses 16,17). Circumcision, not the rite itself, but what it stood for in that calling, was the mark of God's chosen people, chosen to bring blessing to all the peoples on earth (Genesis 12:1-3).[54]

But even in the Old Testament, circumcision was referred to other than in the external, physical act, in such passages as Deuteronomy 10:16: "Circumcise the foreskin of your heart" (see also Jeremiah 4:4; Ezekiel 44:7 and cp. Acts 7:51). Here in Philippians, Paul links circumcision with worship by *the Spirit of God* (or 'worship *God in spirit*').

He does not decry circumcision as a practice, it was after all a necessary requirement for all male Jews and a covenant between them and God on pain of being "cut off from his people" (Genesis 17:9-14). And it formed part of Paul's 'boast' in keeping the Law, that he is about to refer to— "circumcised on the eighth day". This Law of Moses he kept to the letter and hence rendered him "blameless" (Philippians 3:5,6). But that claim was based upon "confidence in the flesh", which the Judaizers were trying to impose upon the Philippians and others no doubt.

The law and the keeping of the Law leading to 'righteousness' had its place, but the 'righteousness ... which comes through faith in Christ, the righteousness that comes from God that depends on faith" (Philippians 3:9), requires no mutilation of the flesh. The true circumcision are those who (Philippians 3:3):

> Worship by *the Spirit of God*
> and glory in Christ Jesus and
> put no confidence in the flesh.

In the verses that follow (4-6 please read), Paul gives a brief history of himself in which, if anyone could claim "confidence in the flesh", he had the greater claim. But at the end of this 'testimony of excellence', all those things which he at one time counted as 'gain', he now considered as "loss for the sake of Christ"; by *comparison with* what he had gained in Christ, he counted them as rubbish (Philippians 3:8).

We must be careful not to think that Paul was referring to the Law as rubbish here, but,

> *All such things which I used to count up* as distinct items with a miserly greed *and reckon to my credit*—these I have massed together under one general head as loss. (Lightfoot *in loco*)

If the Philippians were being pressed to accept circumcision, which involved keeping the whole Law (Galatians 5:2,3), they needed reminding that they were in fact already the true circumcision, and one of the things which demonstrated it was that they "worshipped God *in Spirit*".

2) Salvation:

"Some men came down from Judea and were teaching the brethren, '*Unless you are circumcised* according to the custom of Moses, *you cannot be saved*'... The apostles and elders were gathered together to consider this matter" in the Jerusalem Council.

The outcome of that meeting, after hearing testimonies from Peter and Paul, was that (physical) circumcision was deemed unnecessary for the Gentiles who were turning to God and embracing the Gospel at this time (Acts 15:1-21).

3) Perfection:

"O foolish Galatians! Who has bewitched you? Did you receive the Spirit by works of the law or by the hearing with faith? Are you so foolish? *Having begun by the Spirit, are you now being perfected by the flesh*? ... Every man who accepts circumcision is obliged to keep the whole law ... in Christ Jesus neither circumcision nor uncircumcision counts for anything, but only faith working through love" (Galatians 3:1-3; 5:3,6). Put in the form of a question, Dr. Bullinger interpreted this, "If you have been justified by grace, why are you seeking to be sanctified by works?" (*Word Studies on the Holy Spirit*).

Back in Philippians 3:2,3, Paul's words are reminiscent of the Lord's conversation with the Samaritan woman, where the right 'place' to worship—circumcision and its relevance to belief in Jesus Christ was brought up (John 4:19-24). Here the question that plagued early Christian witness is raised again. Worship here is associated not so much with the 'place' of true worship, but the 'status' of the worshipper; circumcised or uncircumcised. The apostle begins with a warning, "lookout ... lookout ... lookout". He warns them: "Look out for the dogs, look out for the evildoers, look out for those who mutilate the flesh" (Philippians 3:2).

The dogs (*tous kunas*) was a term of reproach used normally by Jews of Gentiles, "by which they stigmatized the Gentiles as impure ... among the Jews of the Christian era it involved chiefly the idea of ceremonial impurity" (Lightfoot). But here Paul 'turns it on its head', reverses the image, and applies it to the Judaizers themselves.

vi) Ephesians and Colossians as parallel epistles

Before looking at these two epistles separately, I draw attention to the fact that they are, in some places in particular, very similar in content. The following are the most obvious passages:

Ephesians 5:18-6:9	Colossians 3:16-4:1
Be filled with the Spirit,	Let the word of Christ dwell in you richly
addressing one another	teaching and admonishing one another in all wisdom,
and spiritual songs, singing and making melody to the Lord with your heart, giving thanks always and for everything to God the Father.	singing psalms and hymns and spiritual songs, with thankfulness in your hearts to God.

Followed by instructions concerning,	**Followed by instructions concerning,**
Wives and Husbands	Wives and Husbands
Children and Parents	Children and Parents
Slaves and Masters	Masters and Slaves

The Holy Spirit and His Ministry

I will come to this later, but here I note that:

"Be filled by (*en*) *the Spirit*" in Ephesians 5:18,

seems to equate to

"Let *the Word of Christ* dwell in (*en*) you" in Colossians 3:16.

And the relationships that follow in both epistles are expressed in virtually the same terms.

D) The Holy Spirit in EPHESIANS

There are fifteen references to *pneuma* in Ephesians, most of which refer to *the Holy Spirit* (although only two actually have the word 'Holy' appended) or His 'gifts' to the believer in the current dispensation. *The Holy Spirit's ministry* for us today in the Body of Christ can be summed up briefly in the following references, with the key words highlighted in bold italics:

- **1:13,14: The Holy Spirit** of promise *seals us* and is the *guarantee* of our *inheritance*.
- **1:17,18:** Paul's prayer for the saints; that God the Father may give you *a spirit of wisdom and revelation in the knowledge of Him* ... that the eyes of your hearts *enlightened* that you may know what is *the hope of your calling ... the riches of His inheritance in the saints ... the greatness of power towards us who believe.*
- **2:18: The Spirit** gives us *access to the Father*.
- **2:22: By the Spirit** we are being *built into a dwelling place for God*.
- **3:4,5: The Spirit** has *revealed more of the mystery of Christ* than He made known to other generations.
- **3:16: The Spirit** *strengthens our inner being so that Christ may dwell in our hearts by faith*.
- **4:3-6:** We are urged to *maintain the unity already made* by the Holy Spirit.
- **4:30:** We are *warned not to grieve* the Holy Spirit of God by whom *we are sealed* for the day of redemption.
- **5:9:** All that is good, right and true is *evidence of the fruit* of the

Spirit. (Some versions have "the fruit of light" instead of "the fruit of the Spirit" as in the *ESV*.)
- **5:18:** We are urged to ***be filled with (or by) the Spirit***.
- **6:17: The word of God** is the **Spirit's** ***sword in the battle against the spiritual forces of evil***.
- **6:18:** ***Keep alert at all times*** in the battle; we should ***pray continually*** **via the Spirit**. He is the sole power.

i) The promised Holy Spirit (1:13,14)

In him you also, when you heard the word of truth, the gospel of your salvation, and believed in him, were *sealed with the promised Holy Spirit*, who is the guarantee (margin "down payment") of our inheritance until we acquire possession of it, to the praise of his glory.

Dr. E.W. Bullinger (*Word Studies on the Holy Spirit*) [55] rendered Ephesians 1:13:

In whom (Christ) ye also (were allotted an inheritance) on hearing the true word of the gospel of your salvation: in whom (Christ) on believing also, ye were sealed (by the Father) with the promised *pneuma* (lit. the *pneuma* of the promise)—*the hagion* [holy].

And his comment on this was: "The first occurrence of *sealing* is in John 6:27[56] and it is attributed to the Father. This gives us the key to this sealing in Ephesians. It is the fulfilment of 'the promise of the Father' (Luke 24:49; Acts 1:4)[57]." He took a promise made originally to the disciples as being 'fulfilled' in Ephesians 1:13. Is this correct?

There is only one Holy Spirit, who can of course make as many promises as He pleases, so there is no necessity to link the promises made to the disciples with the promise of the 'sealing' of the believer in Ephesians. "The promise of the Father" made to the early disciples was to be "clothed with power from on high" (Luke 24:49) and that led to them being able to speak in other tongues and to perform many miracles; we must be careful not to assume that the ministry of "the promised Holy Spirit" in Ephesians gives us the same powers today.

ii) Sealed and guaranteed by the Holy Spirit (1:13,14)

Sealed (*sphragizo*) means "to stamp (with a signet or private mark) for security or preservation" and it occurs twice in Ephesians: guarantee (*arrhabon*) is "a pledge, i.e. part of the purchase money or property given in advance as *security* for the rest" (*Strong*). The other occurrence of 'sealed' is in 4:30: "Do not grieve *the Holy Spirit of God*, by whom you were *sealed* for the day of redemption". In the earlier reference we are sealed "*until* we acquire possession of our inheritance"; in the second we are told that it *looks forward to* a future "day of redemption".

> The Spirit functions as the guarantee of the believers' inheritance, looking forward or vouching for God's full redemption of that for which he has made this down payment. Final deliverance by God means his taking full and *complete possession of those who have already become his*. (Andrew T. Lincoln *Ephesians Word Biblical Commentary*)

What is this inheritance? Ephesians 1:13 has been read two ways. **i)** It could refer to the blessings *given to us* as an inheritance? Or **ii)** is Paul saying that *we are* God's inheritance? This verse reads literally: "The Spirit of promise the holy which is an earnest of *the inheritance of us* to (until) redemption of the possession." And the *NEB* has:

> ... that Spirit is the pledge that *we shall enter upon our heritage*, when God has redeemed *what is his own*, to his praise and glory.

Both aspects of the LORD's inheritance come together in the promises made to Israel in the Old Testament. They were **i)** promised an inheritance in The Promised Land (Genesis 17:8), and **ii)** they were also considered to be the LORD's inheritance. He spoke of them as "my treasured possession ... to be a kingdom of priests and a holy nation" (Exodus 19:5,6; see also Deuteronomy 14:2; Malachi 3:17; 1 Peter 1:1; 2:9). So if both meanings were true of the LORD's relationship to Israel, why not allow both meanings of "the promised inheritance" in our own calling in the Body of Christ: He has *given us* an inheritance; *we are His* inheritance?

However, we look at it, it is important not to forget, that this promise is "to those who believe". This is the link between "hearing" and "sealing and guaranteeing". So we have:

Hearing ... Believing ... Sealing ... Guaranteeing.

This is how *the Holy Spirit's ministry* opens in the Church which is the Body of Christ. We know from the beginning of this epistle exactly 'where we stand' in God's purpose.

iii) Prayer for the saints: 'hope', 'inheritance', 'power' (1:17-22)

Giving thanks for his readers, Paul prays for them,

> that the God of our Lord Jesus Christ, the Father of glory, may give you
> > *a spirit of wisdom and of revelation in the knowledge of him*, having
> > *the eyes of your hearts enlightened*, that you may know:
> > > what is the **hope** to which he has called you,
> > > what are the riches of his glorious **inheritance** in the saints,
> > > what is the immeasurable greatness of his **power** towards us who believe
>
> according to the working of his great might that he worked in Christ when he raised him from the dead and seated him at his right hand in the heavenly places, far above all.

These are the '*gifts of the Spirit*' for the "Church which is the Body of Christ", as Paul names this company of God's people in the verses that follow (1:22,23). They are not the 'gifts' possessed by the Acts church, spoken of by Paul and enumerated by him in 1 Corinthians 12. They are basically threefold—wisdom, revelation and the knowledge of Him (God), and they lead to 'enlightenment' about our hope and calling today.

iv) The hope to which he has called you (1:18)

Shortly after he arrived in Rome, Paul met the leaders of the Jews there and said, "For this reason I have asked to see you and speak with you, since it is because of *the hope of Israel* that I am wearing this chain" (Acts 28:20). He had already defined that hope more specifically when he was before Agrippa in Caesarea as, the "hope ... to which *our twelve tribes* hope to attain" (Acts 26:6,7). Israel's 'hope' is seen prophetically in the closing chapters of Ezekiel (which see) when Israel are finally settled in the Land of Promise and the twelve tribes settled in the portions of that Land allotted to them by the LORD.

At that time, the LORD will set His glory among the Gentile nations (Ezekiel 39:21) and they will "glorify God for his mercy ... and rejoice with God's people" (read Romans 15:8-12). Then the LORD's ancient promise to Abraham as "the father to many nations" will be fulfilled and "all the families of the earth shall be blessed" (Genesis 12:1-3; 17:5; Romans 4:16-18). This was the Gentile 'hope' during the Acts Period, but at that time it was dependant upon the repentance and faithfulness of Israel to the LORD. But as we know now, Israel, as a nation rejected their Messiah and that 'hope' could not be fulfilled. The rest is history.

In Ephesians 1:17,18, Paul is praying for a 'gift' from *the Holy Spirit*, not an attitude of mind. All true wisdom and revelation come from Him; He is the Divine teacher. And in Ephesians 1:18 he is *not* praying that the saints might know a 'hope' such as "the hope of Israel" (above) or the hope the nations on earth. Paul's thoughts are on a Christ who has been raised to the highest pinnacle of glory at the right hand of God in the heavenly places, and he adds later that He has ...

> ... *raised us* up with him and *seated us with him* in the heavenly places in Christ (Ephesians 2:6)

In order to grasp such a hope as this, a hope that places the believer at the very right hand of God, Paul prays that his readers will be given "*a spirit* of wisdom ... revelation ... and knowledge of him" (i.e. of "the God of our Lord Jesus Christ, the Father of glory"; 1:17). This 'revelation' will be clarified when we read on into chapter 3, where Paul speaks of 'secrets' concerning Christ and the Gentiles (see page 218).

v) The riches of his glorious inheritance in the saints (1:18)

Paul has already spoken of *our* inheritance in 1:13,14, of which the Holy Spirit is 'the guarantor'. Now he is praying that his readers might know, "what are *the riches of his glorious inheritance* in the saints"—His inheritance *in us*. This second aspect of 'inheritance' has already been considered in Ephesians 1:13 (page 205). As to *His* inheritance *in us,* compare the two dispensations:

1) **Israel on earth:**

"*The LORD's* portion is his people, Jacob his allotted heritage." (Deuteronomy 32:9)

2) **The "saints" in heavenly places:**

"*His* (*the Father of glory*) glorious inheritance in the saints." (Ephesians 1:18)

vi) The immeasurable greatness of his power towards us who believe (1:19)

The apostle is speaking of a "power" that we can "know", it is the power that God "worked in Christ when he raised him from the dead" (Ephesians 1:20). That 'power' has already (*de jure*), "raised us up with him and seated us with him in the heavenly places in Christ Jesus", so that "in the coming ages (*de facto*), he might show the immeasurable riches of his grace in kindness towards us in Christ Jesus" (Ephesians 2:6,7). Paul piles one strong word upon another, using four synonyms in order to emphasise the nature of the "power" he is trying to get his readers to grasp …

> The immeasurable greatness of his **power** (*dunamis*) towards us who believe, according to the **working** (*energeia*) of the **might** (*kratos*) of his **strength** (*ischus*), which he has wrought in Christ. (Ephesians 1:19,20)

Paul's prayer here is reminiscent of his prayer for the Colossians:

> May you be **strengthened** (*dunamoo*) with all **power** (*dunamis*), according to his glorious **might** (*kratos*), for all endurance and patience with joy, giving thanks to the Father, who has qualified you to share in the inheritance of the saints in light. (Colossians 1:11-12)

In both cases this 'power' is associated with "the inheritance of the saints", but here that inheritance is qualified as having a "share in the inheritance of the saints in light" which, in Colossians 1:13, is interpreted as,

> *delivered from* the domain of darkness and *transferred to* the

kingdom of his beloved Son.

In Ephesians this 'power' is "towards us who believe" (1:19). Paul is praying that believers should not only *know* that 'power' but *appropriate it*. The connection between *the Holy Spirit* and "power" is made again later in Ephesians. Praying for the Ephesian saints, Paul wrote (3:14-19):

> I bow my knees before the Father ... that he may grant you to be *strengthened with power through his Spirit* in your inner being,
>
>> so that Christ may dwell in your hearts through faith—
>> that you, being rooted and grounded in love,
>> may have *strength to comprehend* with all the saints
>> what is the breadth and length and height and depth,
>> and to know the love of Christ that surpasses knowledge,
>> that you may be filled with all the fullness of God.

The connection between *The Holy Spirit* with 'power' (*dunamis*) occurs elsewhere in the New Testament, most notably in the Lord's promise to the eleven apostles, when He said to them,

> "Behold, I am sending the promise of my Father (*the Holy Spirit* John 14:26) upon you. But stay in the city until you are *clothed with power* from on high." (Luke 24:49; see also Acts 1:18)

And Paul began his epistle to the Romans (1:4) by describing Christ Jesus as, "the Son of God *in power according to the Spirit of holiness*", and later (15:13) the apostle spoke of "the *power of the Holy Spirit*" in the context of 'hope'; "May the God of hope fill you with all joy and peace in believing, so that *by the power of the Holy Spirit you may abound in hope*."

The Greek word *dunamis* meaning 'strength, might, power' (*Liddell and Scott*) comes almost straight into English in the word 'dynamite', which gives us some idea of its meaning. In the *KJV* in particular, it is sometimes rendered "mighty works" (Matthew 11:21 etc.) or "miracle" (Mark 9:39; Acts 2:22 etc.).

In Paul's prayer above (Ephesians 3:16), he calls upon the Father to "grant you to be *strengthened with power through his Spirit* in your inner being" so that "Christ may *dwell in your hearts* through faith". Later, in Ephesians 5:18, this subject is addressed as "being filled with *the Spirit*", a passage that has its parallel in Colossians 3:16, "the word of Christ", and yet again, as we shall see, there is a connection between *the Holy Spirit* and the Word of God.

In Colossians 1:27 Paul speaks of this indwelling of "Christ in you" as the climax of a 'mystery', the mystery that was ...

> ... hidden for ages and generations but now revealed to his saints. To them God chose to make known how great among the Gentiles are the riches of the glory of *this mystery*, which is *Christ in you*, the hope of glory.

More on this later (page 218).

vii) Access to the Father (2:18)

Paul now enlightens his readers on the subject of access to God; something the Jews had in Old Testament times, and which continued into the New as long as the temple in Jerusalem still stood, (which it did until A.D. 70 when it was destroyed by the Roman army). Such 'access' to God was one of the privileges that the Jews had over the Gentiles. Paul spoke of it in Romans 9:4,5: "to them (Israelites) belong ... the (Shekinah) glory ... the worship ..." But Paul now says:

> Through him we the both (Jews and Gentiles) have access *in one Spirit* to the Father. (Ephesians 2:18 lit.)

'Access' (*prosagoge*) is used again in Ephesians 3:12. Speaking of "the eternal purpose" that has been realized in Christ Jesus our Lord, Paul continues, "in whom we have boldness and *access* with confidence through our faith in him". Access *in one Spirit* ... made possible for both Jews and Gentiles in Christ Jesus. In 2:18 Paul refers to a situation that has changed; a situation where once the Jews were "near" but the Gentiles "far off" (Ephesians 2:12,13). The privilege of access, enjoyed previously by the Jews, is now relevant for both parties, Jew and Gentile.

viii) Gentile access to the LORD: Old Testament

It has been observed that there are references in the Old Testament where Gentiles had or are envisaged having 'access' to God, much in the same way that Israel did. In 1 Kings 8:41-43 Solomon prayed to the LORD:

> When a foreigner who is not of your people Israel comes from a far country for your name's sake ... when he comes and *prays towards this house* (the Temple), *hear in heaven your dwelling place* and do according to all for which the foreigner calls to you, in order that all the peoples of the earth may know your name and fear you, as do your people Israel.

For example, in the future Millennium see also Isaiah 56:6-8, where the LORD promises that "foreigners who join themselves to the LORD ... will be made joyful in my house of prayer"; it will become "a house of prayer for all peoples". Compare also Zechariah 8:20-23.

However, in the Jewish dispensation into which the Lord came, and Paul and his brethren lived, there was a division made between Jew and Gentile; a (physical) dividing wall in the Temple that drew attention to the difference that still existed *at that time* between the two—a difference of 'status in closeness of access' to the Lord. However, after Acts 28:25-28, in the Post Acts Period, Ephesians 2 shows that that situation changed.

ix) The dividing wall between Jew and Gentile: Acts and post-Acts

The "Gentiles in the flesh" status, up to and including the Acts Period, left all non-Jews ...

> ... alienated from the commonwealth of Israel and strangers from the covenants of promise, having no hope and without God in the world. (Ephesians 2:12)

But now, says Paul, the situation has changed. Under a new dispensation made known by him in this same epistle (3:6), with "the hope of Israel" in abeyance, and the "dividing wall of hostility broken down" (Ephesians 2:14), the Gentiles had a different status.

The "middle wall of partition" (Ephesians 2:14 *KJV*) is a reference to that physical barrier in the Jerusalem Temple that separated Jews from Gentiles, and which was still standing when Paul wrote these words.

The Holy Spirit and His Ministry

Reference to this barrier at that time may have been behind the accusation made against Paul by the Jews when he was in Jerusalem for the last time—"he brought Greeks into the temple and has defiled this holy place" (Acts 21:28).

This physical barrier, or at least a part of it, was unearthed in 1871 during excavations being made on the Temple site. M. Clermont Ganneau, a noted Orientalist and Archaeologist, found a pillar which was believed to be part of this barrier. It was preserved in the Museum of Constantinople at one time. On it was written in Greek the following words:

> NO MAN OF ANOTHER NATION TO ENTER
> WITHIN THE FENCE AND ENCLOSURE
> ROUND THE TEMPLE. AND WHOEVER IS
> CAUGHT WILL HAVE HIMSELF TO BLAME
> THAT HIS DEATH ENSUES.

This 'barrier' represented the priority, privileges and advantages of the Jew spoken of by Paul in Romans 1:16; 2:10; 3:1,2; 9:4,5, and which operated throughout the Acts Period (cp. Acts 21:28,29). That position changed at the end of Acts and today is different, as Paul states unequivocally. The 'status' of the Gentile had changed, whereby Jew and Gentile can approach God on exactly the same terms, as he says:

> Those who once were far off (Gentiles) have been brought near by the blood of Christ ... reconciled (together with the Jews) to God *in one body* through the cross ... *both having access in one Spirit to the Father*. (Ephesians 2:13-18)

Access to the Father is only possible because of Christ's "once for all" sacrifice (Hebrews 9:26), so that *together* we, Jews and Gentiles alike, might *both* be reconciled to God in one body through His cross, *both* having the same access *in one Spirit* to the Father. And further he goes on to state, that this "joint body" of people are being "built together into a dwelling place for God *by the Spirit*". They are the Church which is the Body of Christ.

x) Built by the Spirit into a dwelling place for God (2:22)

The concept of God dwelling 'among' His people (corporate) or 'in' His people (as individuals) is not exclusive to the New Testament. And from what we can deduce from the Scriptures, looked at in human terms, we get the 'sense' that He *wants to* dwell in and among us. He is not remote from His people, nor does He want to be. He had fellowship with our first parents in the Garden of Eden, and even after they had let sin into the world He made a way whereby man may approach Him, and finally be with Him for ever. This goal is not exclusive to the Church which is the Body of Christ, it is true of all callings. But it was only made possible through the one sacrifice, made once for all by Jesus Christ, that dealt with sin (Hebrews 9:26).

In the Old Testament the LORD was 'among' His people Israel when He 'dwelt' firstly in the Tabernacle and later in the Temple. One of the advantages Israel enjoyed over the rest of mankind, was the 'presence' of the *Shekinah*[58] *Glory* among them. "The glory of the LORD filled the Tabernacle"; the LORD promised, "*there* I will meet with the people of Israel" (Exodus 29:42,43; 40:34). Later the *Shekinah Glory* dwelt in the Jerusalem Temple.

Ezekiel in his "visions of God" (1:1; 8:3; 40:2) saw the *Shekinah Glory* leaving the temple at a time of judgement, when "the land is full of blood, and the city full of injustice", when "the LORD has forsaken the land" (9:9-10:18). But that 'glory' was seen returning in Ezekiel's vision, when "the God of Israel ... *will dwell in the midst of the people of Israel for ever*" (43:2-7).[59]

During the Acts Period, Paul, when referring to his brethren as "Israelites" wrote, "to them belong ... *the glory*" (Romans 9: 4). The presence of the *Shekinah Glory* among the people of Israel was one of the many exclusive blessings the LORD had given to them, and it was still relevant when Paul wrote Romans (for the full list see 9:4,5). At this time the Jerusalem Temple was still standing and Israel's status before God was that they were still 'first' (Romans 1:16; 2:10; 3:1,2; 9:4,5).

However, when the Holy Spirit's judgement came upon them at the end of the Acts Period (28:25-28), that status changed and became obvious when Rome destroyed the temple in AD 70. Israel's 'hope' went into abeyance and Paul revealed "the mystery"; the calling of a church whose blessings were all spiritual. (For more detail on this see the author's *The Mystery of Ephesians* OBT.)

Here, in Ephesians 2:22, we read of a different "holy temple" that "grows" as it is being "built by" *the Holy Spirit*. It includes all those believers today within the Church which is the Body of Christ, as Paul says:

> You are ... fellow-citizens with the saints, and of the household of God; And are *built upon* the foundation of the apostles and prophets, Jesus Christ himself being the chief cornerstone; In whom *all the building* fitly framed together, *grows unto an holy temple in the Lord*: In whom you also are *built together for a habitation of God through the Spirit.* (Ephesians 2:19-22 *KJV*)

This temple is made up of believers; its cornerstone is "Christ himself", and it is founded upon "the apostles and prophets". It is a "dwelling place for God *in Spirit (en pneumati* lit.)". Bringing these facts together we have:

The Temple
Cornerstone: Christ.
Foundation: Apostles and Prophets.
Building material: Members of the household of God.
Object: A dwelling place for God.

In the Old Testament the Messiah was foreseen as a "cornerstone ... laid by the LORD in Zion" (Isaiah 28:16; see also Psalm 118:22). During the Acts Period, when "the hope of Israel" was still 'live', Peter, writing to Jewish believers and quoting this passage, told them that they were "living stones being built up as a spiritual house, to be a holy priesthood" (1 Peter 1:1; 2:6-9); an earthly Millennial 'hope' that will one day be fulfilled. The house of the LORD will again be established in Jerusalem, and the Gentile nations will "go up year after year to worship the King, the LORD of Hosts, and to keep the Feast of Booths (Tabernacles)" (Zechariah 14). Such will be the 'presence of the LORD' in relation to the earthly purpose of God, but the calling of the heavenly places is another aspect of His purpose.

In Ephesians, in the context of a people whose blessings are all spiritual and "in the heavenly places" (Ephesians 1:3; 2:6), Christ is also the "cornerstone" of a building, a dwelling place for God.
Christ is the "cornerstone" of a dwelling place for the LORD, whether in relation to a "holy nation" on earth (Exodus 19:5,6;1 Peter 2:9), or a Church in the heavenly places (Ephesians 2:6).

In the Church which is the Body of Christ, our own calling, Christ is "the cornerstone" and "the apostles and prophets" are the foundation of a building that is growing into a temple in which God dwells. But who are these apostles and prophets?

Are they the twelve apostles and prophets who ministered during the Acts Period, to a people whose 'hope' was bound up with an earthly calling, a calling that rested upon an Old Testament promise made to Abraham? It hardly seems so. Those referred to here are surely "apostles and prophets" to whom a revelation of "the mystery of Christ" was given, a revelation that was *"not made known to the sons of men in other generations as it has now been revealed* to his holy apostles and prophets *by the Spirit"*; ministers to the Church which is the Body of Christ (Ephesians 3:4,5).

We may not be able to name many of them as individuals, apart from perhaps including Paul amongst them. We could hazard a guess at Timothy, Tychicus (Ephesians 6:21; Colossians 4:7) and others mentioned in the post-Acts epistles of Paul, such as Titus. But whoever they were, *"the Holy Spirit* is the builder of this holy temple" (Bullinger *Word Studies*).

xi) The Holy Spirit: A revealer of mysteries (3:4,5)

When the Lord was preparing the disciples for their ministry to Israel shortly before He left them, He promised He would give them another "Helper" (*ESV*) "Comforter" (*KJV*)—"*the Spirit of Truth* ... to be with them for ever" (John 14:16,17). His ministry was:

- To bear witness about Jesus (He is the Messiah) and so to "glorify" Him.
- To declare to the apostles "things that are to come".
- To "guide them into all truth", especially things they were not able to bear at that time.
- To "convict the world concerning sin and righteousness". (John 15:26; 16:8,12-14)

The Holy Spirit was given to the Acts 'Church' as both a teacher and a revealer of truth, and whilst these promises recorded by John cannot be automatically assumed to be relevant to us today, it is evident from a reading of Ephesians that the Holy Spirit is just as much a teacher and a revealer of truth to the 'Church' which is the Body of Christ. The most enlightening examples of this are the Holy Spirit's revelations to Paul, and to the apostles and prophets referred to in Ephesians 3. Those revelations were basically twofold (Ephesians 3:3-6 *KJV*):

> **The mystery of Christ** not made known to other generations *as it has now been revealed* to his holy apostles   and prophets *by the Spirit.*
> ***The*** **mystery** concerning the Church made known firstly to Paul, in which both Jew and Gentile are brought together in one 'Body' on equal terms.

These were set out in detail in my booklet *The Mystery of Ephesians* OBT which see.

> **The mystery:** "If you have heard of the *dispensation* of the grace of God which is given me toward you, how that *by revelation he made known unto me **the mystery**,* as I wrote before in few words, By which, when you read..."

> **The mystery of Christ:** "... you may understand my knowledge in ***the mystery of Christ***, which *in other ages was not made known* unto the sons of men, *as it is now revealed* unto his holy apostles and prophets by the Spirit ..."

> **The mystery:** "... That the Gentiles should be fellow heirs, and of the same body, and partakers of his promise in Christ by the gospel, of which I was made a minister ..."

Briefly, distinguishing between the two 'mysteries' here we have:

a) The mystery of Christ

This **'mystery'** concerning the promised Messiah, had been an unfolding revelation throughout the ages. It had been revealed in stages, and recorded in the Scriptures. But Paul tells us that it "was not made known to men in other generations *as it has now been revealed* by the Spirit to God's holy apostles and prophets" (Ephesians 3:4,5). Without claiming to refer to every stage in the unfolding of that mystery, I give below a list of the most obvious. See also the author's *Messiah and His People* OBT for more on this:

> **Genesis 3:15:** The first intimation of a Messiah is in the promise that the seed of the woman would crush the serpent's head.
>
> **John 8:56:** Abraham saw something of the glory of Christ, as Jesus put it, "Abraham rejoiced at the thought of *seeing my day*; *he saw it* and was glad" (*NIV*).
>
> **Acts 2:29-31 (Psalm 16:8-11):** David, knowing that God "would place one of his descendants on his throne" and "*seeing what was ahead*, he spoke of the resurrection of the Christ" (*NIV*).
>
> **Hebrews 8:1,2:** The writer of Hebrews saw Christ as "a high priest, who sat down at the right hand of the throne of the Majesty in heaven, and who serves in the sanctuary, the true tabernacle set up by the Lord, not by man" (*NIV*).

And here,

> **Ephesians 1:10,22,23**: In this latest revelation, Paul reveals Christ as "Head over all things to the church, which is his body", a headship associated with those called under "the dispensation of the mystery".

Intimately connected to this latest revelation of "the mystery of Christ", are believers today, called under the Holy Spirit's latest revelation and described as "the body of Christ". They live under a different dispensation (administration) to that which was being administered during the Acts Period. It is named by Paul as:

b) The dispensation of *the* mystery

Unlike "the mystery of Christ", this 'mystery' *was unknown in past ages*. It was (literally), "*hidden* from the ages in God ... *hidden* from the ages and generations" (Ephesians 3:3,5; Colossians 1:25,26).

Its revelation was entrusted (initially) to Paul alone—"*given to me* for you (Gentiles) ... made known *to me* by revelation" and "to bring to light for everyone what is the plan of this mystery" (Ephesians 3:2,9).

It concerns the calling out of a company of believers known as "the body of Christ", of which He is the Head. Their blessings are spiritual in the heavenly realms, and God's manifold wisdom is declared *through this church*, to the "rulers and authorities" in the heavenly realms, "according to the eternal purpose that he has realized in Christ Jesus our Lord" (Ephesians 1:3: 3:9-11).

Although its members were chosen in Christ before the foundation of the world (Ephesians 1:4 *KJV*), this dispensation was only revealed in the fullness of time in the later ministry of Paul given after Acts 28:25-28. There is nothing in the Old Testament, Gospels, Acts or the epistles written during the Acts Period, that refer to this administration. It was revealed sometime *after* Paul began his imprisonment in Rome (Acts 28:30,31).

It is this "mystery", that seems to have been so misunderstood throughout Christendom, where it has been mixed up with the 'hope' of the Acts church, "the hope of Israel" (Acts 28:20), and no difference made between the ministry of the Twelve and Paul's earlier ministry on the one hand, and Paul's later ministry on the other.

xii) Power through the Spirit so that God may dwell in your hearts (3:14-19)

Paul prays for his readers;

> I bow my knees before the Father ... that he may grant you
> to be strengthened *with power through his Spirit* in your inner being,
> so that Christ may dwell in your hearts through faith—
> that you, being rooted and grounded in love,
> may have strength to comprehend with all the saints
> what is the breadth and length and height and depth,
> and to know the love of Christ that surpasses knowledge,
> that you may be filled with all the fullness of God.

The prayer is breath-taking in vision. The Holy Spirit is "the Giver of all power" (Bullinger), and the goal is that the believer, comprehending the love of Christ, that is beyond knowledge, "may be filled with all the fullness of God". The concept of the indwelling of the Triune God in His fullness in the believer is expressed in three ways in Ephesians:

- that Christ may dwell in your hearts through faith (3:17)
- that you may be filled with all the fullness of God (3:19)
- that you may be filled by the Spirit (5:18)

So we have God the Father (3:14,19), Christ (3:17) and the Holy Spirit (5:18) dwelling in and filling us with God's fullness. In practical terms what does that mean? To say He is filling us with 'spirit' is somewhat nebulous, so this will be looked at when we consider Ephesians 5:18, as will the rendering of the Greek preposition in the phrase *en pneumati* as "by the Spirit" (see page 224).

xiii) The unity of the Spirit ... the bond of peace (4:3-6)

Paul urged the Ephesians and all who read this epistle:

> Endeavour to keep the unity of the Spirit in the bond of peace. There is:
> > one body, and *one Spirit*—even as you are called in
> > one hope of your calling;
> > one Lord, one faith, one baptism,
> > one God and Father of all, who is above all, and
> > > through all and in you all. (*KJV*)

A sevenfold unity, that has *already been made by the Spirit,* must be kept diligently by believers. For this, all will need, "grace according to the measure of the gift of Christ" (Ephesians 4:7). In the passage that immediately precedes this "unity of the Spirit" (4:1,2), Paul urged his readers to "walk in a manner worthy of the calling to which you have been called" and that walk, amongst other things, is characterised by:

> humility ... gentleness ... patience ... forbearance in love ... eagerness to maintain that unity

None of these virtues suggests weakness of character, although that is how the world might see them. They are based on a proper evaluation of oneself and a realisation of one's own dependence on the grace of God and the worth of one's brothers and sisters in His eyes. (Andrew T. Lincoln *Word Biblical Commentary in loco*)

xiv) Unity in 'the Church which is the Body of Christ' (3:6; 4:3,4,13)

'Unity', Greek *henotes*: *Strong's Concordance* gives its meaning as 'unanimity, unity'. Underlying its meaning is the idea of *one* individual 'unit' made up of *many equal parts* that constitute *a whole*. There are only two references to the word 'unity' used here, in the New Testament:

> Walk in a manner worthy of the calling to which you have been called ... eager to maintain *the **unity** of the Spirit* in the bond of peace. (Ephesians 4:3)

> He gave the apostles, the prophets, the evangelists, the shepherds and teachers, for the work of ministry, for building up of the body of Christ, until we all attain to the ***unity*** *of the faith and of the knowledge of the Son of God*, to mature manhood, to the measure of the stature of the fullness of Christ. (Ephesians 4:11-13)

Although the word 'unity' is not used in Ephesians 3:6, we have there *effectively*, 'the unity of the body':

> This mystery is that "the Gentiles are fellow heirs, *members of the same body,* and partakers of the promise in Christ Jesus through the gospel".

So we have a threefold 'unity':

- ***The unity of the Spirit***: All believers today *should maintain this unity*, they are fellow heirs, and have an inheritance in Christ. (Ephesians 1:13,14; 4:3)
- ***The unity of the faith***: All believers today *should attain to the unity of the faith and of the knowledge of the Son of God.* (4:13)
- ***The unity of the body***: All believers today *are part of one and the same body.* (4:4)

The sevenfold 'unity of the Spirit' (Ephesians 4:4-6) may be seen under two heads:

> **The Trinity:** One Spirit; One Lord; One God and Father of all.
> **The One Body of believers:** One hope of our calling; one faith; one baptism

The "one baptism" here refers to one of two ways in which the believer is seen as *identified with Christ*:

> In him (Christ) you were circumcised with a circumcision made without hands, by putting off the body of the flesh by the circumcision of Christ, *having been buried with him in baptism.* (Colossians 2:11,12)

This is part of a sevenfold identification with Christ revealed by the apostle in Romans and Ephesians. It is largely beyond the remit of this study, but I set out below the seven 'stages' of that identification that demonstrate our oneness with Christ in every step of His act of salvation, that He went through for us believers. (See the author's *Paul's Letter to the Romans* OBT pages 71,72 for more on this.)

Identification with Christ in the everyday life of the believer (Romans 6 and 8) in five steps:

- Crucified with Him (6:6)
- Dead with Him (6:8)
- Buried with Him (6:4)
- Quickened with Him (8:11 *KJV*)
- Raised with Him (6:5)

And additionally, in the Church which is the Body of Christ,

- Ascended with Him, and
- Seated with Him in the heavenly places (Ephesians 2:6).

xv) Grieving the Holy Spirit (4:30)

Paul first reminded the Ephesians that the Holy Spirit has sealed them for that future day, when their redemption reaches its fulfilment in the receiving of their inheritance (Ephesians 1:13,14). He then warned them of their conduct in the present life:

> Let no corrupt talk come out of your mouths, but only such as is good for building up and fits the occasion, that it may give grace to those who hear. And do not grieve *the Holy Spirit of God,* by whom you were sealed for the day of redemption. (Ephesians 4:29,30)

The Unity of this body of believers, the Church, is made by the Holy Spirit, and we are urged to 'keep it *in the bond of peace*'. Hence anything that does not tend to the building up of that body grieves Him. Here Paul highlights "corrupt talk", but it may be anything that disturbs that unity. The most obvious example in the Scriptures of such grievance is found in the attitude and actions of the people of Israel as recorded in Isaiah 63:9,10:

> In his love and in his pity he (the LORD) redeemed them; he lifted them up and carried them all the days of old. But they rebelled and *grieved his Holy Spirit*; therefore he turned to be their enemy.

We must not forget that the LORD was referring here to a 'redeemed' people. And yet, with all their experience of the LORD's blessings upon them, their deliverance from Egypt and His watching over them in the wilderness, they rebelled, and He effectively became their enemy, and they suffered accordingly (see Hebrews 3:7-11).

Whilst the position of the Christian today may be very different from that generation of ancient Israel, Christians can live a way of life, or act towards one's 'brothers' or 'sisters', in a way totally alien to what is required of a redeemed people. And when the apostle warned his readers not to 'grieve' the Holy Spirit, he set it in a context of "putting away falsehood ... anger ... giving opportunity to the devil ... honest work ... bitterness ... wrath ... slander and malice", reminding them that they were "sealed by the Holy Spirit for the day of redemption" (Ephesians 4:25-32; see also 1:13,14).

Elsewhere the apostle had said of a Christian's way of life: "If your brother is *grieved by what you eat*, you are no longer walking in love." This specific example may not be very relevant today, but the principal is the same; that of "putting a stumbling block or hindrance in the way of a brother" by one's own 'freedom' (Romans 14:13-15).

In addition to "grieving" *the Holy Spirit*, but similar in principle, are the "quenching" of *the Holy Spirit* (1 Thessalonians 5:19), and "resisting" *the Holy Spirit* (Acts 7:51). Whilst the last of these quotes was a deliberate act by a "stiff-necked people" *against the Holy Spirit*, in Ephesians 4:30 it is more that the sins of believers affect other Christians, offending God and so standing in the way of the work of *the Holy Spirit* in the building up of the Church of God (cp. Ephesians 2:22; 4:2,3).

xvi) Be filled by the Spirit (5:18)

In his book *The Giver and His Gifts*, Dr E. W. Bullinger has taken great pains to consider whether in the phrase, *alla plerousthe en pneumati*, the preposition *en* should be translated "with" or "by"; and he concludes that it should be rendered, "be filled by the Spirit",[60] which I have adopted. But filled with what?

Some might say "spirit", which is somewhat nebulous. Apart from the *KJV* which has "Ghost" in places, there is only one reference in most versions of the New Testament where *pneuma* is rendered other than "Spirit" or "spirit" (John 3:8 "wind")[61], and that is hardly the meaning in Ephesians 5:18!

Looking back over the ministry of *the Holy Spirit* in the Old Testament, we see that when the Spirit of God came upon individuals, He conveyed a 'gift' to them. Both Joseph and Moses were given the 'ability' to rule over people, as were Saul (initially; later the Spirit left him) and David. Others had the 'gift' of prophecy (Samuel, Isaiah, etc.) and particularly interesting was Bezalel, who was given *the skill* to be a fine craftsman. *The Spirit of God* never 'filled' these individuals with some ethereal thing called 'spirit', but with some 'concrete' knowledge or ability to do God's work. And so it is here. But used generally of all believers, as Ephesians 5:18 suggests, what is it? Let Scripture interpret itself.

It has been remarked how Ephesians and Colossians run parallel to each other in some respects, in particular in the following sections of the epistles which repeat here (page 202):

Ephesians 5:18-6:9	Colossians 3:16-4:1
Be filled with the Spirit,	Let the word of Christ dwell in you richly

The Holy Spirit and His Ministry

addressing one another and spiritual songs, singing and making melody to the Lord with your heart, giving thanks always and for everything to God the Father.	teaching and admonishing one another in all wisdom, singing psalms and hymns and spiritual songs, with thankfulness in your hearts to God.

Followed by instructions concerning, Wives and Husbands Children and Parents Slaves and Masters	**Followed by instructions concerning,** Wives and Husbands Children and Parents Masters and Slaves

For my purpose here, I note that

"Be filled *by the Spirit*" in Ephesians

is parallel to

"Let *the Word of Christ* dwell in you" in Colossians.

That is, being filled by the Spirit *equates to* the Word of Christ dwelling in you.

Without discounting that the Holy Spirit of God may give to a believer 'any gift' as He wills, in this context what *the Holy Spirit* wants to fill all believers with is "the Word of Christ". Granted that there may be a subtle difference, a nuance, intended here, I doubt anyone would argue that "the Word of Christ" is not one and the same as "the Word of God". I take these two expressions as being essentially the same—the *God-breathed Scriptures* (2 Timothy 3:16).

In the personal comments of Paul, whose death seems imminent in his second letter to his "son" Timothy, he lays emphasis upon the importance of: "*The sacred writings*, which are able to make you wise for salvation through faith in Christ Jesus" (2 Timothy 3:15). These he later identified as

> *All Scripture is breathed out by God* and profitable for teaching, for reproof, for correction, and for training in righteousness, that the man of God may be competent, equipped for every good work. (2 Timothy 3:16,17)

The Holy Spirit fills the believer with "the Word of Christ", not for their own aggrandisement, so they can demonstrate great knowledge and ability, but in order to produce from them "every good work".

xvii) The Spirit's sword is the word of God (6:17)

"The whole armour of God" (Ephesians 6:10-20) has, I don't doubt, been made into many a fine sermon, and it deserves more space than I can give it here. But part of this study concerns "the sword *of the Spirit, which is* the word of God", where once again the link between the Holy Spirit and the word of God is seen.

It has often been observed that "the sword of the Spirit" is the only offensive weapon in this list of armour parts, and in this context used only as we,

> Stand against the schemes of the devil ... wrestle not with flesh and blood, but against the rulers, against the authorities, against the cosmic powers over this present darkness, against the spiritual forces of evil in the heavenly places. (Ephesians 6:11,12)

It was used by the Lord against the devil and his temptations, when three times He overcame that evil one's efforts to trap Him into displaying His powers as the Son of God before the correct time. He did so by quoting from the Scriptures (Matthew 4:1-11).

References to armour in relation to such as righteousness and salvation are found in the Old Testament, as well as elsewhere in the New: "He put on righteousness as a breastplate, and a helmet of salvation on his head" (Isaiah 59:17; cp. 11:5), and "Put on the breastplate of faith and love, and for a helmet the hope of salvation" (1 Thessalonians 5:8).

The 'sword' is associated with the 'mouth', the 'breath' and the 'lips'. For example, in the book of Revelation, the rider on the white horse, called "the Word of God", uses "the sword of his mouth" to wage war with the nations (19:13,15). This is reminiscent of Isaiah 11:2,4, which speaks of the Messiah, and His judgement on the wicked just prior to the Millennium:

> *The Spirit of the LORD* shall rest upon him ... He shall strike the earth with *the rod of his mouth*, and with *the breath of his lips* he shall kill the wicked.

In these passages, judgement is described as "the Spirit of the LORD" striking with "the rod of his mouth", and "the breath (spirit) of his lips"

xviii) The Holy Spirit's 'Sword', the Adversary and the Battleground (6:10-20)

In contrast to all the enemies and battles we read of in Old Testament times that took place on earth, or are prophesied to come, "We do not wrestle against flesh and blood ... but against *the spiritual forces* of evil in the heavenly places" (Ephesians 5:12). This conflict is likened to 'wrestling', which, just as the use of a sword suggests, is 'at close quarters'.

This battle is not taking place 'light years away' so as to have little or no relevance to us, even though the phrase, "in the heavenly places" might seem to suggest so. It was real enough for Paul to urge believers *living on earth* to be equipped by God for the conflict.

J. Armitage Robinson's paraphrase of the whole passage, Ephesians 6:10-20 *Epistle to the Ephesians,* is well worth reading. As Paul wrote:

> My final injunction concerns you all. You need power, and you must find it in the Lord. You need God's armour, if you are to stand against the devil. We have to wrestle with no human foe, but with the powers which have the mastery of this dark world: *they are* not flesh and blood, but *spirit*; and they wage their conflict in the heavenly sphere. You must be armed therefore with God's armour.
> Truth and righteousness, as you know, are His girdle and breastplate; and in these His representative must be clad. In the confidence of victory, you must be shod with the readiness of the messenger of peace. With faith for your shield, the flaming arrows of Satan will not discomfit you. Salvation is God's helmet,

and He smites with *the sword of His lips*. Your lips must *breathe* perpetual prayer. Prayer, too, is your watch, and it will test your endurance. Pray for the whole body of the saints: and pray for me, that my mouth may be opened to give my own message boldly, prisoner though I be.

xix) The battlefield: In the Heavenly Places

There are five occurrences of the expression, *en tous epouraniois*, and it is found only in Ephesians in the Scriptures:

- **1:3:** Blessed us in Christ with every spiritual blessing *in the heavenly places*.
- **1:20:** God's great might worked in Christ when he raised him from the dead and seated him at his right hand *in the heavenly places*, far above all rule ...
- **2:6:** God ... made us alive with Christ ... raised us up and seated us together with him *in the heavenly places* in Christ Jesus ...
- **3:10:** Through the church the manifold wisdom of God ... made known to the rulers and authorities *in the heavenly places*
- **6:12:** we wrestle against ... the rulers ... authorities ... cosmic powers over this present darkness ... spiritual forces of evil *in the heavenly places*.

Questions arise: Are "the heavenly places" the same 'place' or 'sphere' where our blessings are? We are seated with Christ, a 'place' described as "far above all rule and authority and power and dominion, and above every name that is named" (Ephesians 1:20,21). Apart from the feeling that this cannot be so, I join the many commentators who have struggled to give some kind of answer to this. I do not believe I have the answer, but I make the following observations which may help.

In Solomon's prayer of dedication of the first Temple he said:

> But will God indeed dwell on the earth? Behold, the heaven and *the heaven of heavens* cannot contain thee; how much less this house that I have built. (1 Kings 8:27 *KJV*)

The *ESV* has "the highest heaven", apparently in an attempt to give

Solomon's words their full force. *Moffatt* has "The very heaven, the height of heaven itself". I suggest that just as "the Most Holy Place" of all in the Temple on earth came to be called, "the Holy of Holies", giving it a status above "the Holy Place"; see the two 'sections' in Hebrews 9:1-8.

So, whilst I am not saying there are only two sections in the heavenly places, it too may have some form of division that separates the throne where Christ is seated for above all from a disputed lower 'area of conflict'. In the latter "the spiritual forces of evil" are defying God and attempting to stand between Him and His people.

To get all the references to "heavenly places" (above) to make sense in this context, I refer the reader to the *de jure* and *de facto* argument. *De jure* is the believer's presence in the heavenly places *by right*: *De facto* is the believer's *actual* presence there in the future. *At present* the believer is *effectively* (*de jure*) in the heavenly places, and so,

- Has every spiritual blessing *in the heavenly places.* (1:3)
- Has been raised with Christ from the dead and is seated with Him at His right hand *in the heavenly places.* (1:20; 2:6)
- And the Church is now and will continue to demonstrate God's manifold wisdom to the spiritual powers *in the heavenly places.* (3:10)

The *de facto* experience, actually being *in the heavenly places* awaits the future winning of the battle and the culmination of God's purpose in Christ.

E) The Holy Spirit in COLOSSIANS

There are only two references to *pneuma* in this epistle and neither seems to refer directly to *the Holy Spirit*, although in the first the *ESV* and *KJV* have a capital 'S'. They are:

> Epaphras our beloved fellow servant ... a minister of Christ on your behalf ... has made known to us your love *in the Spirit.* (Colossians 1:7,8)
> Though I am absent in body, yet I am with you *in spirit*, rejoicing to see your good order and the firmness of your faith in Christ. (Colossians 2:5)

The second usage is familiar to us even today and is equivalent to saying, 'I am sorry I cannot be with you but I am thinking of you, my thoughts are with you, I am with you in spirit.' But the first is capable of more than one meaning. Bullinger (*in loco*) refers it to "the original gift of *pneuma hagion*" to the believer, and refers to Romans 5:5:

> *God's love* has been poured into our hearts *through the Holy Spirit* who has been given to us.

And he commends an earlier edition of the *KJV* 1611 which uses a small 's' in Colossians 1:8. However, in Romans 15:30, Paul makes an appeal to his brethren:

> By (*dia*) our Lord Jesus Christ and by (*dia*) *the love of the Spirit* ... strive together with me in your prayers to God on my behalf, that I may be delivered from the unbelievers in Judea ...

Bullinger takes *dia* as meaning "by means of". Hence he concludes, "'the love of the Spirit' is the Genitive of origin; and means that this love (Romans 15:30) is the gift of the Spirit, 'the love of God', which He, the Spirit, sheds abroad in our hearts". (Readers might note that this is another verse where the Trinity is implied.)

However, we read these verses, God's presence and love is with the believer through the ministry of *the Holy Spirit*, and He may be called upon in "prayers to God" both individual and corporate (cp. Romans 8:26).

Chapter 17
Paul's final witness: The Holy Spirit in the Pastoral Epistles

The three so called 'Pastoral Epistles', 1 & 2 Timothy and Titus, present us with the same difficulty as to when they were written as Philippians did. Do they belong within the Acts Period or were they written post-Acts 28? Lightfoot's remark is succinct:

> They have occupied almost every conceivable position in the systems of different critics. This circumstance is in itself a sufficient proof of the difficulties which beset the question, and might perhaps lead us to despair of a solution. (*Biblical Essays*)

Nevertheless, he concluded, "they cannot be placed within the compass of the history contained in the Acts, and they must have been written after the other letters of the apostle, towards the close of his life". This has become the weight of opinion. It means of course, that they were written after the full knowledge of the Mystery of "the Church which is the Body of Christ" was revealed to Paul.

Timothy came to be looked upon by Paul as his "true child in the faith" and was appointed by Paul to lead the church in Ephesus (1 Timothy 1:2,3). Titus, also addressed by Paul as "my true child in a common faith" had been left in Crete to put things in order in the churches there and "appoint elders in every town" (Titus 1:4,5).

Spirit/spirit (*pneuma*) occurs four times in 1 Timothy, three times in 2

Timothy and once in Titus. (1 Timothy 4:12 is omitted in later versions following 'all the critical texts'.)

A) The Holy Spirit in TITUS

The one reference in Titus emphasises that the Christian should be *constantly looking* to the influence of *the Holy Spirit* in their life. It has also been observed that it gives us one of the most 'elegant' descriptions of the Trinity in the New Testament.

Washing of regeneration, renewal of the Holy Spirit (3:4-6)

Paul wrote:

> God our Saviour appeared, he saved us, not because of works done by us in righteousness, but according to his own mercy, by the washing of regeneration and *renewal of the Holy Spirit*, whom he poured out on us richly through Jesus Christ our Saviour, so that being justified by his grace we might become heirs according to the hope of eternal life. (Titus 3:4-6)

The apostle makes it clear that 'salvation' and 'justification' are by God's 'mercy' and 'grace'; works are excluded here. Paul also refers to the passage as a trustworthy "saying", as though Titus would be familiar with it; perhaps part of an early Creed (Titus 3:8). The passage has been described as being:

> One of the most elegant descriptions of the Trinity in the New Testament. It shows the three members of the Godhead actively involved in the salvation of sinners: *God the Father* as the planner and initiator (v.4); *Jesus Christ* as the agent of redemption (v.6), and *the Holy Spirit* as the instrument of regeneration and renewal (v.5). (William D. Mounce quoting C. Spicq *Word Biblical Commentary*)

"Washing" (*loutron*, the act of washing) is a metaphor of the cleansing power of conversion—"regeneration" the new birth (cp. John 3:1-15). In the only other reference in the New Testament it is associated with "the word"—"the washing of water *with the word*", a metaphor here of Christ's cleansing of the church, so that it might be "holy and without blemish" (Ephesians 5:26).

"Renewal of the Holy Spirit". The Greek *anakainosis* occurs in this form elsewhere only in Romans 12:2, where it is put in contrast to, "conforming to this world":

> Be transformed by the *renewal* of your mind, that by testing you may discern what is the will of God, what is good and acceptable and perfect.

The context in Titus requires that it is to be understood as a *once-for-all renewal* since it refers to the one act of salvation "through Jesus Christ our Saviour" (v.6). Conversion is both a negative cleansing ('washing') and a positive re-creation ('renewal') in a person.

B) The Holy Spirit in 1 TIMOTHY

What follows was possibly words of an early Christian Creed or Hymn that may have originated to warn against those who were teaching that Jesus Christ **did not** "come in the flesh". (Compare 1 John 4:2,3.)

> Great indeed, we confess, is the mystery of godliness:
> He (God)
> **i)** was manifested in the flesh,
> **ii)** justified by the Spirit
> **iii)** seen by angels
> **iv)** proclaimed among the nations,
> **v)** believed on in the world,
> **vi)** taken up in glory. (1 Timothy 3:16)

As a Christian hymn, their arrangement has been seen in three main ways; one stanza of six lines, two stanzas of three lines or three stanzas of two lines. I favour the third as it brings together:

> **i)** & **ii)** flesh and Spirit
> **iii)** & **iv)** angels and the nations;
> **v)** & **vi)** present belief in the world, and glory where Christ now is (*de jure*) with His church (far above all).

However, the clause that concerns us in this study is literally, "justified in (or by, Greek *en) the Spirit*" and Bullinger refers this to Christ's resurrection. "Jesus our Lord ... was delivered up for our trespasses and *raised* for our *justification*" (Romans 4:24,25). Here Paul links *resurrection* and *justification* together when referring to man's salvation.

It is not often remarked upon that in providing salvation for man through the death and resurrection of Christ, God's own righteousness was demonstrated. He could not summarily wipe out or gloss over sin, it had to be paid for ("the wages of sin is death", Romans 6:23). And so for us to be "justified by his grace as a gift" required:

> The redemption that is in Christ Jesus, whom God put forward as a propitiation by his blood, to be received by faith. *This was to show God's righteousness ... so that he might be just and the justifier* of the one who has faith in Jesus. (Romans 3:23-26)

The resurrection of Christ "justified" (*ESV* "vindicated") God in what He did as God incarnate, and the Spirit gave witness to Him who "was descended from David *according to the flesh* and was declared to be the Son of God in power *according to* **the Spirit of holiness** *by his resurrection from the dead*" (Romans 1:3,4). This was "the mystery of godliness", observed by angels, and, after His ascension into glory, proclaimed and believed on in all the world.

But we must not lose sight of the fact that these words were written in the context of living a life of "godliness". He had set them in the context of, "If I delay (to come to you), you may know *how one ought to behave* in the household of God, which is the church of the living God, a pillar and buttress of the truth" (1 Timothy 3:15).

They were also said in contrast to some whom Paul refers to in his second letter to Timothy who, "had the *appearance of godliness*, but denied its power" (1 Timothy 3:5). William D. Mounce rightly observed, "This hymn presents pure theology upon which the practical aspects of ministry are based" (*Word Biblical Commentary*).

i) The Holy Spirit and deceitful spirits: (4:1)

In general, Christians believe in the existence of *the Holy Spirit* even if they hold different opinions on His nature and Being and actions. But do they believe that "evil spirits" exist, or do they consider them the fantasy of a more 'primitive' age without the benefits of our knowledge today? Today, do they belong only to the séance and the claims of mediums?

Paul certainly believed in them as 1 Timothy 4:1-4 shows, referring to them as "deceitful spirits." And under various names they appear elsewhere in the Scriptures (*KJV*):

Old Testament: "familiar spirits" (Leviticus 19:31; Isaiah 19:3 etc.).
New Testament: "unclean spirits" (Matthew 10:1; Luke 6:18 etc.).
"wicked spirits" (Matthew 12:45).
"evil spirits" (Luke 7:21 etc.).
"seducing spirits" (1 Timothy 4:1).
"spirits of devils" (Revelation 16:14).

The "deceitful" or "seducing" spirits in 1 Timothy 4:1,2 are associated with "the teaching of demons, through the insincerity of liars whose consciences are seared (branded as with a hot iron)". They speak through human beings, just as *the Holy Spirit* does (e.g. the prophets cp. 1 Peter 1:10-12). And it is probable that Paul had particularly in mind those in Ephesus, referred to earlier in his epistle (Ephesians 6:11-12). He had in fact left Timothy there to challenge them (1 Timothy 1:1-7).

This development is reminiscent of Paul's words to the Ephesian elders on his last fateful journey to Jerusalem, when he warned them that, "after my departure fierce wolves will come in among you, not sparing the flock" (Acts 20:17-38). And, insofar as Paul is identified with his message, it may reflect Paul's words in his second epistle to Timothy, where he warned that "all who are in Asia turned away from me". He spoke also of being "deserted" and "rejected", but not by the Lord (2 Timothy 1:15; 4:16,17). It is in this same epistle that he urges Timothy to "guard the good deposit entrusted to you" (2 Timothy 1:14). To what was he referring?

C) The Holy Spirit in 2 TIMOTHY

Paul's second letter to Timothy was probably the last New Testament writing. Paul's martyrdom undoubtedly followed this letter, as his words in 2 Timothy 4:6 suggest—"The time of my departure has come." And the general atmosphere of the last part of Paul's letter is somewhat depressing, speaking as it does of a turning away from him and rejection of his "sound teaching" (4:3), although Paul himself remains upbeat as he contemplates receiving "the crown of righteousness" (4:8).

i) The Good Deposit: (1:14)

> Follow the pattern of the sound words that you have heard from me, in the faith and love that are in Christ Jesus. *By the Holy Spirit who dwells within us*, guard the good deposit entrusted to you. (2 Timothy 1:13,14)

Dr. Bullinger's comment here is:

> This deposit was the wondrous Secret or 'Mystery' received by *pneuma hagion*, and specially committed in the first instance to the Apostle Paul; (see Ephesians 3:2,3). In 1 Timothy 1:11 he calls it 'the gospel of the glory of the blessed God which I, even I, was entrusted with ... the revelation of the Mystery or Secret concerning 'Christ and the Church.' (*The Giver and His Gifts*)

To grasp the significance of this "good deposit" in the context of Paul's ministry in general, and its relevance for today, let us look back to his experiences on his arrival in Rome and what *the Holy Spirit* committed to him, and, through him to us. For a more detailed consideration of this, look under Paul's letter to the Ephesians (page 203), but I give here a short resume.

ii) Acts 28:16-31 and the Good Deposit

Following Paul's arrival in Rome, he was placed under house arrest "at his own expense", but with a certain amount of freedom, insofar that he was able to "welcome all who came to him, proclaiming the kingdom of God ... with all boldness and without hindrance" (Acts 28:23,30-31). He was evidently able to write and send letters to the churches. Two such letters written at this time were Ephesians[62] and Colossians.

In the first of these he claimed that:

> The stewardship of God's grace that *was given to me* for you, how the mystery was *made known to me by revelation*, as I have written briefly ... that the Gentiles are fellow heirs, members of the same body, and partakers of the promise in Christ Jesus through the gospel. (Ephesians 3:2,3,6)

Paul is claiming here (rarely given its full weight in commentaries) that "the mystery was *made known to me* by *revelation*". Such claims are either figments of the apostle's imagination or Bible truth. I believe it is the latter.

(We might recall here the words of Agrippa when Paul tried to convince him of the resurrection of Christ and its prophetic fulfilment—"Paul, you are out of your mind; your great learning is driving you out of your mind", to which Paul replied, "I am not out of my mind … I am speaking true and rational words", Acts 26:24,25.)

If Paul is speaking "true and rational words" in Ephesians, then his claim is surely true; especially this claim to have been the first to whom "**The Mystery**" was unfolded. (See the author's *The Mystery of Ephesians* OBT for more on this.) He is neither making a false claim nor boasting of his greatness. He was an apostle who had had many 'revelations' from the Lord (2 Corinthians 12:7), so why doubt him here?

So when he wrote his second and last letter to Timothy, the personal element is again present:

> Follow the pattern of the sound words that you have ***heard from me***, in the faith and love that are in Christ Jesus. *By the Holy Spirit who dwells within us*, guard the good deposit entrusted to you. (2 Timothy 1:13,14)

He wrote later in the same epistle: "What you have ***heard from me*** in the presence of many witnesses entrust to faithful men who will be able to teach others also." And Timothy was warned *to guard* the good deposit, "*by the Holy Spirit who dwells within* us". Paul "entrusted it" to Timothy and, as stated above, he in turn was to:

> Entrust it to faithful men who will be able to teach others also. (2 Timothy 2:2)

And so by this progression, Paul's gospel would "make all 'men' see what is the dispensation of the mystery which from all ages has been hidden in God who created all things" (Ephesians 3:9 *Revised Version*).

"The good deposit" is the body of truth called **The Mystery** based upon the salvation that is in Christ Jesus, and concerning the Church which is the Body of Christ. Paul defined it as part of, "The pattern of sound words that you have heard *from me*". He does not say, 'heard from *all the apostles*', but "heard *from me*". Paul is not suggesting that the other apostles are not teaching sound words, and it is not a show of conceit on his part. His words are said in a context of some who "will not endure sound teaching" (2 Timothy 4:3,4) and the sad observation that "all who are in Asia turned away from me" (2 Timothy 1:15).

This "good deposit" was to be passed on as Paul instructs. This is the only Scriptural 'Apostolic Succession' that I know of. It was *the ministry of the Holy Spirit*; entrusted to Paul, Timothy and hence to 'able and faithful men'. Did it ever get beyond Timothy?

iii) The Good Deposit: Epilogue

Dr. Bullinger made a sad observation on the critical texts in regard to *paratheke* "deposit" as referring to "the Mystery":

> The very confusion in the Greek text over the passages which have to do with the Mystery is a sad proof of the fact that it was given up in the Apostle Paul's own lifetime (as is stated in 2 Timothy 1:15).

Was that true? What do we know of this from the history that followed the death of the last apostles? It was not until the fourth century that Paul's writings were brought together with the other New Testament books to form what we know today as "the Scriptures". And, as Stuart Allen in *The Early Centuries and the Truth* BPT wrote:

> From the age of the Apostolic Fathers, one or two of the Gospels were known, and the epistles of Paul, as a whole ... What actually happened after the martyrdom of the Apostle Paul? We do know for certain that the body of Truth given by revelation of the Lord Jesus to him, was passed on to his son in the faith, Timothy. What happened to Timothy? Alas, we cannot say, for the earliest Christian literature does not mention him.

How did Timothy fare at this time, if indeed he was not martyred together with Paul? There is no record of him at this early stage. So what happened when such as Paul and Timothy passed off the scene? Some of those mentioned in the final chapter of 2 Timothy may have survived for some time; Luke, Mark, Prisca and Aquila etc. (2 Timothy 4:9-12, 19-21), but a few years down the line, a catastrophe was awaiting the Christian community—the destruction of the Jerusalem Temple by the Romans in A.D.70. This was to be the catalyst that led to a deepening separation between Jewish and Gentile Christians and, as far as we can deduce from what reliable writings we have from this time, a complete misunderstanding of "The Mystery" that Paul wrote of in Ephesians. This misunderstanding had an influence on the development of the Christian Church to the present day, and was to be far reaching in its scope.

For a detailed consideration of this development see the author's *The Mystery of Ephesians* OBT pages 84-105.

Also on the Holy Spirit

The Work of the Spirit in an Age of Grace
by Michael Penny

Within Christendom there is a wide variety of teaching on the work of the Holy Spirit. Anyone who has studied the subject from the pages of Scripture will not be surprised by this, for as we progress through the Bible we find that the work of the Spirit changes. Thus our view of the Spirit and His work will depend upon which parts of Scripture we focus on.

After Christ's ascension, for the next thirty or so years, there was a profusion of overt action from the Spirit, but what about after that? That is what this booklet considers. What was the work of the Spirit *after* the period of time covered by the Acts of the Apostles?

To answer that question, we need to study the Spirit in the last seven letters of Paul; Ephesians, Colossians, Philemon, Philippians, Titus, 1 & 2 Timothy. These were the letters Paul wrote after Acts 28:25-28, after the nation of Israel had lost its central position in God's plan, and after God had turned to the Gentiles, independently of Israel. In these letters we have essential teaching for this age of grace in which we live.

****

Available as an eBook from Amazon and Apple
and as KDP paperback from Amazon.

About the Author

Brian Sherring was born in Isleworth, Middlesex, England in 1932. Following a technical education, he took an engineering apprenticeship and worked for some years as a design draughtsman in agricultural engineering. He was onetime Assistant Principal of The Chapel of the Opened Book in London and wrote regular articles for *The Berean Expositor* and several booklets. He then spent some 25 years in the food import business and worked with farm animals at weekends as a hobby. He lives with his wife in retirement in Surrey and is now a regular contribut *Search* magazine.

He has written many Bible Study Booklets and the following four major books:

- *Paul's Letter to the Romans: Background & Introduction*
- *The Mystery of Ephesians*
- *Messiah and His People.*
- *The Ten Commandments*

More information on these four books is given on the next pages.

Information about the numerous Bible Study Booklets written by Brian Sherring can be seen on **www.obt.org.uk** (the website of The Open Bible Trust) or you can use this url:

http://www.obt.org.uk/brian-sherring

Also by Brian Sherring

Paul's Letter to the Romans:
Background & Introduction

This book sets Paul's letter to the Romans in the context of both the New Testament and his other letters. It gives the reader a good basis for a detailed study of the epistle.

It was written from Greece some three years before Paul arrived in Rome (Acts 20:2-3). This means that it was written *before* the judgement Paul pronounced upon the Jewish leaders in Rome (Acts 28:25-28). That is *before* Paul wrote Ephesians and Colossians in which new teachings are revealed about a heavenly calling, about Gentile and Jewish equality, and about the abolishment of the Law of Moses. It is essential when reading Romans, not to read back into it such teaching as these, and the author does an excellent job of explaining Romans in its correct historical context.

The Mystery of Ephesians

In Ephesians 3:3 Paul mentions a 'mystery', and states that he had written about it briefly, i.e. earlier in the letter. So ... What is this 'mystery'? ... Why have so few Christians heard about it? ... And why do some, who have heard about it, reject it? ... Even oppose it?

With great clarity, Brian Sherring explains that the Greek word translated 'mystery' does not mean something 'mysterious' but refers to a 'secret', and this 'secret' is an important one. It relates to all mankind, and God had just revealed it to Paul and wanted Paul to make it known far and wide ... which is just what he did in writing Ephesians.

Messiah and His People

In this book, Brian Sherring takes the reader through the Bible and the unfolding portrait it paints of the Messiah, the Christ, the Redeemer.

He starts off in Genesis 3, where we learn of the seed of the woman who is to crush the serpent's head, and as we progress through time, slowly more and more is revealed about this One. He is to descend from Abraham and be of the house of David. He is to be born of a virgin and be born in Bethlehem.

He is to combine the offices of Prophet, Priest and King. From Ephesians 1 we learn that in the end He is to be head over all things and Philippians 2 states He is to have that Name which is above every name.

The Ten Commandments

In spite of an increasing lack of knowledge of the Bible in Britain, the Ten Commandments are probably still the best-known set of laws in the western society. They lie behind our justice system and, in Christian society, form an outline of what God requires of mankind. They are of course, only an outline, or skeleton, that needs to be expanded—and that is just what this book does.

****

The above four are also available as perfect bound paperbacks from

www.obt.org.uk

and from

The Open Bible Trust, Fordland Mount,
Upper Basildon, Reading, RG8 8LU, UK.

They are also available as eBooks from Amazon and Apple
and as KDP paperbacks from Amazon.

Subject Index

A Doxology: The fellowship of the Holy Spirit	172
A kingdom of priests and a holy nation	129
A letter from Christ written with the Spirit of the living God	166
A warning for readers of the KJV	133
Access to the Father	210
Acts 28:16-31 and the Good Deposit	236
An important decision: 'Spirit' or 'spirit'?	19
Anointing and Sealing	165
Anointing, the Spirit of the Lord and "The Lord's anointed"	39
'Apostolic mistakes'	106
Authority to forgive sins: binding and loosing	94
Authorship and date of John's Gospel	65
Background and context of the New Testament	43
Be filled by the Spirit	224
Blasphemy against the Holy Spirit	61
Built by the Spirit into a dwelling place for God	213
Conscience and The Holy Spirit	30
Conscience: 'Light' and 'responsibility'	27
Conscience: The word as used in the Scriptures	26
Corinthians: First Epistle	151
Corinthians: Second Epistle	165
David's Son and David's Lord: A Conundrum	63
Destination of the Gospel of John	67
Ephesians and Colossians as parallel epistles	202
Epistles to the circumcision: Peter and James	127
Expectancy of the coming of the Messiah	47
Fellowship of the Spirit	
Galatians and Romans	175
Gentile access to the Lord: Old Testament	211
Gifts of the Spirit during Acts	121
Gifts of the Spirit during the Gospel and Acts Periods	115

Glory: Its meaning in Scripture	169
God's Spirit in God's temple	156
Greater works than these because I go to the Father	85
Greece: The Epistles to the Corinthians	149
Grieving the Holy Spirit	222
He will guide you into all the truth	89
Heirs of God ... fellow heirs with Christ	186
His commissioning and warning to His disciples	60
'If you are willing to accept it'	55
Impasse: Israel rejected and Paul turns to the Gentiles	193
Israel's feasts reflect their history in type	111
Jesus anticipates His coming sacrifice	80
Jesus; The Holy One of God	77
John and baptism with fire	57
John chapters 14-16	83
John the Baptist: God's messenger	54
John's Epilogue (chapter 21)	81
John's epistle v. John's Gospel	133
Life in the Spirit	184
Living Water = the Holy Spirit	78
Luke's record and the course of the Acts	101
Macedonia: The Epistles to the Thessalonians	144
Man' and 'the natural man'; Definitions	21
No condemnation ... no separation from God's love in Christ	184
No longer a slave but a son ... crying Abba! Father!	181
Old Covenant letter v. New Covenant *Spirit*	167
Old Testament gifts of the Spirit	38
One door closes; another door opens	192
One Spirit, many gifts, a warning and a goal	161
Other Tongues at Pentecost	116
Our judgement and the Spirit of God	158
Paul and the laws of life	185
Paul Entrusted with the Gospel to the uncircumcised	175
Paul's authority in relation to the apostles of the circumcision	176
Paul's conscience and anguish of heart for his brethren	189

Paul's final witness: The Holy Spirit in the Pastoral Epistles	231
Paul's letter to Philemon	195
Paul's priestly service to the Gentiles	190
Pentecost in the context of the New Testament	114
Pentecost: Its history and significance	108
Pentecost: Why Pentecost?	107
Post-resurrection: "Receive the Holy Spirit"	80
Power and authority given to the apostles pre-Pentecost	115
Power through the Spirit so that God may dwell in your hearts	219
Prayer for the saints: 'hope', 'inheritance', 'power'	206
Prophecy rather than tongues	120
Receiving the Holy Spirit	177
Redemption and the blood of Christ	136
References to the Holy Spirit in Hebrews	134
References to the Holy Spirit in John's Gospel	69
References to the Holy Spirit in Revelation	141
References to The Holy Spirit in the Acts Period	102
Romans and Corinthians	117
Sanctification of God's people	147
Sealed and guaranteed by the Holy Spirit	205
Sharing in the Holy Spirit	136
Spirit, the words of Jesus and eternal life	77
Spirit/spirit and 'the calling to which you are called'	20
Spirit: Translations and usage	18
Standing firm in one spirit	197
The apostles are sent forth	97
The Baptist reveals the Messiah to Israel	70
The battlefield: In the Heavenly Places	228
The birth and early days of John and the Messiah	50
The Body of Christ: During the Acts and post-Acts Periods	163
The Book of The Revelation of Jesus Christ	141
The curse of the law and the promise to Abraham	178
The dating of all the New Testament epistles	126
The Day of the Lord	110

The depths of God and the mind of Christ	152
The Dispensation of the Mystery	218
The dividing wall between Jew & Gentile: Acts & post-Acts	212
The Epistle of Jude	130
The Epistle to the Galatians	175
The Epistle to the Romans	182
The fruit of the Spirit	181
The Good Deposit	236
The Good Deposit: Epilogue	238
'The Great Commission' (so called)	92
The groaning creation and the waiting with patience	187
The Hebrew and Greek words for 'Spirit' and 'spirit'	18
The Holy Spirit and 'all men'	21
The Holy Spirit and deceitful spirits:	235
The Holy Spirit and the individual believer in Acts	105
The Holy Spirit and the love of God	183
The Holy Spirit and the prayer of the believer	188
The Holy Spirit and the Preparation of the apostles for their coming mission (John 14-16)	83
The Holy Spirit and the promises: A summary (John 14-16)	91
The Holy Spirit and the Word of God in Corinthians	151
The Holy Spirit and the world of 'men'	21
The Holy Spirit at work during the Acts Period	103
The Holy Spirit between the Testaments	41
The Holy Spirit during the Acts Period	101
The Holy Spirit in 1 Timothy	233
The Holy Spirit in 2 Timothy	236
The Holy Spirit in Colossians	229
The Holy Spirit in Corinthians	149
The Holy Spirit in Ephesians	203
The Holy Spirit (*pneuma*) in Galatians)	177
The Holy Spirit in Hebrews	133
The Holy Spirit in John's Gospel	65
The Holy Spirit in Luke's history of The Acts of the Apostles	192
The Holy Spirit in Philippians	195

The Holy Spirit in relation to 'anointing' and 'sealing'	165
The Holy Spirit in relation to the 'old self' and the 'new self'	153
The Holy Spirit (*pneuma*) in Romans	182
The Holy Spirit in the Gospel of Luke	50
The Holy Spirit in the Gospel of Matthew	53
The Holy Spirit in the man of dust	22
The Holy Spirit in the New Testament	43
The Holy Spirit in the non-Pauline Acts Epistles	126
The Holy Spirit in the Old Testament	35
The Holy Spirit in the Pauline Acts epistles	143
The Holy Spirit in the Pauline Acts epistles	175
The Holy Spirit in the Synoptic Gospels	49
The Holy Spirit in Thessalonians	144
The Holy Spirit in Titus	232
The Holy Spirit is a Person	7
The Holy Spirit is God	8
The Holy Spirit spoke through the O.T. prophets	135
The Holy Spirit within 'the Trinity'	9
The Holy Spirit: A brief summary	16
The Holy Spirit: A revealer of mysteries	216
The Holy Spirit: An unfolding revelation	14
The Holy Spirit: Man and his conscience	24
The Holy Spirit: Who is He?	7
The Holy Spirit's 'Sword', the Adversary and the Battleground	227
The hope to which he has called you	207
The immeasurable greatness of his power towards us who believe	208
The Lord will judge His people	139
The Lord's ministry in John	72
The ministry of Jesus in the Synoptics	60
The Mystery of Christ	217
The Name of Jesus Christ	157
The Prison epistles of Paul	195
The promise of "another Helper"	84

The promised Holy Spirit	204
The prophecy of Joel	109
The restoration of the kingdom to Israel	45
The riches of his glorious inheritance in the saints	208
The Spirit given without measure	73
The Spirit of God and the Word of God	33
The Spirit of God: Post-Moses	37
The Spirit of God: Pre-Moses	36
The Spirit of Jesus Christ and Paul's deliverance	196
The Spirit of the Lord: 'Freedom' and degrees of 'glory'	171
The Spirit's sword is the word of God	226
The temptation of Jesus	59
The Three Epistles of John	131
The Trinity in the New Testament	11
The Trinity in the Old Testament	11
The Trinity: Different 'roles'	15
The (true) circumcision worship by the Spirit of God	199
The Truth: Then and now	90
The Twelve Apostles and their authority	92
The Twelve: Final instructions	97
The Two Covenants: Old and New	137
The unity of the Spirit … the bond of peace	220
Thessalonians and Corinthians	143
Thessalonians: The First Epistle	145
Thessalonians: The Second Epistle	146
"This is My beloved Son"	58
Three categories of 'man'	29
Tongues are a sign for unbelievers	119
Tongues following Pentecost: Acts Period	117
Tongues: Purpose and place	118
Twelve apostles, twelve thrones of judgement	95
Unity in 'the Church which is the Body of Christ'	220
Was John Elijah?	54
Washed, sanctified, justified: The Name and the Spirit of God	157
Washing of regeneration, renewal of the Holy Spirit	232

Who wrote Hebrews and to whom was it written?	134
Worship in spirit and truth	74
"You must be born again"	72

Bibliography

Bible Versions quoted:
ESV; *KJV*; *The Revised Version*; *New King James*; *NEB*; *Moffatt*.
The Septuagint (*LXX*) Greek version of the Hebrew Old Testament.
The New Greek Interlinear New Testament.

OBT publications consulted:
Ozanne Charles: *The Sabbath and Circumcision*;
  The Wife the Bride and the Body.
Penny Michael: *40 Problem Passages*;
  The New Covenant! Who is it with? When is it for?;
  The Fruit of the Spirit;
  Galatians Interpretation and Application.
Penny Sylvia: *Salvation: Safe and Secure*.
Sherring Brian: *Apocalypse*;
  Jesus God and Man;
  Messiah and His People;
  The Mystery of Ephesians;
  Christians: Their Message and Their Witness;
  The Gospel of John and the Samaritans.
  Paul's letter to the Romans: Background and Introduction.

Other works consulted:
Allen Stuart *The Early Centuries and the Truth* The Berean Publishing Trust.
Barrett C.K. *The Gospel according to St. John* SPCK.
Bonar Andrew *Leviticus: Geneva Series of Commentaries* The Banner of Truth Trust.
Bruce F.F. *The Acts of the Apostles* The Tyndale Press.
Bruner Frederick Dale *The Theology of the Holy Spirit* Hodder and Stoughton.
Bullinger E.W. *The Companion Bible*.
  Word Studies on the Holy Spirit (formally *The Giver and His Gifts*) Kregel.
Dunn James D.G. *Romans: Word Biblical Commentary*.
Kruse Colin 2 Corinthians *Tyndale Commentaries*.
Lincoln Andrew T. *Ephesians: Word Biblical Commentary*.
Lightfoot J.B. *Biblical Essays* Macmillan (1893).

St. Paul's Epistle to the Philippians Macmillan. 1891.
The Apostolic Fathers (edited by J.R. Harmer 1926) Macmillan.
Macgregor C.H.C. *The Gospel of John: The Moffatt New Testament Commentary* Hodder and Stoughton.
Moffatt James *An Introduction to the Literature of the New Testament* International Theological Library.
Morris Leon: *1 Corinthians: Tyndale New Testament Commentaries*.
Mounce William D. *The Pastoral Epistles: Titus: Word Biblical Commentaries*.
Murray Beasley G.R. *Baptism in the New Testament.* Paternoster Press.
The Gospel of John:Word Biblical Commentary.
Robinson J.A.T. *Redating the New Testament* SCM Press Ltd.
The Priority of John SCM Press Ltd.
Robinson J. Armitage *St. Paul's Epistle to the Ephesians* Macmillan 1922.
Sparks H.F.D. *A Synopsis of the Gospels* Adam and Charles Black.
Stott John R.W. *1 John: Tyndale New Testament Commentaries*.
Strachan R.H. *2 Corinthians: The Moffatt New Testament Commentary.*
Thiselton Anthony C. *The First Epistle to the Corinthians: The New International Greek Testament Commentary*
Warrington Keith *The Message of the Holy Spirit: The Bible Speaks Today Series.* Paternoster Press.
Wenham John *Redating Matthew, Mark and Luke* Hodder and Stoughton.
Welch C.H. *Just and the Justifier* Berean Publishing Trust.
Westcott B.F. *The Gospel According to St. John* John Murray 1898.
The Epistle to the Hebrews Macmillan 1898.

Bible 'Tools':
A Critical Lexicon and Concordance to the English and Greek New Testament E.W. Bullinger.
Concordance to the Bible Alexander Cruden.
The Englishmen's Greek Concordance of the New Testament G.V. Wigram.
The Englishman's Hebrew Concordance of the Old Testament G.V. Wigram.
Greek-English Lexicon Liddell and Scott.
Englishman's Hebrew Concordance to the Bible James Strong.
The New Bible Dictionary Inter Varsity Press.
New Testament Synonyms Richard Chenevix Trench Macmillan 1865.

Also referred to:
The Concise Oxford Dictionary;
The International Websters Dictionary.
Common Worship (Church of England).

Additional (superscript) Notes

[1] The word *prosopon* is rendered in the *KJV* 'face' (Matthew 6:16; 16:3 etc.); 'person' (Matthew 22:16; Luke 20:21; 2 Corinthians 1:11etc.); 'before' (Acts 13:24; 2 Corinthians 8:24); 'outward appearance' (2 Corinthians 10:7); 'presence' (2 Corinthians 10:1; Hebrews 9:24); 'fashion' (James 1:11).

[2] In the context of Jeremiah 31 which differentiates "Israel" from "Judah" (the Northern Kingdom from the Southern Kingdom)-verse 9- "Ephraim" (largest of the ten Northern tribes) seems to stand for *all* ten tribes of Israel.

[3] It has been observed that there is no evidence either in the Scriptures or in early Christendom that this formula was ever used, and it has been suggested that it belongs to the future 'Kingdom Age', i.e., The Millennium.

[4] I first came across this title in the writings of C.H. Welch, although it may pre-date him.

[5] A full exposition of this passage can be found in C.H. Welch's book *The Testimony of the Lord's Prisoner* BPT. See also the author's *The Mystery of Ephesians* OBT.

[6] For more on this passage see the author's book *The Mystery of Ephesians* OBT.

[7] The word occurs three times in the *KJV* (Acts 17:29; Romans 1:20; Colossians 2:9). In other versions the Greek is rendered: "the divine being", "divine nature", "deity" (e.g. *ESV, NIV*). In the Romans reference, *Moffatt* has "invisible nature".

[8] The few places where the O.T. text is in Aramaic are Ezra 4:7-6:18; 7:12-26; Jeremiah 19:11; Daniel 2:4-7:28.

[9] Readers may find others. Here I am referring to these Scriptures: John 8:9; Acts 23:1; 24:16; Romans 2:15; 1 Corinthians 8:7,10; 1 Timothy 3:9; 4:8; Hebrews 9:22.

[10] See *The Companion Bible* notes on Isaiah 45:18 and Genesis 1:2. Also *Theories of Creation* Sylvia Penny OBT.

[11] "Holy Spirit" in the O.T. occurs only in Psalm 51:11; Isaiah 63:10,11.

[12] "Contend with man". *The Companion Bible in loco* following the Septuagint, Arabic, Syriac and Vulgate versions, has "remain in man". The KJV has "strive with man".

[13] *The Companion Bible* works this out as 2348 B.C., although not all are agreed on this. It may also look back to the ancient prophecy of Enoch (who was "translated" before the birth of Noah). This was recorded

by Jude and concerned a future "coming of the Lord" in judgement upon the ungodly (Genesis 5:21-24; Jude 14,15).

[14] Prophets: Elijah and Elisha (1 Kings 19:16; 2 Kings 2:9,15). Priests: Aaron and his sons (Exodus 30:30): Kings: Saul and David (1 Samuel 24:6; 2 Samuel 23:1). In its verbal form it occurs many more times (66).

[15] For more on the practice and significance of "anointing" see the author's *Messiah and His People* OBT.

[16] "Messiah" is a translation of the Hebrew word *mashiach* and the Greek word *Messias*. It is translated as such only twice in the *KJV* Old Testament, and in some versions (e.g. *ESV, NIV*) "an anointed one" (Daniel 9:25 & 26). It occurs also only twice in the New Testament in its Aramaic form, "Messias" *KJV* and "Messiah" *ESV* (John 1:41; 4:25). The Hebrew *mashiach* actually occurs some 40 times in the Old Testament, and is used of Prophets, Priests and Kings.

In the Greek translation of the Old Testament (*LXX*) it is always translated by the word *christos:* Saul was "the LORD's *anointed*" and David, "the *anointed* of the God of Israel" (1 Samuel 12:3,5; 2 Samuel 5:3) . It is also used of Cyrus, king of Persia who was, in a sense, a 'redeemer' of Israel (Isaiah 45:1,13): "Thus says the LORD to *his anointed*, to Cyrus ... He shall build my city and *set my exiles free*".

[17] Apocrypha: Fourteen books of the Septuagint (*LXX*) in the Latin Vulgate, but not in the Canonical Hebrew Scriptures, nor in the Authorised (King James) Version (*Webster's New International Dictionary*).

[18] See for example, F.F. Bruce in his *Commentary on the Greek Text of the Acts of the Apostles* in loco, Tyndale 1965. He saw this as a 'spiritual kingdom'.

[19] Recorded in Matthew 3:13-17; Mark 1:9-11; Luke 3:21,22; John 1:29-34.

[20] For a comparison of these two genealogies, see *The Companion Bible* Appendix 99.

[21] The word 'power' is the Greek *dunamis*, a word translated elsewhere "mighty works" and "miracles" (Matthew 13:54; Luke 19:11) and yet "John did no *miracle*" (John 10:41 *KJV*). The word here is actually *semeion* ('sign') and is so translated elsewhere in John (*ESV* and other versions).

[22] The Day of the Lord. This expression, first used in Isaiah 2:12, is the first of twenty occurrences in the Old Testament, sixteen of which have *yom Jehovah* (LORD). In the New Testament it must be seen in contrast to 'man's day', an expression Paul uses in 1 Corinthians 4:3

when he says to them, (lit.) "It is a very small thing to me that I am judged by you or by *man's day (anthropines hemeras)*" and which still reflects the present situation, "when man exalts himself, and bows God out of the world he has created" (*The Companion Bible*).

"The Day of the LORD" was anticipated by Israel as a future day of *Jehovah's visitation.* In the first reference to it Isaiah says:

"*The LORD of Hosts has a day* against all that is proud and lofty, against all that is lifted up—and it shall be brought low ... and the haughtiness of man shall be humbled, and the lofty pride of men shall be brought low, and *the LORD alone shall be exalted in that day*". (cp. Isaiah 13:6,9-22)

And Paul, writing during the Acts Period, said:

"You are fully aware that *the day of the Lord* will come like a thief in the night. While people are saying, 'There is peace and security' then sudden destruction will come upon them." (1 Thessalonians 5:2,3; cp. 2 Peter 3:10)

This future day of judgement can be seen in Malachi's prophecy: "Who can endure the day of his coming, and who can stand when he appears" (3:2): a passage that reflects John the Baptist's warning to the Pharisees and Sadducees; "who warned you to flee from the wrath to come" (Matthew 3:7).

[23]This is one of the big 'Ifs' in the New Testament that introduces a condition and puts the onus on the hearer—"If *you* are willing to accept it". Another 'If', very relevant to an understanding of the Acts Period, although perhaps not so often noticed, was when Peter, addressing his own people shortly after the Day of Pentecost, said:

"Men of Israel ... God glorified his servant Jesus, whom you delivered over and denied in the presence of Pilate, when he had decided to release him ... you killed the Author of life whom God raised from the dead."

"Now brethren, I know that you acted in ignorance ... *Repent therefore*, and turn again, *in order that* your sins may be blotted out, *in order that* times of refreshing may come from the Lord, *and that* he may send the Christ appointed for you, whom heaven must receive until the time for restoring all the things about which God spoke by the mouth of his holy prophets long ago". (Acts 3:13-21)

The imminence of the Messiah's return is seen in much of the writings that belong to that **period**, but it was *conditional* on the *national* repentance of Israel, which never happened. In the same way, the Lord was saying that John the Baptist could be the fulfilment of the prophecy of the coming of Elijah before the coming of the Messiah—IF.

[24] The early return of Christ was expected throughout the Acts Period beginning with the promise made to the twelve apostles at the Ascension (Acts 1:11), quickly followed by Peter's words shortly after Pentecost (3:19-21) and found in the epistles written during that period e.g. 1 Corinthians 10:11; 15:51 "we shall not all sleep"; 1 Thessalonians 4:15 "we who are alive, who are left until the coming of the Lord"; Hebrews 10:25; James 5:7-9; 1 Peter 4:7; 1 John 2:18. Also in Paul's last letter during this period Romans 13:11,12 "the night is far gone; the day is at hand"; 16:20 "The God of peace will soon crush Satan under your feet".

[25] See the author's *The Gospel of John and the Samaritans* OBT.

[26] See *The Companion Bible* Appendix 176, which lists the signs in structural form.

[27] "The idea of the lamb as typifying the Messiah, not found in the other Evangelists, is only explained by recalling the Messianic expectations of the time." Lightfoot *Biblical Essays* page 149.

[28] This is the only place in John's Gospel where the expression, "the kingdom of God" is used. See Stuart Allen's book, *The Kingdom of God in Heaven and on Earth* (Berean Publishing Trust) for a detailed study of this subject.

[29] This book has now been published under the name, *Word Studies on the Holy Spirit*. See Bibliography.

[30] Some might doubt whether this was a 'miracle' at all. Fish do accumulate in shoals, and it could be claimed that it was just a matter of knowing where they could be found, which any experienced fisherman would have known. But unless there was a miraculous element involved here, and it was another "sign" that "Jesus is the Messiah", I doubt John would have recorded it.

[31] As an example of this, even after the disciples' hopes had been dashed by the crucifixion and death of Jesus, the two disciples on the Emmaus Road said of Him, "*We had hoped* that he was the one *to redeem Israel*" (Luke 24:21). And after His miraculous rising from the dead, and as the apostles stood together on the Mount of Olives, the last question they asked Him before His ascension was, "Lord, will you at this time *restore the kingdom to* Israel?" (Acts 1:6). This was still their 'hope'—Israel's redemption, Israel's restored kingdom, the consolation of Israel.

And yet in spite of this there have, and continue to be, those who have said (or implied) that the apostles who asked this question had completely misunderstood why the Messiah had come and what His purpose was. They say, 'Was He not speaking of *a spiritual* kingdom?' 'Did He not come to build a spiritual Church?' 'Surely the apostles had misunderstood the Lord?' 'It was surely not to restore an earthly kingdom to Israel on earth!' (See F.F. Bruce in his *Commentary on the Greek Text of The Acts of the Apostles*. Tyndale 1965.)

[32] *Parakletos*, John 14:16, 26; 15:26; 16:7 "Helper" (*ESV*) "Comforter" (*KJV*): 1 John 2:1 "Advocate" (*ESV* and *KJV*).

[33] I have placed these epistles during the Acts Period in an order based on the nature of their content.

[34] The nearest 'succession' of ministry in the New Testament is contained in Paul's instruction to Timothy: "Follow the pattern of the sound words that you have heard from me ... and what you have heard from me in the presence of many witnesses *entrust to faithful men who will be able to teach others also*" (2 Timothy 1:13; 2:2).

[35] For a detailed exposition of 'The Great Commission' see *40 Problem Passages* by Michael Penny and *Paul's Letter to the Romans* by the author both OBT.

[36] This figure is subject to differences of opinion on whether certain references refer to 'Spirit' or 'spirit' (see page 102).

[37] See for example, F.F. Bruce in his *Commentary on the Greek Text of the Acts of the Apostles* in loco, Tyndale 1965.

[38] I used to imagine that the twelve apostles conducted twelve 'open air meetings' in the twelve languages, but Peter spoke to all, so it must have been a language known to all, and Greek at this time was the *lingua franca*.

[39] It also appeared in a series of articles in *Search* numbers 188-199.

[40] I take "all" here, to refer to the twelve apostles, ignoring the chapter break and reading straight on from 1:26. "Matthias was numbered with the eleven apostles ... they were all together in one place."

[41] Greek was established as the *lingua franca* during the dominance of Greece in the days of Alexander the Great's father. Although Hebrew is the language of the Old Testament, hardly anyone spoke it at this time. Judeans spoke either Greek or Aramaic. At Pentecost, I think it more likely that Peter spoke in Greek rather than Aramaic, since some of the Jew of the Dispersion may not have understood Aramaic.

[42] See Anthony C. Thiselton's book *The First Epistle to the Corinthians* for a detailed list of these (see Bibliography).

[43] There is a tendency to think of the church in Corinth as being largely Gentile. That may have been so, but when we read of the Gentile position at this time such as Paul has set out in Romans 11, the Jew

still possessed all the privileges and advantages (Romans 3:1,2; 9:1-5), and had priority at that time (Romans 1:17; 2:,10). The Gentiles were but "wild shoots" grafted into the olive tree of Israel; the Jews were the "natural branches" (Romans 11:17-21). And privilege carries with it responsibility. Hence the quotation is addressed initially to them.

[44] 'Asia', as used in the New Testament, does not refer to the Continent of Asia as we understand it today, but to a province, Asia Minor (approximately equivalent to Western Turkey today).

[45] Paul's letter to the Philippians is taken in this study to belong post-Acts 28, although not all would agree with this. Some believe that it was written from Caesarea during Paul's two-year confinement there (Acts 24:27).

[46] "In the likeness of our image". *The Companion Bible* takes this to be the figure of speech *Hendiadys*, 'one thing not two', which I believe is better than "in our image, after our likeness".

[47] *Two Natures in the Child of God* is the title of a booklet by E.W. Bullinger (OBT) first published in 1907.

[48] The various aspects of 'salvation' were also considered in *Search* numbers 188 to 199 (June 2015 to April 2017). Now published in the book *Seven Aspects of Salvation* (OBT).

[49] In modern times we might recall the attempts made by some to be more holy by such as flagellation.

[50] This is based upon two years in Caesarea where Paul was held in custody (Acts 24:27) plus "many days" (25:13) and the voyage to Rome with its shipwreck etc.

[51] Romans chapter 8: Occurrences of *pneuma*: (1),2,4,5,5,6,6,9,9,9, 10,11,11,13,14,15,15,16,16,23,26,26,27, *KJV.* I have put verse one in brackets because it is omitted in later versions on textual grounds.

[52] This word is used in the Septuagint (*LXX*) of the *support* given to Moses by the 70 elders who were given a share in the "spirit" that the LORD had put upon Moses (Numbers 11:16,17).

[53] This quote is based on the Septuagint (*LXX*) version of the Old Testament.

[54] This may throw some light on those who "say that they are Jews and are not, but are a synagogue of Satan" (Revelation 2:9). Why would they want to be Jews unless there was some advantage in being so?

[55] This work was originally published under the title *The Giver and His Gifts* 1905.

[56] In some copies this reference is given incorrectly as xi 27.

[57] In some copies this reference is given incorrectly as Acts i:9.

[58] *Shekinah* is a Hebrew noun meaning 'dwelling' or 'settling'. It is first found in Rabbinic literature but not in the Hebrew Bible.

[59] It is beyond the remit of this study to interpret these passages here, but they would seem to point to a time when Israel's 'hope' *as a nation* has been set aside (the present situation), and to their future blessing (the Millennium) when they are re-settled in the Land promised to them (see Ezekiel chapters 47 & 48) and their temple is rebuilt.

[60] His argument is complicated, involving as it does whether the case of the noun *pneuma* should be read as Genitive or Dative. Summing up he writes:

If it were the *pneuma* with which we were to be filled, *pneuma* would necessarily be in the Genitive case, and the Greek would have been "filled of the Spirit". *But it is not*! It is in the Dative case (emphasised by the preposition *en*) denoting the One who fills. So that the rendering "filled with the Spirit" is quite misleading. The capital 'S' is correct, for it is the Holy Spirit who is meant. But He is *the Filler*; and it is with His gifts and graces and "power from on high" that *He fills* the children of God.

[61] In 1 Corinthians 14:12 the *KJV* has "spiritual (gifts)".

[62] The absence of the name 'Ephesus' in some manuscripts has led to the belief that this epistle had a far wider circulation than the Ephesian church, and that what we have here is just one of a number of copies that were distributed at the time.

****

Publications of The Open Bible Trust must be in accordance with its evangelical, fundamental and dispensational basis. However, beyond this minimum, writers are free to express whatever beliefs they may have as their own understanding, provided that the aim in so doing is to further the object of The Open Bible Trust. A copy of the doctrinal basis is available on **www.obt.org.uk** or from:

THE OPEN BIBLE TRUST
Fordland Mount, Upper Basildon,
Reading, RG8 8LU, UK